The Complete

DOG

OWNER'S MANUAL

The Complete
DOG
OWNER'S MANUAL

AMY MARDER, V.M.D.

FOG CITY PRESS

Published by Fog City Press
814 Montgomery Street
San Francisco, CA 94133 USA

Conceived and produced by Weldon Owen Pty Limited
59 Victoria Street, McMahons Point, NSW, 2060, Australia
A member of the Weldon Owen Group of Companies
Sydney • San Francisco

This edition 2004

The Iams Company Complete Dog Owner's Manual.

FOG CITY PRESS
Chief Executive Officer: John Owen
President: Terry Newell
Publisher: Lynn Humphries
Managing Editor: Janine Flew
Design Manager: Helen Perks
Editorial Coordinator: Jennifer Losco
Production Manager: Caroline Webber
Production Coordinator: James Blackman
Sales Manager: Emily Jahn
Vice President International Sales: Stuart Laurence

Project Editor: Greg Hassall
Designer: Robyn Latimer
Picture Researcher: Karen Burgess

Written by Amy Marder except
Training Your Dog by Debra Horwitz
A Guide to Breeds by Lynn Cole

THE IAMS COMPANY
The Iams Company, makers of Eukanuba® and Iams® Cat
and Dog Foods, has a vision to be recognized as the world leader
in cat and dog nutrition. With a strong foundation of core beliefs
about culture, customers, products and people, The Iams Company
is committed to enhancing the well-being of cats and dogs by
providing world-class quality foods.

Iams, Eukanuba, the paw print design, and the composite Iams Company
and paw print design are trademarks of The Iams Company registered
in the U.S. Patent and Trademark Office. The color rhodamine red
is a trademark of The Iams Company.

For more information about the care and feeding of your pets, contact
The Iams Company at 1-800-525-4267 or www.iams.com.

A catalog record for this book is available from the
Library of Congress, Washington, DC.

ISBN 1 74089 313 1

Color reproduction by Colourscan Co Pte Ltd.
Printed by SNP LeeFung
Printed in China

A Weldon Owen Production

CONTENTS

INTRODUCTION

I't's common knowledge that the simple act of petting a dog can make people healthier and happier. It's even been suggested that people who own dogs lead longer, fuller lives. For thousands of years, dogs have provided people with companionship and protection. Today millions of proud dog owners around the world are testimony to this unique relationship.

The Complete Dog Owner's Manual provides present and prospective dog owners with the information they need to care for their pet. From choosing the right dog, to feeding tips, to health care and training essentials, this book is filled with sound, practical advice. Also included is a detailed guide to the world's most popular dog breeds, providing helpful information about the feeding, grooming and exercise requirements of these breeds.

For those people who already own a dog, this book will be an invaluable reference. For those who are deciding what kind of dog fits their needs, it will be an inspiration. Remember, a dog's love is a great privilege, and with it comes a genuine responsibility. As dog owners, we must ensure that every care is taken to make our pets' lives as happy and fulfilling as possible.

From the dog lovers at The Iams Company

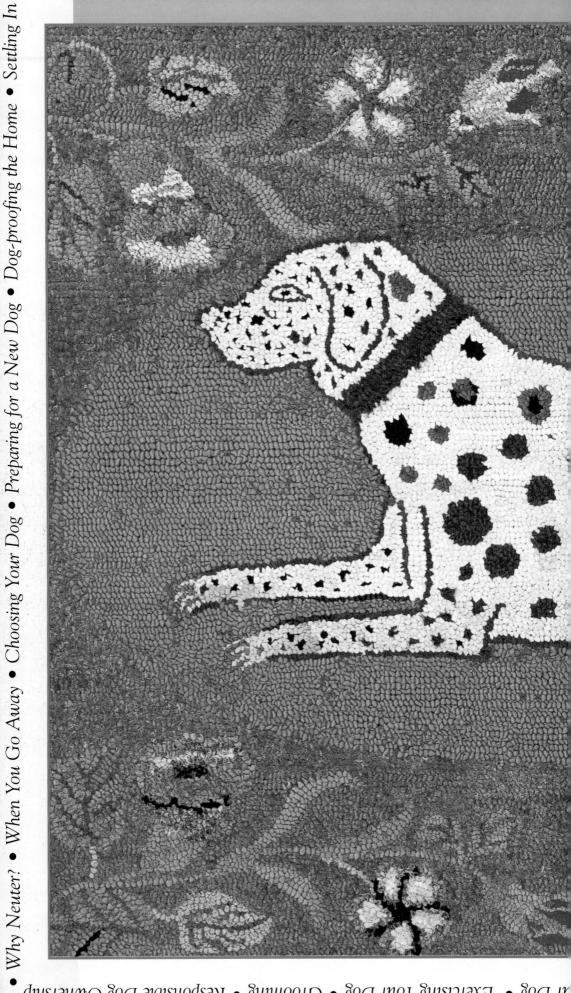

YOU AND YOUR DOG

*The fidelity of a dog is a precious gift
demanding no less binding moral
responsibilities than the friendship
of a human being.*

KONRAD Z. LORENZ (1903–89),
Austrian ethnologist and writer

CHOOSING YOUR DOG

The relationship between a person and a dog can be one of life's most rewarding experiences. To give this relationship the best chance of success, choose your pet carefully. Consider your lifestyle, your home environment and your family needs.

THE RIGHT CHOICE?
Lively and playful, the Jack Russell Terrier is an ideal pet for a family with plenty of time and energy.

KNOW YOUR BREED
Before choosing a dog, learn as much as you can about the different breeds. Go to dog shows to see representatives of the breeds that catch your interest. Talk to breeders, handlers and judges for their invaluable opinions.

Too often, a dog is chosen with little forethought and does not live up to an owner's expectations—with heartbreaking consequences. The key to a successful relationship between you and your pet is to make the right choice in the first place.

FAMILY MATTERS
Before taking on the responsibility of a dog, make sure that the whole family is willing to care for the new pet. Feeding, play, exercise, training and grooming are all essential canine needs and take time.

If you don't have this time, perhaps a cat or smaller animal would be a better choice of pet. Also, make sure that no one in the family is allergic to dogs. Too many dogs are given up each year because of an allergy that was overlooked.

Consider the overall costs of owning a dog. Think about the price of food, leashes, toys and veterinary care, not to mention the replacement of demolished household items. You may also need to build a fence or hire a dog-walker.

Once it is firmly established that there are enough committed caretakers, it's time to consider exactly what kind of dog you want.

ROOM TO MOVE
If you choose an active breed, such as this Golden Retriever, make sure you allow your dog plenty of exercise each day.

THE RIGHT DOG

Learn as much as you can about the characteristics of different breeds so you can narrow your choices to those that best fit your needs.

Although dogs vary from individual to individual, dog breeds tend to have distinct appearances and behave in distinct ways. For example, the sporting breeds were bred for long hours in the field and tend to need a lot of exercise. Therefore, a retriever may not be the best choice if you live in an apartment. However, if you live in the suburbs and have a large fenced yard, a retriever may be perfect.

For apartment dwellers, a less active breed may be best. The giant breeds, like Great Danes and New-foundlands, require little exercise. The toy breeds can get much of the exercise they need right in the hall of your apartment. But be careful, as some are quite noisy.

Coat length should also be considered when deciding upon a breed. Long-coated dogs, such as Chow Chows and Keeshonds, have beautiful thick coats but they require a good deal of grooming to keep them that way. Short-coated dogs, such as Labradors and Dalmatians, require less grooming but tend to shed hair all year round. The breeds that don't shed, such as Bichon Frises and Poodles, need to be clipped regularly—an additional expense if this is done professionally.

Think about the climate your dog will be living in. The Arctic breeds, such as Huskies and Samoyeds, have thick coats and tend to be uncomfortable in hot, humid climates. On the other hand, Greyhounds get very chilled in cold climates. If conditions are extreme where you live, choose a dog whose coat type permits easy adaptation.

You should also consider gender. In general, males can have more behavioral problems and are more aggressive than females. While dogs of either sex make wonderful compan-ions, first-time dog owners or families with children might want to look for a female first. Males and females make equally good watchdogs.

Don't forget the mixed breeds, for they often make great, loving pets. The breeding of genetically similar dogs can result in diseases, such as hip dysplasia, and behavioral problems, such as aggression. Adopting a mixed-breed dog is one of the best ways to avoid inherited diseases. Although it is not as easy to predict the adult appearance or behavior of a mixed breed, most are very appealing and many are in need of homes.

SUITABLE DOGS FOR CHILDREN

If young children are part of the family, you may want to consider these playful and friendly breeds:

- West Highland White Terrier
- Welsh Corgi
- Golden Retriever
- Labrador Retriever
- Beagle
- Shetland Sheepdog

BE AWARE
Children under three may be unintentionally rough with their pets. Dogs, too, can be rough with very young children. Even those breeds listed above require training and positive early experiences with children to be reliable.

GROWING UP TOGETHER
While this Australian Kelpie makes a wonderful companion for these children, don't buy a dog for a child on condition that the child alone must care for it. A dog by itself will not teach your child responsibility; you must be willing to accept responsibility when necessary.

PUPPY OR OLDER DOG?

While puppies have obvious appeal, chewed shoes, housetraining and the other rigors of puppyhood are not for every family. Some people will wisely choose to adopt an older dog.

WHEN ADOPTING A DOG, TRY TO FIND OUT:

- Why was the dog given up?
- Where did he come from?
- How many homes has he already had?
- Is he housetrained?
- Is he used to children?
- Is he used to other pets?
- Is he friendly to people?
- Does he like to be petted?
- Has he had his shots?
- Does he obey commands?
- Does he look healthy?

PUPPIES GROW UP
Remember that a puppy will quickly grow up into an adult dog. In many breeds, such as the Weimaraner (below), the size difference is great.

Puppies and adult dogs have different needs and make different demands of their owners. Think carefully before choosing your pet.

ADOPTING A DOG
Don't adopt a dog, whether from a shelter or another family, just because you feel sorry for it. Although many adult dogs up for adoption make wonderful companions, some may have been given up because of behavioral problems that might not be obvious. Try to obtain an accurate history of the animal (see box). If you choose carefully, an adult dog may be perfect for you. In addition, you will be providing a home for an animal that really needs one.

WHAT ABOUT A PUPPY?
If you get a puppy, you will have more control over his learning during those crucial first few months of life. If you have children, your puppy will grow up with them, learning to be tolerant and unafraid of children in general.

Try to get your new puppy between six and eight weeks of age. It's important for the development of social behavior that a pup stays with his mother and littermates until this time. However, as a six- to eight-week-old puppy is in the midst of the so-called "period of socialization" (between three weeks and three months of age), it's just as important that you start to bond with your new pup now.

Choose your puppy from a healthy litter. Make sure all the puppies appear bright, alert, active and well-fed. If possible, arrange to meet the puppy's parents and other adult relatives. This will indicate what your puppy is likely to look like and how he'll behave when he grows up. Make sure he has been provided with kindness, attention and good nutrition. Watch how the puppies interact with each other. Play with them and pick up each one individually. Although the runt of the litter might be the cutest, he may also have medical and behavioral problems.

WHERE TO LOOK
If you are looking for a pure-bred dog, whether a puppy or an adult, find a well-respected breeder. Responsible breeders are aware of the problems of their breed, keep careful records, and try to breed for both good health and good temperament. Some backyard, or hobby, breeders are less likely to understand the problems that may arise and

how to prevent undesirable traits from being perpetuated in their breeding programs.

Your veterinarian, local breed club or national kennel club should be able to direct you to a good breeder. Although a puppy from a good breeder may be more expensive than those from other sources, when you consider that you may have your dog for ten or more years, it's a pretty good investment.

The best place to find a mixed-breed dog is at your local animal shelter. Animal "pounds", often associated with humane organizations, are shelters run by individual city or town councils. Many shelters are well organized and supervised by trained staff. Some, however, are poorly run. To get more information about the shelters in your area, talk to your local veterinarian or call your local animal control officer.

Always check out the shelter yourself. The animals should look healthy, clean, and well cared for. The staff should be able to answer your questions about individual animals and help you to choose the one best suited to you. Make sure you know what kind of dog you are looking for before you visit the shelter.

Many of the dogs in the shelter are there because their previous owners didn't choose an animal that really suited their lifestyle. Take the time to make an informed choice and you will be rewarded with the joy of a loving companion for many years to come.

CHOOSE WISELY
When selecting a dog from a shelter, take the time to make an informed choice, finding out as much as you can about the dog's history before committing yourself.

A HEALTHY PUP

When choosing a puppy, examine him carefully from head to toe to make sure he is bright and healthy.

SKIN
Under the coat: not oily, no flakes or dandruff, no scabs or lumps.
Belly: usually free of hair, pink, no sores or pimples.

BODY
Strong and symmetrical, (i.e. no signs of poor growth).

ANUS
Clean and dry, not red or irritated.

EARS
Clean, free of discharge, not red or odorous.

FUR
Clean and shiny, little or no shedding when stroked, no fleas.

EYES
Clear, bright and expressive, free of discharge, and not red.

LEGS
Walks and runs effortlessly, puts even weight on all four legs, no lameness.

NOSE
Usually cold and wet, but not running.

MOUTH
Gums pink, teeth white, pleasant-smelling "puppy breath."

PREPARING FOR A NEW DOG

Your new dog will bring you many years of love, companionship and happiness. By preparing the home for your dog in advance, you will make the first days of your relationship easy for both of you.

YOUR NEW PUP
This Australian Shepherd pup is as defenseless as he is adorable. When your new pup arrives he will rely on you absolutely for all his basic needs. Don't let him down.

COZY COMPANIONS
Whether you are preparing for an adult dog, a pup or even an entire litter, make sure they have some-where warm, clean and comfortable to sleep. These Pekingese pups look right at home in their basket.

Before your new pup arrives, you will need to prepare your home for him. Think about his basic needs. Where will he sleep? How will you take him out for exercise? What will he play with?

BEDDING

The first thing that your new dog will need is a comfortable bed in a place of his own. For a puppy, a box turned on its side and lined with soft, washable bedding, or a chew-proof pad inside a pen is perfect. For an adult dog, a durable dog bed (the bean bag type) or soft blanket would be greatly appreciated. Find a quiet, warm area away from drafts but close to the family. Dogs need an area where they can sleep undisturbed whenever they are tired. Young puppies sleep up to 20 hours a day!

A traveling pen or crate is also a worthwhile investment for a puppy. If you buy one large enough for your puppy when fully grown, you can continue to use it for trips throughout his life. A crate or pen also makes the chore of housetraining much easier (see pp. 66–7) and will stop your puppy from getting into trouble when you're not there to supervise him.

ACCESSORIES

Your dog will also need his own set of food and water bowls. Try to find the kind that is designed for his breed, so that he can eat and drink without submerging his nose or ears. Choose flat-bottomed bowls, because they are less likely or be knocked over. Put the bowls either inside your dog's pen or close to his bed.

Other essentials you can buy in advance are a collar, leash and identification tag. This tag must be worn at all times and should be inscribed

food bowls

extendable leash

leather collar

identification tag

with your name, address and telephone number. While you are at the pet supply store also be sure to pick up some safe chew toys, a soft bristle brush and a cleaning solution for the inevitable accidents that even mature dogs may have while adjusting to a new home.

COLLARS & LEASHES

The range of collars and leashes available for dogs can be mind boggling. The first type of collar you will need is a plain buckle collar, either made of nylon or leather, which your dog can wear at all times. Leather or nylon collars and leashes are ideal for mature dogs. As puppies continuously outgrow their collars and tend to chew on leashes, the nylon varieties are preferable. Attach the identification tag to the collar to ensure that you will be contacted if your dog gets lost. Even if your dog has a tattoo or microchip (see p. 30), he should still wear a tag.

When you fit your dog's collar, it should be loose enough to be comfortable but not so loose that he will be able to slip out of it. You should be able to fit two fingers under a collar that's the right size. Other types of collars are used for training and for dogs that pull when on a leash. Choke chains and pinch collars should be used

only by experienced owners or under the supervision of a dog trainer. If used improperly or with excessive force they may cause injury (see box). A harness that goes around the body is useful for walking some dogs.

There is also a wide variety of leashes available. Leashes are generally made of leather, cotton or nylon. Leather leashes are the most expensive, but they last longer and are gentle on the hands. Thick nylon is strong and inexpensive, but is less flexible than leather. Short, lightweight nylon leashes are the best choice for puppies. They're also inexpensive, so if a puppy chews his, it costs less to replace. An extendable leash is another worthwhile investment. Usually made with a comfortable plastic handle, these leashes give dogs freedom to explore while remaining attached to their owners. If an owner needs the dog to be close by, the dog can be easily reeled in.

BASIC ACCESSORIES

There are a number of essentials that you should buy in advance of your new pet's arrival. Make sure that you are ready from the outset to be the best owner your dog could possibly hope for.

USING A CHOKE CHAIN

When using a choke chain, make sure you put it on correctly. When applied the right way, the chain will automatically loosen when you stop pulling. When put on back ard, it will not loosen when you stop pulling. Do not leave a training collar on an unattended dog.

DOG-PROOFING THE HOME

Puppies and dogs can get themselves into a lot of trouble around the average house and yard. Before your new dog moves in, make your home safe for him.

A NOSE FOR TROUBLE

Puppies, such as this Norwegian Elkhound, are naturally curious creatures and will try to eat almost anything they come across. Make sure you remove dangerous materials from the house and avoid growing potentially poisonous plants in the garden, such as the Poinsettia (below).

POISONOUS PLANTS

The following house and garden plants can be toxic to dogs if chewed up or eaten in sufficient quantities:

- Poinsettia (leaves)
- Azaleas and rhododendrons (green leaves)
- Dumb cane (leaves)
- Japanese yew (needles, bark, seed)
- Oleander (leaves, stems, bark)
- English ivy (fruit)
- Mushroom (*Amanita* species)
- Precatory bean (seeds)
- Castor bean (seeds)

Dog-proofing the home is a lot like child-proofing—it basically means removing anything that may be a danger or at risk of being broken. To prevent electric shocks or a nasty bump on the head from a heavy appliance, unplug electrical cords or secure them out of reach. A dangling cord is an irresistible temptation to a young pup. Keep all cleaning compounds and other dangerous materials in a secure place. Insect sprays, rodent poisons, antifreeze and even some common plants (see box) can be poisonous if ingested by a dog.

If you have a yard, check the fencing to see that it is secure enough to keep a dog inside. If there are any holes, fix them. For a small dog, a fence that is four feet (1.2 m) high should be adequate, while a six-foot (1.8 m) fence will hold most large dogs. Bear in mind that some dogs, such as terriers, are natural diggers and will dig under a fence if it

is not well secured. Make sure the gate shuts firmly and that a small dog is not able to squeeze under it. An asthetic alternative is to install an invisible electronic fence. While this will not keep out canine intruders, it will keep your pet from roaming, even if he is a climber. Swimming pools or ponds should always be covered or fenced.

You may prefer to use an outdoor pen. If so, make it

large enough for a good game of fetch. If you plan to keep your dog in the pen for several hours at a time, provide a dog house for shelter from the elements. A large working dog, such as a Mastiff or a Great Dane, might be more comfortable outside in a kennel than inside the house.

There are many different designs but any kennel should be sufficiently large for the dog to move around freely inside. Consult a local expert for advice about a kennel design that will suit your needs. The first few times you let your new dog out into your yard or kennel, do not leave him alone. Dogs can be Houdinis if left unattended.

CHEWING

When puppies are between three and six months of age, their new teeth begin to emerge, causing them pain. Chewing on a hard object may relieve some of this discomfort. Giving your

puppy a nylon chew toy that has been stored in the freezer overnight will soothe the pain. Even when they are not teething, puppies love to chew, and it makes no difference to them whether they're chewing a toy, your shoes or the legs of a kitchen table. So get some "chew" toys that will satisfy your dog's need to chew. They will also help exercise his jaws and clean his teeth. A variety of nylon bones, rope bones, rawhides and fleece toys will keep your dog busy for hours. Buy new ones or rotate the old ones every week so that they remain interesting.

Also get some toys that you can use when you play with your dog. Balls, frisbees and tug toys are favorites. Teach your dog to play fetch with both the balls and frisbees. Play tug-of-war with your dog only after he has learned to release his toys on command (see p. 79).

GIVE A DOG A BONE
Pups, and even older dogs, love to chew, so a good way to protect your household belongings is to provide your dog with a safe alternative. Rope and nylon bones (above left and right) are good to fetch, tug and chew.

ROOM TO MOVE
Very large dogs, such as these Great Danes (left), may knock things over and be unable to move about comfortably if kept in the house. Some dogs may be just as happy in a dog house (right) in the yard.

19

SETTLING IN

The first few weeks of your new relationship may require some effort and, at times, a lot of patience. However, once your new dog has settled in you'll wonder how you ever got by without him.

When you first bring your new puppy or dog home, he will probably be somewhat confused and apprehensive. Before you bring him inside, take him to the place that will be his permanent toilet area. If he "performs" for you, praise him but don't be too upset if he doesn't get the message just yet. Housetraining takes time and patience (see pp. 66–7), so don't give up.

Once indoors, restrict your pup to one room. Let him sniff around and familiarize himself with his surroundings. Introduce him to his bed and food and water bowls. Be gentle with him. Praise him for little things, such as being bold, playful and beautiful. Don't speak harshly or punish your new dog yet. He needs to trust, not fear you during the first few days. You'll have plenty of time to train him after the adjustment period.

Try not to have friends around to the house until your new pet has settled in. Let him get used to you and your family first, before introducing him to strangers. Teach your children to be gentle and quiet around the new dog, especially if

BE PATIENT
Housetraining won't take place overnight and a few mishaps around the house are to be expected at first. Don't punish your new pet—just clean up the mess and vow to supervise him more carefully next time.

A SOFT TOUCH
Teach your children to be gentle with their new pet. Dogs can be wonderful playmates for children, but they are not toys. Children under the age of three should never be left unsupervised with a dog, no matter how trustworthy it is thought to be.

he's a puppy. Children must learn that puppies are not toys and need to be left alone when resting or eating.

MEETING OTHER PETS

Introduction to the household's established pets should be made gradually and under constant supervision. Many older dogs and cats resent the arrival of a puppy, so never leave them alone together at first, unless the puppy is inside a protected pen. Let the established pets sniff the newcomer through the pen. Always give your older animals the most attention, never allowing them to feel that they are being replaced. Also, to prevent "food wars" feed the animals separately until they are comfortable with each other.

For the first few nights, put them in a crate; your new dog or puppy will probably be homesick and lonely. He may whimper and cry, but try not to go to him every time he makes a noise. If you have a puppy, he may settle down if you imitate his mother's companionship by wrapping a ticking clock and hot water bottle in his bedding. Many people find that bringing their puppy's bed and crate into their bedroom at night also helps the puppy to settle in.

PLAYTIME

Most puppies try to play with their owners as they would play with other dogs. They jump up, chase, growl and bite. Play is necessary for the proper social development of puppies, but they need to be taught how to play with people (see p. 64). If your pup starts to bite, say NO! and turn away from him. If he gets uncontrollable, either leave him alone in a room or confine him in his crate until he calms down.

ADJUSTING TO COLLARS & LEASHES

A puppy should start to wear a collar right away. Because many puppies are afraid of collars, the first time you put the collar on give him his favorite treat. Puppies will take a little time to adjust to collars and leashes, so start with short periods and gradually increase the time that your puppy wears his new garb. After a few days, he won't even pay attention to the collar, and after a few weeks he'll miss it if you take it off! However, you may want to remove the collar when you put your puppy in a crate. Sometimes, collars can get caught on the crate wires.

Have your puppy drag the leash around the house for short periods so he won't be afraid of it. When you take him out for his first walks, don't tug him. Instead, go wherever he wants to. In the beginning, your puppy will be walking you. Later, get your puppy to chase you while on leash and play "follow the leader" games.

TIME FOR A WALK
If your new dogs associate their leashes with enjoyable activities, such as walks and games, they will soon learn to love them. These Australian Cattle Dogs know they're about to be taken for a walk.

ARE WE FRIENDS YET?
Be sure to supervise your new dog around other household pets until they are comfortable with each other.

21

FEEDING YOUR DOG

Dogs love to eat and owners love to feed them. Feeding your dog a nutritious and well-balanced diet in the proper amounts is one of the most important things you can do to keep him happy and healthy.

Although dogs are omnivores, they are best fed as carnivores, with a diet based on protein, fat, carbohydrates, minerals and vitamins. A dog must have fresh water at all times to maintain proper levels of body fluids and ensure that body wastes can be eliminated efficiently.

THOSE LUCKY DOGS

People and pets have different nutritional needs. The low-fat diet that is healthy for us is not the best for our dogs.

CONVENIENT AND COMPLETE

Easy to store and economical to feed, dry foods are the most commonly fed form of dog food. Choose one that has been tested on dogs and suits your dog's stage of life. On the label, it should carry the words "nutritionally complete and balanced."

puppy food

dry dog food

VARYING NEEDS

A dog's nutritional needs vary according to life stage and lifestyle. Working dogs, pregnant bitches and young pups have higher nutritional needs than sedentary house pets or older animals. The package label will state that the food has been tested according to feeding protocols established by the Association of American Feed Control Officials (AAFCO). Dog foods must carry this information on the label.

TYPES OF FOOD

Commercial dog foods come in three basic types (dry, semi-moist and canned), and three quality levels (generic, popular and premium). They differ in convenience, cost, moisture content, ingredients and palatability.

Choose a nutritionally balanced food that meets your dog's needs. For instance, all-meat products are extremely palatable but will not provide your dog's daily vitamin and mineral needs. Canned foods contain about 75 percent water, plus a variety of meat, fish and cereal-based products. They are highly palatable and digestible, but their energy content is relatively low, so large dogs require a greater quantity of food to supply their needs.

Semi-moist foods contain only about 15 to 30 percent water, as well as meat, cereals, vegetable proteins, fat, sugars and colorings. Their energy content is higher than canned foods, so smaller amounts can be fed. Dry foods have the highest energy content and contain only about 10 percent water. Manufacturers have developed techniques to create dry foods that taste good to dogs, since a balanced diet is of no use unless the dog eats it.

Generic or private label pet foods, available in some grocery and discount stores, may contain only the bare minimum nutrients your dog needs, and the ingredients will vary as market prices change. While these foods seem low in price, their low nutritional value means that larger quantities must be fed.

Popular pet foods are the brands available in local grocery stores. Most are made to variable formulations. This means that the ingredients in a particular brand may vary from batch to batch, based on price and availability of ingredients. Check the label certifying that AAFCO feeding trials were used.

Premium foods have been developed to give your dog optimal nutrition. They are available through veterinarians and specialty feed and pet stores. Highly digestible, quality ingredients are used. Most such foods are made to fixed formulations, so the ingredients will not vary. Although premium foods are more costly than popular brands, less food needs to be fed on a per-weight basis, because of the higher-quality ingredients. This means cost per serving is comparable to many popular brands of pet food.

WHEN TO FEED

Whether you feed your dog at regular times or make food available throughout the day depends on the type of food you use, your dog's age and health, and whether he tends to overeat. A dog that is overweight or has health problems, such as a history of bloat, should be fed according to a schedule recommended by the veterinarian. Each dog should be fed individually to make sure he receives his fair share of food. Free-choice feeding is best reserved for trim, healthy dogs that are fed dry foods and don't overeat.

HOW MUCH?

Don't overfeed your dog. The amount of food a dog needs varies according to breed, size and activity. Food formulated for an active young dog will not make a sedentary old one healthier—just fatter.

Cold weather, strenuous exercise, hard work and stress (such as lactating) increase a dog's caloric needs; a sedentary life decreases them. Read the instruction on the label of your dog food for guidelines to the amount of food for his body weight, and adjust for his level of activity.

OPTIMUM BODY WEIGHT
Check your dog regularly for weight gain or loss—you should be able to feel the ribs along his sides. Adjust his food intake accordingly.

DAILY NEEDS
A tiny Maltese needs only about 250 calories a day, while a fully grown Rottweiler may need 2,400 calories—more than most people! When working, Alaskan Malamutes (below) and other sled dogs need more than 10,000 calories per day to maintain their body weight and energy levels.

EXERCISING YOUR DOG

As a dog owner, providing your dog with plenty of exercise is a key responsibility. Not only will your dog love the activity, but it will keep him happy and healthy. So, however busy you are, always make time to exercise your pet.

HOP, SKIP AND JUMP
Small toy breeds, such as the Pomeranian (above), can get much of the exercise they need inside an apartment.

A GENTLE STROLL
A daily walk on a leash is enough to keep many breeds of dog happy and healthy.

As a species, dogs are naturally very active and playful. Their wild relatives spend most of their day hunting for food, defending their territory and playing with each other. Pet dogs, on the other hand, are given all the food they need (usually more) and are often confined for most of the day. As a result, 25–44 percent of them tend to become overweight, out of shape and lazy. Lack of exercise can also lead to boredom, which makes many dogs destructive. The key to a happy, healthy dog is exercise.

EXERCISE REQUIREMENTS
All dogs enjoy exercise and play, but the actual amount and type varies according to their age, breed and state of health. Before buying a new dog, get to know the different breeds and the amount of exercise they require. Many breeds, particularly the sporting, herding and working dogs, need regular vigorous exercise. If you are a busy professional who only has the time for a short, daily walk, it would be irresponsible to take on one of these breeds unless you can arrange for someone to exercise the dog. You would be better off with a toy dog or one of the less active breeds.

In general, you should try to give your dog some type of exercise every day. If you have questions about your dog's fitness for exercise, see your veterinarian before starting an exercise program. He or she can check your dog for any health problems that may be aggravated by exercise (such as heart and joint problems) and give you suggestions for a safe exercise regimen. Those breeds that are prone to bloat (see p. 51) should not be exercised immediately after meals.

FORMS OF EXERCISE

Walking is the best all-around form of exercise, providing cardiovascular conditioning and muscle toning. When walking a dog in public, always use a leash. An extendable leash allows your dog plenty of freedom to explore, but also gives you short-leash control when necessary.

If your dog is old, out of shape or has health problems, start with a 15-minute walk on a leash each day and gradually increase the duration. For young, healthy dogs, leash walks alone may not provide enough exercise. For these dogs, vigorous off-leash activities should be added. However, dogs should only be allowed off the leash if they obey commands and only in safe areas where regulations permit. If your dog enjoys playing with other dogs, organize for them to meet up and play together.

Jogging or running is another way to exercise energetic, healthy dogs, but use common sense when taking a dog for a run. Don't run with a dog until its skeleton is mature and avoid running on very hot days. You should also try to stick to soft surfaces to protect your dog's footpads.

Playing games is one of the best ways to both stimulate your dog's mind and provide vigorous exercise. In addition, it allows you to establish your leadership in an enjoyable way. Games of fetch with balls, Frisbees or sticks are excellent ways to give your dog a good workout without getting yourself too sweaty. The sporting breeds, such as retrievers and spaniels are naturals at fetch and easily give up objects. Other breeds, such as terriers, are more likely to hold onto things no matter what. All dogs, however, can be taught to drop an object on command (see p. 79).

When playing fetch, choose a toy that your dog likes to put in its mouth. Fleece toys, soft frisbees, squeaky toys or soft balls are good choices. Avoid small or smooth balls which can be swallowed and don't pick something edible, such as rawhide.

Tug-of-war games are enjoyed by most dogs and can be combined with a game of fetch as a reward for retrieving. Don't play tug, however, until your dog knows how to drop on command. Otherwise he may get overexcited and become aggressive.

FRISBEE FUN
Young, active dogs need plenty of vigorous exercise to stay in shape. Playing games such as frisbee with your dog will make these sessions more fun for both of you.

TAKING THE LEAD
When walking your dogs in public, make sure they are firmly under your control. Just imagine the trouble if these Italian Greyhounds got away.

GROOMING

Regular grooming not only helps your dog look and smell good, but also keeps his skin and coat in top condition. Make grooming sessions part of your dog's preventive health program.

A DOUBLE COAT
The Samoyed (right) has a thick undercoat that sheds twice a year, requiring extra grooming.

TURNING OVER A NEW LEAF
Dogs clean themselves naturally by rolling on the ground, but their owners may have other ideas.

A PROUD OWNER
Some breeds require a great deal of grooming. Here, a pin brush is being used to keep this Afghan's long coat looking beautiful.

Dogs keep themselves clean by rubbing and rolling on the ground and licking or scratching themselves. Often, however, this is just not enough to meet the human definition of clean. Moreover, many of the things that dogs choose to roll in may smell unpleasant to humans. Regular grooming will keep your dog looking good and make life around the house more pleasant for everyone.

BRUSHING

Brushing removes loose dirt from a dog's coat as well as dead hair, which would eventually either be shed or become matted. Brushing also distributes skin oils throughout the coat, keeping it shiny.

When you brush your dog, try as much as possible to brush in the direction that the hair grows. Exceptions are when you run into tangles or when you want to fluff up certain areas, such as the ruffs on a dog's chest.

Dogs with different types of coats have different grooming requirements. In general, short-haired dogs, such as Boxers, Doberman Pinschers and Labradors, need to be brushed only once or twice a week and tend to stay fairly clean. However, many of them shed heavily. On the other hand, dogs with long, curly or wiry coats need daily brushing.

Dead hairs can be removed from shorthaired dogs with a soft bristle brush or rubber brush. Wire slicker brushes may be required to remove the dead hairs from dogs with short dense coats, such as Labradors.

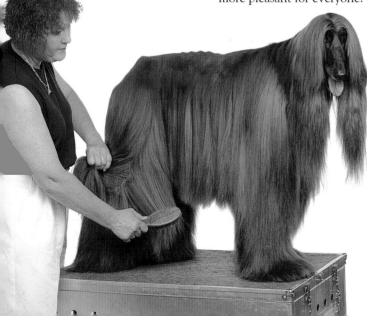

THE LION CLIP

The lion clip was developed to lighten a dog's coat for swimming while protecting the joints and major organs. It is now a popular show clip for certain breeds.

Löwchen

Standard Poodle

Slicker brushes and pin brushes are used to groom longhaired dogs, such as Afghans. However, some long-coated dogs, such as Yorkshire Terriers, have no undercoat to protect their delicate skin, so be gentle. Use a comb to get any tangles out of the feathers and use scissors to carefully trim the hair on the feet and ears. Pay particular attention to hair that grows between the toes and around the opening of the ear canal.

Curly-coated dogs, such as Poodles, do not shed and may develop mats in their hair if their coats are not groomed regularly. For such dogs, use a slicker brush daily to prevent matting and have the coat clipped every six to eight weeks. While some people enjoy clipping their dogs themselves, others prefer to use a professional groomer.

A slicker brush will remove dead hair from the coat of wirehaired dogs, such as many of the terriers. These dogs also need to be either stripped (with your hands or a stripping knife) or clipped every two to four months.

Stripping, which involves pulling the dead hairs from the dog's coat, keeps the coat stiffer, whereas clipping will make it softer. Also trim any long hairs around the face, feet and ears with scissors.

REMOVING MATS

If you encounter a mat in your dog's coat while grooming, first try to remove it by gently untangling it with your fingers and then combing through it. If you can't untangle it, use scissors or a mat splitter to cut into the center of the mat. Try to put your fingers between the mat and your dog's skin to prevent cutting the skin.

comb

combined bristle and pin brush

scissors

NEAT WHISKERS

This Schnauzer's wonderfully styled eyebrows and mustache are the result of careful trimming.

NAIL CLIPPING

A dog's nails need to be trimmed about every two weeks. Dogs that regularly walk on concrete wear down their nails and need less frequent trimming. Use a sharp trimmer and have some styptic available to stop bleeding just in case you cut the quick.

A dog's nail is shaped like a crescent. It is widest where it attaches to the skin and narrows to a curved point at the end. The quick, or nail-bed, contains the nail's nerves and blood supply and runs down the center of the nail. If the quick is cut, it hurts and bleeds, so keep the trimmer well away from it. The pink quick can be seen clearly in dogs with white nails. If your dog has black nails, you can be sure you are far away from the quick if you take off only the thin, curved tip of the nail.

quick

recommended cut

GROOMING SESSIONS

Your dog's grooming sessions should always be enjoyable. Start with a gentle massage and plenty of praise. Then do your home health examination to check for any trouble spots (see p. 40). If the dog is restless or nervous, feed him a treat. After the examination, start grooming from head to toe.

Clean any discharge from your dog's eyes with a soft cotton ball moistened in lukewarm water. If the ears are dirty or there is any sign of discharge, clean the flap and ear opening with a cotton ball moistened with a little alcohol or mineral oil. Do not poke a cotton-tipped swab down the ear canal because this can pack debris against the ear drum rather than removing it. Clean your dog's teeth with a wash-cloth, gauze pad or toothbrush and canine toothpaste. Don't use human toothpaste—it foams and can make a dog sick.

Use a flea comb to check for fleas or ticks (see p. 45). Clean any dirt or discharge from between the toes with a cotton ball moistened in warm water. Trim your dog's nails if necessary (see box) and smooth off any rough edges with a nail file. You should also trim the dewclaws (a fifth digit on the inside of the leg).

WARM-WEATHER WASHING

If you have a large dog and the weather is warm enough, it can be fun to wash him outside under a hose. Make sure that you don't turn the hose up too strongly or you might scare him.

BATHING YOUR DOG

Routine grooming will keep most dogs' coats clean and healthy. Baths are necessary, however, when your dog is very dirty or when there is a medical problem, such as parasites, dandruff or infection. No dog should be bathed more than once a month, unless recommended by a veterinarian, and many dogs need bathing only a couple of times a year. Too much bathing may dry out a dog's coat and skin and strip away its natural waterproofing. A good alternative to bathing is to brush dry shampoo through your dog's coat from time to time.

Before you begin a bath, make sure that you always brush your dog thoroughly. Then put a drop of mineral oil or eye ointment in each eye and cotton in his ears if he'll tolerate it. Choose a warm, draft-free area for the bath—a bathtub is fine if you use a rubber mat to prevent slipping. Very small dogs can even be washed in the kitchen sink. During warm weather, dogs can be washed outside in the yard under a hose.

When bathing, always use lukewarm, not hot, water. Try to use a shampoo specially formulated for dogs, but if you can't find one, use a mild dishwashing liquid. Never use a household cleanser or laundry detergent.

Lather the dog's body and head, being careful to avoid getting soap in the ears or eyes. Give the dog a good massage so that the suds get all the way down to the skin. Once the coat is well lathered, thoroughly rinse the dog, being sure to remove all the shampoo. Any shampoo left on the dog may irritate his skin, causing itching and attracting dirt. Let your dog shake and then dry him with a large towel.

Make sure to dry his ears thoroughly with cotton to prevent infection. A hair dryer, set on a warm or cool setting, dries a dog very well. However, some dogs are disturbed by the noise. After a bath, it is normal for your dog to run around the house like a puppy, trying to dry himself on everything. To avoid this and keep him clean for at least a little while, try to entertain him with his favorite toy until he has dried off.

A PERFECT FIT
A small dog can be washed easily in a bucket or bathtub. Just be gentle and use lukewarm water.

NATURAL WATERPROOFING
After a wash, a dog can shed much of the water from its coat with a quick shake (below). The coats of many dogs, such as Saint Bernards (left), have natural waterproofing properties that bathing too frequently may damage.

RESPONSIBLE DOG OWNERSHIP

Your responsibilities as a dog owner should be to keep your dog happy and healthy, while making sure that he is a well-behaved member of your local community.

WORTH SPOILING

Love, admire and respect your dog for who he is: your companion and a wonderful and intelligent member of the canine species.

KEEP IT CLEAN

Always clean up after your dog in a public place. There are a number of products available to help you do this simply and hygienically.

Responsible dog ownership is a matter of common sense and common courtesy. Remember, your dog depends on you and deserves the best care you can provide.

LOCAL LAWS

Laws regarding dog ownership vary from place to place. It is common for owners to be required to keep their dogs on a leash in public places and certain breeds may also be required to wear muzzles. Familiarize yourself with any local laws and obey them. While dogs may be allowed to exercise off the leash in certain locations, never let your dog loose without supervision.

Most towns and cities in the U.S. require that dogs be licensed or registered, and many also require that dogs be vaccinated for rabies. In addition, your dog should always wear an identification tag on his collar. In Britain, registration and rabies vaccinations are not required, although dogs must wear a collar and tag in public at all times. For permanent identification, have a veterinarian inject a computer microchip under your dog's skin or have him tattooed. Both procedures are relatively painless.

When walking your dog in public, make sure that you always clean up after him. In many U.S. cities, and throughout Britain, it is now an offense not to do so. If possible, train your dog to defecate on your own property before the walk.

CROPPING AND DOCKING

The cropping of ears and the docking of tails are becoming increasingly controversial practices and you should be aware of any regulations regarding them in your country. The cropping of ears to make them erect is actually forbidden by some national kennel clubs including The Kennel Club of Britain. The docking of tails, which is traditional for many breeds and involves removing part of the tail shortly after birth, is still allowed, but be aware of kennel club regulations regarding such practices. If you are in any doubt, contact your national kennel club (see p. 222).

If you are not planning to breed professionally, then it is both sensible and responsible to neuter your dog. Neutering not only addresses the growing problem of pet overpopulation but also has beneficial effects on your dog's health and behavior (see pp. 32–3).

A GOOD CANINE CITIZEN

You must train your dog from an early age to behave well around people and other dogs. All dogs should be taught to obey the basic commands and to walk on a leash without pulling. Allow your dog off the leash only where regulations permit.

Avoid tying your dog up in the yard away from people for long periods. Such isolation can lead to barking and aggression problems. If your dog is noisy and likely to disturb the neighbors, don't let him out in the yard between 10 pm and 7 am. If your dog does bark a lot when alone, consult a veterinarian or animal behaviorist.

HEALTH & GROOMING

Your dog depends on you to fulfill his basic needs, so don't let him down. It is up to you to make sure he is adequately fed, housed, exercised and kept in general good health.

Feed your dog a balanced premium diet and provide plenty of fresh water at all times. Try to exercise or play with your dog for at least 20 minutes a day. Regular exercise and play will keep him healthy and also stop him from being lonely or bored. This, in turn, will help avoid many behavioral problems.

It is your responsibility to provide regular veterinary care for your dog. Annual vaccinations and check-ups are essential for good health and also to prevent the transmission of diseases to people and other dogs. In addition, always keep your dog clean and groomed. This will not only keep your dog looking good but will also control skin parasites, which can lead to health problems that can even be passed on to people.

IT'S NOT WORTH THE RISK
If you think your dog may be aggressive, keep him firmly leashed and muzzled in public at all times, even if you are not required to do so by law.

DANGEROUS DOGS

Unlike the U.S., Britain has national legislation to control dogs in public. The Dangerous Dogs Act (1991) specifies that three breeds, the Fila Brazileiro, Dogo Argentino and Japanese Tosa, are totally banned. A fourth breed, the American Pit Bull Terrier, is allowed only under severe restrictions. It must be registered, neutered, tattooed, microchipped and has to carry insurance. It cannot be bred or imported and, when in public, it must be muzzled, leashed and handled by a person over 16 years of age at all times.

WHY NEUTER?

If your dog is not of breeding quality or you're just not interested in taking on the responsibility of breeding, then neutering your dog at an early age is best for both of you.

A GREAT RESPONSIBILITY
As adorable as puppies may be, there are too many of them. When they grow up, many will find themselves in humane society shelters (above) because their owners were not prepared to care for them. Neutering helps to prevent this tragic situation.

Neutering is the term for the permanent surgical sterilization of an animal. In females, the procedure is often called spaying and it involves the removal of both the ovaries and uterus. In males it is usually referred to as castration or altering and involves the complete removal of the testicles. Because there are so many myths about neutering, dog owners often fear the procedure. The following facts should ease your mind and convince you that neutering is the wisest decision.

THE CASE FOR NEUTERING
Each year, thousands of dogs are put to sleep in animal shelters because no one wants them. Many of these dogs are the result of accidental breeding. The only way to halt this tragedy is to stop allowing our pets to breed, and the safest and most effective way to achieve this is to neuter. By not adding to the population of dogs, the chance that homeless pets will find homes is increased.

With current methods of veterinary surgery, both forms of neutering are quick and relatively safe and painless procedures. Furthermore, the health benefits are significant.

WHY NEUTER A MALE?
Castration has significant health benefits for a male dog. It prevents prostate disease, a serious problem for older male dogs, and virtually eradicates the chances of testicular cancer or infection.

Neutering can also modify many behavioral problems.

It eliminates the sex hormone testosterone which is responsible for such "male behaviors" as mounting, urine marking (leg lifting), fighting and roaming. Not only is your dog less likely to fight with other male dogs, but he is also less likely to be picked on. Because neutered males have less desire to roam and search for females, they are less likely to be hit by cars.

Contrary to popular belief, castration will not make a male dog calmer, although it will remove the cause of much of his frustration. Only maturity, exercise and good training will calm an active young dog.

WHY SPAY A FEMALE?

Spaying removes the primary source of the female sex hormones estrogen and progesterone. If you spay a female dog before her first heat, she has virtually no chance of developing breast cancer. Spaying also eliminates her chances of developing cancer or infection of the uterus.

Unlike castration, spaying has little effect on behavior. However, spaying does prevent the irritability and occasional aggression that females experience during heat and the period of false pregnancy that often follows the heat (see pp. 84–5).

Spaying also means that you won't have to contend with blood stains on your carpets and furniture from the discharge that occurs during heat. In addition, it will spare you the burden of persistent neighborhood males sitting outside your door waiting expectantly for your female.

MYTHS & FACTS

A popular myth about neutering is that neutered pets become psychologically depressed. In fact, most neutered pets are more loving and playful since they are no longer preoccupied with mating. Another myth is that neutered animals become fat and lazy. Although neutered dogs do require fewer calories, they will easily maintain their trim physique when placed on a proper diet and exercise program. Obesity is far more often caused by overfeeding and inactivity than neutering.

Some owners also worry that neutering will reduce their dog's basic instinct to defend his or her territory, turning their once-vigilant watchdog into a wimp. Again, there is no truth in this.

It's never too late to neuter your dog. Although best done before puberty, studies show that neutering has the same effect on behavior and reproduction at any age. There is no need to let your dog go through a heat cycle or have a litter before being neutered.

There is really no reason not to neuter your dog. The procedures are affordable and readily available, with many humane societies offering low-cost neutering programs. The cost of the operation is certainly much less than the cost of raising an accidental litter of puppies or paying the medical bills for problems that neutering can easily prevent.

ONE THING ON HIS MIND
It is very difficult to confine an unneutered male dog—they tend to have only one thing on their minds if there are females around and many become restless and destructive.

NAKED AGGRESSION
Neutered dogs are unlikely to pick fights or be picked on by other dogs—reason enough to have your dog neutered.

WHEN YOU GO AWAY

During vacations, many dog owners wonder whether or not to take their dog with them. While taking your dog away can be a wonderful experience, the difficulties may outweigh the benefits for both of you.

ON THE ROAD
If traveling by car, taking your dog on vacation with you needn't be a problem. However, make sure he is restrained and that he has plenty of fresh air and water.

HOME AWAY FROM HOME
A traveling case is ideal for carrying a small dog whether you are making the journey by car, bus, train or airplane.

Before deciding whether or not to take your dog on vacation with you, consider the condition of the dog, the mode of transportation and the nature of the destination. Dogs who get nervous or carsick when they travel, those who are sick or aggressive and females in heat are all best left at home.

If you are not intending to travel by car, your options will be limited. In many countries, trains and buses will not accept dogs as passengers or cargo unless they are specially trained to assist handicapped people. While most airlines do allow dogs to travel on board, those over 10 inches (25 cm) tall are usually required to travel in the baggage compartment.

Consider your destination. The hotel or campground you're going to may not allow dogs. Also, are you willing to involve your pet fully on your vacation? While dogs love to go camping, most don't enjoy being cooped up all day in a strange hotel room while their owners are out sightseeing.

If you're traveling to another country, think long and hard before taking your dog, especially if it's only going to be a brief trip. Many countries require a dog to be quarantined, sometimes for up to six months.

TRAVELING WITH DOGS
If you really want to take your dog along on vacation, by all means do so, but make sure you prepare properly (see box). To help prevent travel sickness, feed a light meal no later than two hours before the trip, and provide constant access to water. If this doesn't relieve the nausea, ask your veterinarian about medication for future trips.

Most dogs do not need tranquilizers when traveling. In fact, a tranquilized dog traveling in the baggage area of a plane may have difficulty breathing. If you feel that your dog really should be sedated, consult your veterinarian. Always test tranquilizers at home before your trip.

TRAVELING BY CAR

When traveling by car, make sure that the dog is restrained. Dog seatbelts, crates and barriers prevent a dog from disturbing the driver and reduce the risk of injury from sudden stops or accidents. Stop every few hours to allow your dog to stretch his legs, relieve himself and drink some water. Try to follow your pet's normal routine as closely as possible. Feed at least two hours before driving, and feed less, as he will be less active while traveling. If carsickness is a problem, feed at the end of the day.

Never leave your dog inside a closed car on a warm day. Temperatures inside the car rise dangerously high within minutes, and can lead to heatstroke (see p. 55). If you must leave your dog in the car, park in a shady area. Keep your dog restrained and open the windows and sun-roof as wide as you can.

TRAVELING BY AIR

Check with each airline because fees and regulations vary, but most airlines require health certificates signed by a veterinarian within ten days of departure. The space allotted for animals is limited and reservations must be made in advance. While some airlines may allow a small dog to travel in a carrier under the seat, larger dogs must travel in the baggage area. Either way, you'll need a container approved by the airline.

To reduce the stress of flying try to book a non-stop flight and avoid traveling during peak travel times or extreme weather conditions.

BOARDING & KENNELING

If you decide to leave your dog behind, then you must choose where he will stay. If you can get someone to feed, walk and keep your dog company, then he can stay right in his own home. Another option is to try to get a person to live in your home while you're away. There are also many pet-sitting services that are reliable and insured.

If leaving your dog in your home is not feasible, there are many reputable kennels that will take excellent care of him. To find a good one, get references from friends or your veterinarian. Be sure to take a thorough tour of the facility, including the housing, feeding and exercise areas. There should be someone on the premises at all times and a veterinarian available if needed. When you drop your dog at the kennel, bring a favorite bed or blanket, his own food and a couple of his toys. Having the things he's used to will make the transition easier.

WISH YOU WERE HERE
If you decide to take your dog away with you, make sure that you include him in as many activities as possible. If you are going to leave him tied up in a room, he may as well be at home or in a kennel.

PREPARING FOR A TRIP

To satisfy local laws and to make your pet as comfortable as possible, always organize the following before going on vacation with your dog:

- A current health certificate, proof of vaccination and medical history.
- Have your dog checked by a veterinarian before you go and ask about any diseases you might encounter that your dog might not be protected against.
- Any medications that your dog regularly needs.
- Your dog's leash and collar with an identification tag, and his license.

- Food and water bowls.
- A supply of regular food and treats to last the whole trip.
- Plenty of water, preferably from home.
- Grooming tools, including a flea comb.
- Toys and a favorite bed or blanket.
- Photos of your dog in case he gets lost.
- Clean up materials.

HEALTH CARE

*You may catch the glance of a dog
sometimes which seems to lay a kind of
claim to sympathy and brotherhood.*

RALPH WALDO EMERSON (1803–82),
American essayist, poet and philosopher

HEALTH CARE

✚

Making sure that your dog lives a long and healthy life means providing not only a well-balanced diet and plenty of play and exercise, but also good preventive health care. This program should begin at puppyhood and continue throughout your dog's lifetime.

After obtaining your puppy, you should visit a veterinarian as soon as possible. Ask your dog-owning friends to recommend a good doctor or call your local humane society or veterinary association for a referral. At the first visit, your veterinarian will give your puppy a thorough physical examination to make sure she is healthy, will check her feces for intestinal parasites and will set up a vaccination schedule for you to follow.

CHECKING A DOG'S HEART RATE

To count your dog's heart rate, gently place your fingers on the chest inside of the dog's elbow. Press lightly and you will feel the beats. A normal rate is between 80 and 140 beats per minute.

VACCINATION

Puppies are susceptible to several life-threatening contagious diseases that are easily prevented through vaccination. Most vaccines are given two or three times at three-to-four week intervals until the puppy is 12 to 14 weeks old (see chart, p. 39). The vaccines are given several times because most puppies carry temporary protection (antibodies) from their mothers that may interfere with their ability to develop their own protection. Most vaccines are boostered annually. Bear in mind that your puppy is not fully protected until she has received all of her puppy vaccines. If your puppy is not fully immunized, don't take her places where she will come into contact with unvaccinated dogs.

Depending on where you live and what your dog is likely to be exposed to, your veterinarian may also recommend vaccines for Lyme Disease, a tick-transmitted disease that affects many body systems, and Coronavirus, another intestinal viral disease that can be serious for puppies.

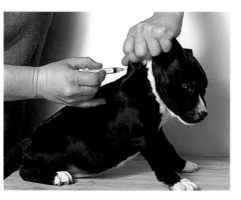

An intranasal form of the kennel cough vaccine is often recommended for dogs who are going to be housed with other dogs (as at dog shows or in boarding kennels). Your veterinarian may also suggest an oral heartworm preventive, although this is not a vaccine.

VITAL SIGNS

Most dogs are not complainers and will hide their discomfort. It's up to you to observe your dog's behavior and vital signs and know when to seek help.

A dog's normal heart rate is between 80 and 140 beats per minute. The heartbeat can be felt by placing your hands around the chest just behind the elbow and gently pressing. To check for respiration, look for movement in the chest. If a dog is unconscious and appears lifeless, place a thread or hair in front of the nose to detect the slightest flow of air.

The normal body temperature for a dog is between 101 and 102.5°F (38–39°C). To take your dog's temperature just put a dab of lubricating jelly on the tip of a rectal or digital thermometer and carefully insert it about 2 inches (5 cm) into the rectum. Hold on to the thermometer throughout and read it after two minutes. Anything over 103°F (39.5°C) is a fever and deserves immediate attention.

Most feverish dogs have poor appetites, are inactive and have a "dull" look to their eyes. They tend to have warm, dry noses, but so do many healthy dogs, so your dog's nose is not a good barometer of a fever. The only sure way to tell if your dog has a fever is to take her temperature.

BETTER SAFE THAN SORRY

Vaccines for many of the common canine diseases are given together in one injection. These days, vaccination is such a quick and simple procedure, why take a chance on your pet's life?

VACCINATION SCHEDULE

DISEASE	AGE AT FIRST SHOT	AGE AT SECOND SHOT	AGE AT THIRD SHOT	BOOSTER
Distemper	6-10 weeks	10-12 weeks	14-16 weeks	12 months
Infectious canine hepatitis (CAV-1 or CAV-2)	6-8 weeks	10-12 weeks	14-16 weeks	12 months
Parvovirus infection	6-8 weeks	10-12 weeks	14-16 weeks	12 months
Bordetellosis	6-8 weeks	10-12 weeks	14-16 weeks	12 months
Parainfluenza	6-8 weeks	10-12 weeks	14-16 weeks	12 months
Leptospirosis	10-12 weeks	14-16 weeks	—	12 months
Rabies	12 weeks	64 weeks	—	12 or 36 months*
Coronavirus	6-8 weeks	10-12 weeks	12-14 weeks	12 months

Source: American Veterinary Medical Association (AVMA).   *check with your veterinarian as to type of vaccine

THE HEALTHY DOG

U se your grooming sessions to give your dog "home health examinations." Early detection of any physical health problems will help your veterinarian treat them more successfully. Start the examination by giving your dog a whole body massage. Begin with the head and neck area and gently progress down to the tail and feet.

WARNING SIGNS

Always consult your veterinarian if something in your home health exam doesn't seem right or if you notice any of the signs below:

- Loss of appetite accompanied by not acting "right" for more than a day.
- Trouble eating or mouth pain.
- Sudden weight loss or weight gain noticed by weighing or by a rib check.
- Prolonged gradual weight loss.
- Fever.
- Pain.
- Vomiting more than three times. Call veterinarian immediately if bloody or dark.
- Diarrhea for more than a day. Call veterinarian immediately if bloody.
- Change in bowel habits for more than a day.
- Coughing or labored breathing.
- Sneezing for more than a day.
- Excessive drinking for more than a day.
- Increased urination, sudden accidents in the house, difficult urination, straining, bloody urine or decreased urination.
- Excessive salivation.
- Sluggishness, unwillingness to exercise or behavior changes for more than a day.
- Excessive scratching or itching, including ear rubbing or head shaking.
- Lameness for more than a day.
- Seizures or convulsions.
- Eye discharge for more than a day. Squinting or discomfort immediately.

• Run your hands through your dog's coat. Healthy fur is shiny and will not fall out excessively when you do this. Look for any bald spots.

• Notice the skin under the fur. Normal skin is clean and has no flakes, scabs, odor or grease. Look around for any fleas, flea dirt (flea excrement, which looks like coarse black pepper) or ticks.

• Examine your dog's tail end. The anal area should be clean, dry and free of lumps. If irritated, your dog may have diarrhea or the anal sacs may be blocked.

• Check your dog's legs and paws. Feel for any lumps or painful areas.

• Look for cuts on your dog's pads or damage to the nails. Do the nails need trimming?

• Look into your dog's eyes. They should be bright, clear and free of discharge. There should be no redness, squinting (sign of pain) or cloudiness.

• Check inside your dog's ears. They should be pink, painless and free of discharge. Any odor, swelling, tenderness or discharge means trouble.

• Normal canine noses are usually cold and wet, but they are free of discharge. A warm, dry nose may be normal if it is not accompanied by other signs of illness.

• Find out if your dog is dehydrated by gently picking up the skin on the neck. Normal skin is soft and rapidly falls back into place. Dehydrated skin is stiff and remains elevated.

• Your dog's teeth should be white. If they are yellow or brown, they probably need to be professionally cleaned.

• Carefully check inside your dog's mouth. The gums and tongue should be pink (some dogs have black pigment spots, which are normal). Paleness or change of color to red, blue or yellow is a sign of disease. Any lumps in the mouth are abnormal.

• Feel for your dog's ribs. If your dog is fit, you should be able to feel the ribs. Overweight dogs have an obvious fat layer. Underweight or ill dogs have very prominent ribs. A pot belly in an overweight animal may be normal, but is not if the dog is thin over the rest of the body.

• If your dog has "doggy breath," there is probably some gum or dental disease. But kidney and digestive problems are also a possibility.

• Notice your dog's breathing. It should be regular and comfortable. Dogs normally pant when they are hot, excited or stressed.

41

HEALTH PROBLEMS

✚

No one knows your dog as well as you do, so if you think she might be sick or depressed, don't hesitate to seek immediate veterinary help. Remember, your dog depends on you.

A PORTLY POODLE
Just like people, many dogs get fat simply from eating more calories than their bodies need. This overweight poodle probably feels as unhappy as it looks.

STAYING IN SHAPE
A brisk walk every day is a simple way to make sure that your dog does not become overweight.

🐾 OBESITY
Obesity is the number-one nutrition-related disease in dogs. Sometimes a metabolic disease, such as hypo-thyroidism, triggers obesity. In most cases, however, the extra weight is simply due to dogs eating too much and exercising too little. As with people, extra weight can cause or exacerbate a number of medical problems, including skin disorders, arthritis, diabetes and heart disease.

The easiest way to tell if your dog is overweight is to do a rib test (see box). If there is a weight problem, your veterinarian can design a good weight-reduction program.

A typical weight-reduction program both reduces your dog's intake of calories and increases her exercise. Calories can be cut either by feeding your dog less (usually about 60 percent of current intake) or by initiating a special low-calorie diet. Avoid high-fiber diets. Divide her meals into two or three daily portions so she won't feel so hungry. If she's used to snacks between meals, make them low-calorie ones, such as dog biscuits specially made to go with her reducing diet.

Regular exercise is a vital part of any weight-loss program. Starting with short sessions of five or ten minutes, try to work up to 30 minutes of active play or brisk walking every day. Be sure to slow down or stop if either of you gets tired. Monitor your dog's progress by feeling for her ribs and weighing her every week

THE RIB TEST

You should not be able to see the ribs. Run your hands down your dog's sides and feel for them. If they are not obvious, your dog is plump. Looked at from above, she should have a definite waistline. From the side, her tummy should not be lower than her rib cage. If your dog is overweight, consult your veterinarian for a safe and effective way to tackle the problem.

or two. If you're diligent, you'll be pleasantly surprised to see how fast that extra weight comes off!

COUGHING & SNEEZING

All dogs cough and sneeze occasionally, but if the problem is frequent or persists for more than one day, visit your veterinarian. Persistent sneezing could be due to allergies. If it is accompanied by a thick nasal discharge from one nostril, a dog could have breathed in a foreign body or have a nasal tumor.

Coughing that appears suddenly in a healthy dog may be due to kennel cough, the canine equivalent of our cold. A typical kennel cough looks and sounds like gagging, and often brings up a small amount of phlegm. Owners often think that their dog has something caught in its throat. Coughing due to kennel cough may last up to two weeks.

Persistent coughing, especially at night, may be caused by a failing heart. Many dogs experience heart failure as they get older. When the heart no longer pumps efficiently, fluid builds up in the lungs and sometimes in the abdomen. The dog may not only cough but also experience difficult or rapid breathing, have an enlarged abdomen and be reluctant to do any exercise. In severe cases, the dog's gums and tongue may take on a bluish color and the dog may have fainting episodes. Heart failure is a deadly disease but can be successfully treated with medication if caught early.

Older dogs also frequently cough when they have bronchitis, which is easily remedied with medication. Young toy dogs frequently cough because of a collapsing trachea, an inherited defect of their windpipe. This problem can be quite severe in some dogs, and in such cases surgery may be necessary to correct the defect.

BREATHING TROUBLE
Some toy dogs, such as the Yorkshire Terrier (above), can cough and have difficulty breathing. This may be due to an inherited defect of the windpipe.

HOW TO WEIGH A DOG

The best way to weigh a dog is to pick her up and step on the bathroom scales. Then you simply subtract your own weight from the total, leaving you with the weight of the dog. If you own a small dog or puppy, this is a very simple procedure. However, if your dog is large, be sure to lift her correctly. Crouch down to gather up your dog (below) and rise slowly, using your legs, not your back (right).

A STITCH IN TIME
Many skin problems, particularly those caused by external parasites, can be avoided by keeping your dog clean and healthy.

SKIN PROBLEMS
This mixed-breed dog is suffering from severe skin problems. In most cases, such suffering can be avoided by looking for the early signs of irritation and seeking immediate advice from your veterinarian.

Skin Problems

Skin conditions are probably the most common canine medical problems that veterinarians treat. The problem can be as mild as dry skin or as serious as a severe infection. Signs of skin disease include scratching, dandruff, hair loss, redness, odor, pimples, scabs and lumps.

Severe scratching, rubbing and licking can lead to skin infections. If licking is confined to one area, a painful infection, called a "hot spot," can develop. Parasites, such as fleas, are responsible for many itches, but some dogs scratch because they are allergic to things they have eaten, touched or inhaled. If your dog is scratching, first look for fleas (see p. 45). If there are no signs of fleas, consult your veterinarian. Meanwhile, a cool bath may help. Dandruff, sometimes accompanied by scratching, is often caused by

dry skin. To combat this, especially during winter, feed a diet with an adequate fat level and adjusted omega-3 fatty acids. If the flakiness is accompanied by a dull or greasy coat and a bad odor, a skin disorder called seborrhea may be the cause. Your veterinarian can determine the cause of the problem and prescribe the proper treatment.

Hair loss can be caused by parasites (mites), fungal infections, such as ringworm, or hormonal imbalance. Fortunately, most hair-loss problems in dogs are treatable.

Redness, pimples and scabs, sometimes accompanied by scratching and a bad odor, may be signs of a skin infection known as pyoderma. Your veterinarian can prescribe antibiotics and special medicated baths.

A lump on or under your dog's skin could be a cyst, tumor or abscess. Cysts are usually painless and may be filled with fluid. Tumors vary in size and shape. Those with an unusual shape or color or that grow quickly may be malignant. Abscesses (localized infections) are painful and may be hard or soft in places. Have your veterinarian check any lumps found.

Lice

These biting insects are visible as they crawl over your dog's skin. Their white eggs, called "nits," are also easy to see in your dog's hair. If your dog is scratching and you see either lice or eggs, ask your veterinarian to recommend a safe insecticidal shampoo. Dog lice are easy to get rid of and are not contagious to people.

FLEAS: A COMMON PROBLEM

These small, flat, hopping insects are by far the most common skin parasites that plague dogs. Their bites lead to scratching and chewing, most notably on the dog's back at the base of the tail. Many dogs are allergic to flea saliva and develop severe itching all over the body. Dogs may also acquire tapeworms from ingesting fleas.

If your dog is scratching, look for evidence of fleas. Use either a fine-toothed flea comb or your fingers and search for the insects under the fur in the rump area or between your dog's hind legs. Also look for coarse, black "flea dirt" (a combination of digested blood and flea feces) in the coat. Flea dirt will turn red if placed on a moistened tissue.

Because fleas live both on and off your dog at different stages of their life cycle, eradication can be difficult. Effective treatment requires that you eradicate fleas not only from your dog and other pets, but also from your house and yard. Start by bathing your pets (any dog shampoo will kill fleas). When dry, use a flea comb to pick up any stragglers. Launder your pets' bedding and thoroughly vacuum your house, discarding the bag afterward. There are many safe and effective insect-control products available to help you get rid of fleas. Consult your veterinarian for advice.

Ticks

Although a tick bite itself usually causes little or no skin irritation, the danger of ticks is in the diseases they carry, such as Lyme Disease and Tick Paralysis.

If your dog has been romping through grassy fields or woods, use a flea comb to carefully check for ticks. These insects look like flat, brownish seeds, but can swell to the size of a small grape when engorged with blood. If you find any, remove them as soon as possible to reduce the chances of disease transmission.

First kill the tick by covering it with petroleum jelly or rubbing alcohol. Grasp the tick as close to the skin as possible with tweezers then gently pull it out, making sure you remove the head. Try not to squeeze the tick when removing it. Many flea-killing products will also kill ticks, but there are products specifically for tick prevention. Consult your veterinarian for advice.

Mites

These microscopic parasites live under the skin. Two of them, Demodex and Sarcoptes, cause mange. Demodex mites are found in the hair follicles of all dogs. At times, when a dog's immunity wanes, the mites multiply and cause hair loss. Most cases are resolved naturally, but some spread and develop into severe infections.

Unlike Demodex mites, Sarcoptes mites are highly contagious. They burrow under the skin, causing intense scratching, crusting and hair loss, especially on elbows and ears. People may also be bitten by these mites.

If your dog is suffering from hair loss or obvious skin irritation, your veterinarian will be able to diagnose mites by examining a tiny scraping of your dog's skin under a microscope. Depending on the diagnosis, treatment may consist of baths or an oral or injectable parasiticide.

FLEA COMBS

These very fine-toothed combs are designed to pick out fleas from a dog's fur. They can also be used to search for ticks.

SEARCHING FOR TICKS

If your dog has been playing outdoors, use a brush or comb to check the fur thoroughly for ticks. Make sure you check the ears.

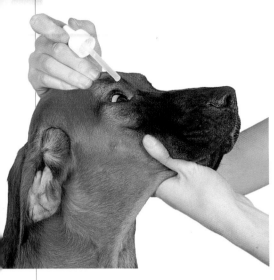

ADMINISTERING EYEDROPS

Your veterinarian may prescribe eyedrops to treat certain eye problems. To administer eyedrops, hold your dog's head firmly and apply a few drops to the corner of the eye. If your dog is uncomfortable, you may need someone to help hold his head still.

CATARACTS

Cataracts are a common problem, particularly in older dogs, and make the center of the eyes appear white or opaque (right). If severe, they may require surgery.

EYES

The canine eye is very much like the human eye, and every part is subject to problems that can affect the ability to see. The most common eye problems produce discharge, redness and pain. Signs of pain are tearing, squinting and holding the eye closed. Conjunctivitis is probably the most common cause of eye discharge and redness in dogs.

"Pink eye" is not the same disease that human children contract. In dogs, the conjunctiva, or lining of the eyelid, becomes swollen and red and may be itchy. The discharge may be clear or yellow, thick or thin. Conjunctivitis can be caused by allergies, environmental irritants (such as pollution), or bacterial or viral infections. Sometimes the inflammation leads to blockage of the tear ducts in the corner of the eye, causing the tears to flow over the lower lid and onto the face. Conjunctivitis is easily treated by drops or topical ointments obtained from your veterinarian. To clean the discharge from around your dog's eyes, soak with lukewarm water and gently wipe with clean cotton ball.

Redness and a very thick eye discharge, sometimes green, is seen in dogs who are unable to produce enough tears. Known as "dry eye," or keratoconjunctivitis sicca, this condition can lead to permanent corneal damage and loss of vision if not treated. Your veterinarian will prescribe medication.

Redness, pain and discharge may also be signs of glaucoma, a condition caused by too much pressure within the eye. Many dogs with glaucoma become depressed because of the pain. Because glaucoma can rapidly lead to blindness, any dog suspected of having it must be treated immediately.

Cataracts, or opacities of the lens, are common in dogs and make the center of the eye look white. Cataracts may be present at birth or develop with age. They are often caused by diabetes. If cataracts grow large, they begin to obstruct vision and may need to be removed by a veterinary ophthalmologist. However, some cloudiness of the lens is a natural part of aging in dogs. Called lenticular sclerosis, or hardening of the lens, this condition doesn't significantly interfere with a dog's vision.

PREVENTING PERIODONTAL DISEASE

Following these simple steps will ensure that your dog's mouth remains healthy and smelling good.

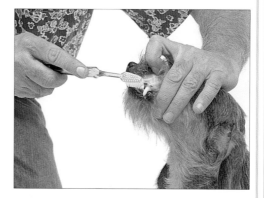

- Check your dog's teeth each time you groom. Brush your dog's teeth at least twice a week, using a gauze pad, wash cloth or child's tooth brush. Use the flavored toothpastes made especially for dogs, not human brands.

- Have your dog's teeth checked once a year by your veterinarian. If there's significant tartar build-up, your dog's teeth may need professional cleaning, usually done under anesthesia.

- Feed your dog dry food or hard dog biscuits every day and provide a hard toy or bone to chew on.

Retinal diseases also lead to impaired vision in dogs. Progressive retinal atrophy (PRA) is an inherited disease affecting many breeds, the first symptom of which may be trouble seeing at night. Unfortunately, total blindness follows and there is presently no treatment. However, other diseases that cause impaired vision do respond to treatment. If you notice any sign of vision loss in your dog, see your veterinarian at once.

Cat's claws and tree branches often cause corneal injuries in dogs. A dog with a corneal injury will hold her eye closed and tear excessively. If left untreated, the damaged area can become infected and ulcerated, resulting in blindness.

Inherited abnormalities of the eyelids can also lead to corneal damage. Some eyelids roll abnormally in or out or have eyelashes that grow in the wrong direction, toward the eye. Most of these problems, however, are easily corrected by surgery.

🐾 MOUTH

While dogs do not usually get cavities, more than 80 percent of them get periodontal disease (an infection of the gums and supporting structures of the tooth) by the time they are three. The disease starts with a build-up of bacteria, plaque and tartar on the teeth. The gums and supporting structures of the teeth then succumb to infection, resulting in tooth loss. If not treated, the infection can spread and eventually lead to kidney, liver and heart problems.

Periodontal disease can be prevented with regular dental care (see box) and is reversible if treated in its early stages. The first sign of dental disease is usually bad breath. Other signs may be drooling, reluctance to eat (especially hard food), nasal discharge and a swollen jaw or cheek. Dogs have doggy breath only if there's a problem. While dental disease is the most common cause of halitosis, other causes include diabetes, kidney and liver disease.

A HUNTING PAST
Although our pet dogs rarely hunt like their wild relatives, they still have the same set of sharp, shredding teeth.

47

EARS

A dog's ear is made up of four parts, all of which are subject to disease: the ear flap, the external ear canal, the middle ear and the inner ear.

The ear flap often gets injured and may bleed profusely. If your dog's ear flap is cut, apply firm pressure right over the injury with a towel, prevent your dog from shaking her head and see your veterinarian as soon as possible. Another common problem of the ear flap, especially in older dogs, is a soft swelling called a hematoma. Possibly caused by excessive head shaking, hematomas require professional treatment as soon as possible. Excessive delay will cause needless pain and possibly deformity.

Perhaps the most common ear disease in dogs is inflammation of the external ear canal (otitis externa). A dog with otitis externa shakes its head, scratches and rubs the affected ear. The ear is usually painful when touched, has a discharge and an unpleasant odor.

Ear mites are a common cause of otitis externa, especially in puppies. Often spreading throughout a litter, the mites cause itching and a thick, dark, gritty discharge. This discharge can be cleaned out with a few drops of mineral oil and a cotton ball, but medication will be required to rid your dog of all the mites.

Otitis externa may also be caused by bacterial or yeast infections. In addition, allergies and seborrhea may be contributing causes. Flop-eared dogs and dogs that swim often get ear infections. To increase the aeration of a flop ear, clip the hair on the ear flap and around the opening. If your dog likes to swim, see your veterinarian for a solution to put in the ear canal to dry it out after a dip. If your dog shows signs of ear disease for more than two days, see your veterinarian.

Infections of the external ear can spread to the middle and inner ears causing more serious problems, including nerve damage, a head tilt, loss of balance and deafness. Treatment must be immediate to prevent permanent damage. Deafness can be inherited and is very common in dogs that are all or primarily white, such as Dalmatians. Some degree of hearing loss is also common in older dogs.

ORTHOPEDICS

Arthritis

Osteoarthritis, also known as degenerative joint disease, is the most common type of arthritis occurring in dogs. It may affect any joint and is very common in older dogs. Arthritis

CLEANING A DOG'S EAR

Clean your dog's ears only if they are dirty, waxy or if there is discharge—overcleaning can actually cause problems. Use a cotton ball, not a cotton-tipped swab—these may pack debris against the ear drum.

FINE TUNED

Your dog's ear is an intricate and sensitive organ. Dogs are able to hear sounds of much higher frequencies than humans—50,000 to 60,000 cycles per second compared to only 20,000 cps in people.

may develop because of an inherited malformation (such as hip dysplasia), an old injury or from normal wear and tear.

The first sign of arthritis may be that your dog is stiffer than usual after a rest, but as she moves around the pain seems to go away. Treatment starts by determining the cause, so a trip to the veterinarian is paramount. For routine osteoarthritis, a combination of anti-inflammatory medication (such as buffered aspirin), proper exercise and weight reduction (if your dog is overweight) is usually recommended. Extra weight can put unnecessary stress on your dog's damaged joints.

Hip Dysplasia

Hip dysplasia is an inherited defect that causes abnormal positioning of the bones of the hip joint. With time, the hip often becomes painful and arthritis develops. Although hip dysplasia affects almost every breed of dog, the large breeds are the most severely affected. Diagnosis is made through examination and X-rays, and treatment may involve surgery to reconstruct the joint, removal of the heads of the hip bones or the insertion of an artificial

hip. Medical therapy is the same as for arthritis.

Back Pain

Just like people, dogs can suffer from back problems. One of the first signs of back pain is a reluctance to climb stairs or to jump up onto furniture. Your dog may also cry out in pain when touched or lifted. While many back problems are due to nothing more than sore muscles, some are the result of slipped spinal disks. Mild slippage may cause discomfort only, but more severe slippage can cause partial or complete paralysis.

Although any breed of dog can suffer back problems, long-bodied, short-legged dogs, such as Dachshunds and Corgis, are the most prone. If the dog is overweight, the risk is greatly increased. You should see your veterinarian at the first signs of back pain. Treatment for muscle soreness usually consists of strict rest, muscle relaxants and a course of anti-inflammatory drugs. Severe disk disease requires immediate surgery.

EASING THE PAIN
Slipped disks that cause pain in the neck are a common problem. If your dog is affected, you can help by raising her food bowl off the ground so she doesn't have far to bend. It is also increasingly possible to find a veterinarian trained in chiropractic techniques for dogs.

A MATTER OF BREEDING
Dogs have been selectively bred to accentuate certain features. The Dachshund's short legs (below) were developed so the dog could chase badgers down burrows, but this design has made it vulnerable to back problems.

dwarfed legs

dwarfism affects disks in back

GASTROINTESTINAL PROBLEMS

Worms

Intestinal worms and parasites are extremely common in dogs. In fact, most puppies are born with worms or get them soon afterward with their mother's milk. Most cause few problems in their hosts, but some can cause disease in humans. Sometimes you will be able to see the adult worms in your dog's feces, but generally your veterinarian will need to do a special microscopic examination of the feces to see if your dog has worms. Only then can the proper medication be prescribed to rid your dog of a specific type of worm. Fecal examinations should be a routine part of your dog's yearly physical exam.

ROUNDWORMS

Roundworms are a common problem in puppies.

COMMON INTERNAL WORMS AND PARASITES

WORM	EXPLANATION	DETECTION	PROBLEMS	TREATMENT
Roundworm	Puppies acquire them from their mothers before thay are born. Infection can occur at any age due to ingestion of eggs.	Look like spaghetti in puppy's feces. Eggs also seen in microscopic examination of feces.	Usually mild vomiting and diarrhea. In large numbers can cause weight loss, dull coat and pot belly. Eggs can also infect humans.	Medical treatment, often at time of vaccination.
Hookworm	Inhabit intestine where they ingest blood. Dogs may be infected through mother's milk, through penetration of the skin or by ingesting immature worms.	Invisible to naked eye so fecal examination is required to detect worms or eggs.	Anemia and diarrhea. Contaminated dirt can infect barefoot humans.	Prevention by maintaining good hygiene. Medical treatment required for elimination.
Whipworm	Inhabit large intestine. Caused by unhygenic living conditions.	Worm or eggs usually found by a microscopic exam.	Diarrhea, sometimes with blood and mucus.	Maintain hygiene. Prescription medicine for elimination.
Tapeworm	Inhabit small intestine. Infection through ingestion of carrier (usually fleas but also rabbits and rodents).	Segments of worms visible in feces or dried, rice-like pieces around anus.	Usually harmless.	Prevention by controlling fleas. Prescription medicine for elimination.
Coccidia	Infection caused by unhygenic, crowded living conditions.	Microscopic fecal examination.	Diarrhea.	Maintain hygiene. Easily treated by medication.
Giardia	Infection through drinking contaminated water.	Microscopic fecal examination.	Diarrhea. May also infect humans.	Maintain hygiene. Easily treated by medication.
Heartworm	Carried by mosquitoes and inhabit the heart.	Simple blood test.	Typical signs of heart disease: coughing, rapid breathing, exercise intolerance, weight loss, sudden death.	Prevention by monthly pill.

Vomiting

It's normal for dogs to vomit. How else would they protect themselves from all the junk they pick up and eat? Dogs vomit when they overeat, or when they eat things they're not used to. A simple change in diet or a snack stolen from the garbage can cause a dog to vomit. Dogs also often vomit after feasting on grass, one of their favorite delicacies. Many dogs eat grass regularly.

The best way to settle your dog's stomach if she has just vomited a few times is to give her a rest. Don't feed her for 12 hours. Once she stops looking queasy, give her small amounts of water. You might want to start with ice cubes for her to lick so that she doesn't drink too fast and vomit again. When you reintroduce food, start slowly. There are also special foods you can get from your veterinarian that are highly digestible and can be fed in small portions.

If your dog's vomiting contains blood, if her vomiting continues in spite of being fasted, or if she looks generally unwell, visit your veterinarian right away. Persistant vomiting may indicate poisoning, severe stomach disease, intestinal obstruction, inflammation of the pancreas, kidney or liver failure, infectious diseases (such as Parvovirus or Distemper) or bloat.

Bloat

Bloat, or gastric dilatation and volvulus (GDV), is a true medical emergency, requiring immediate veterinary treatment. During an episode of bloat, the stomach becomes distended with air. It may then rotate so that air cannot escape in either direction. Dogs with bloat retch and try to vomit, but produce nothing. The condition is painful and affected dogs look ill and pant heavily.

If not treated early, bloat leads to shock, often followed by death. Treatment involves decompression and surgery to reposition and secure the stomach. The syndrome is most common in large, deep-chested dogs, such as Great Danes and Saint Bernards.

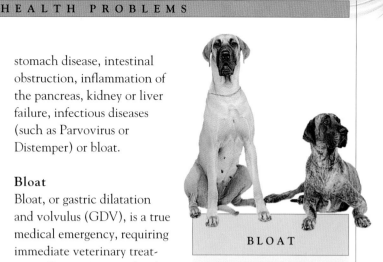

BLOAT

Bloat is a true emergency, requiring immediate medical attention. To reduce the chances of bloat occurring:

- Feed several small meals per day instead of one big one.
- Restrict exercise before and after meals.
- Be aware of the warning signs, such as heavy panting and dry retching, and call your veterinarian immediately.

PREVENTING BLOAT

Bloat can affect any breed, but is most common in large deep-chested dogs, such as Saint Bernards (left). To reduce the chances of bloat occurring, avoid overfeeding these dogs.

stops, begin to feed an easily digestible diet, such as boiled chicken and rice. Over the next few days, mix in her regular food. If the diarrhea doesn't improve within a day, or is bloody, explosive, or painful, see your veterinarian.

Flatulence

Small amounts of gas are a normal product of digestion. Some dogs produce more gas than others. If flatulence is a problem, most of the causes respond quickly to common-sense remedies.

Flatulence is usually caused by overeating, eating too fast, poor-quality diets, changing diet too rapidly or eating garbage. In these cases, the solutions are simple. Try feeding your dog smaller meals, feed a high-quality premium diet, and keep a tight lid on your trash.

Soybeans, found in many commercial dog foods, are a common cause of flatulence. Check the labels on your dog food carefully and avoid soy-based products.

DON'T SHOOT THE MESSENGER
Excessive flatulence is a sign of an abnormal digestive process. If your dog's flatulence is a problem, don't blame her. You can usually reduce the problem by adjusting her diet.

Diarrhea

All dogs get diarrhea at some time during their lives, and the most common cause is diet. Overeating, or eating foods that the intestines aren't used to, will cause diarrhea. Other causes include intestinal parasites, viral diseases (parvovirus), food allergies, digestive disorders, kidney and liver disease and cancer. Most cases of simple diarrhea can be handled at home.

As you do for vomiting (see p. 51), give the intestines a rest. Fast your dog for 24 hours, but provide plenty of water. Once the diarrhea

HOW TO ADMINISTER A PILL

Many common canine health problems respond readily to medication, which will often be supplied by your veterinarian in the form of a pill. Dogs don't like being forced to swallow things so be careful that you administer any pills carefully. Hold the top jaw firmly open, making sure that the dog can't bite you. Then, with the other hand, place the pill as far back on the tongue as you can and push it out of sight. Close the dog's mouth and wait for her to swallow. If she is having difficulty swallowing, stroking the throat may help the pill go down. If your dog has a good appetite, hiding the pill in cheese or peanut butter often works. If your dog is in obvious distress and won't let you hold her muzzle, take her to a veterinarian. It's not worth risking a bite on the hand.

Anal sacs

The anal sacs are situated on either side of the anus, just inside the anal opening. They contain a pungent, fishy smelling fluid, which is normally discharged each time a dog defecates.

Unfortunately, anal sacs often become blocked or infected causing discomfort. If you see your dog dragging her hind end along your carpet or frequently licking her anal area, her anal sacs are probably plugged. Many people mistake an anal sac problem for worms.

Your veterinarian can manually unblock the anal sac opening and empty the sacs. If the sacs are infected, antibiotics are usually necessary. Many dogs need their anal sacs emptied frequently, so, if you wish, your veterinarian can show you how to do it.

URINARY PROBLEMS

Changes in urinary habits

Any sudden changes in a dog's urinary habits merit immediate veterinary attention. Urinary tract infections cause dogs to strain to urinate or to urinate more frequently than usual. Diseases of the prostate gland in male dogs can also cause straining. In both cases, the urine may appear bloody. Some dogs develop stones in their bladder that can block the urethra making urination impossible. If left untreated, urinary blockages can be fatal.

Diabetes and kidney failure (from deterioration of the kidneys), both common diseases of older dogs, cause increased urination and increased thirst. Diabetes can be successfully treated in dogs with insulin injections given at home. Kidney failure is one of the most common causes of death in older dogs. A special diet, adequate fluids and good overall veterinary care will slow the progression of kidney failure and can prolong an older dog's life.

Incontinence

Sometimes a dog will lose urinary control without realizing it; some older spayed females leave puddles while they are sleeping. This type of incontinence responds readily to medication, which your veterinarian can prescribe. Dogs sometimes become incontinent as they grow older. In these cases, more frequent walks will often ease the problem.

KEEPING FIT

Exercise is essential for all dogs, not only young, active ones. A gentle daily walk will keep an older dog trim, fit and happy.

FIRST AID

✚

Knowing how to recognize and react to common emergencies may save your dog's life. But remember, you are not an expert. Your goal should be to prevent further injury and to minimize pain and distress while seeking immediate veterinary care.

A PAINFUL REMINDER
Some dogs love to chase cars and others just have bad road sense. To avoid traumatic injuries or even death, keep your dog leashed in public and fence your yard.

LOOKING FOR TROUBLE
A puppy's natural curiosity can get it into all sorts of trouble. The house and garden are full of things that can cause problems if ingested accidently.

Dogs are lively, curious and adventurous creatures and can get themselves into all sorts of trouble. Unfortunately, it is not uncommon for loose dogs in urban areas to be hit by cars. This kind of traumatic injury can result in fractures, shock, lacerations and bleeding, spinal injuries, internal damage to the chest or abdomen and, sometimes, death.

While this situation is best prevented by keeping your dog leashed or confined to a fenced yard, sometimes a dog will escape and be hit despite your best efforts. If your dog is injured, take her to a veterinarian immediately. However, when you do, make sure you move her carefully (see p. 56).

Dog fights are another common cause of injury, particularly among male dogs. Bite wounds from dog fights can be serious, especially when the attacker is large and the victim is small. Deep wounds must be treated by a veterinarian immediately. Minor wounds are not emergencies, but should be cleaned carefully (see p. 56). Any eye wound should have immediate professional care.

AN UNHEALTHY APPETITE
A dog's love of food will often lead it to trouble, especially in the kitchen. If your dog gets too close to the stove, there is a serious risk of it being burned by hot pots, splashes of hot cooking oil or naked flames. Electrical burns are also common in puppies and young dogs who think it's fun to chew electrical cords (see p. 57).

Again, prevention is the best policy. Keep your dog away from the stove when you are cooking and keep electrical cords unplugged or out of reach at all times.

Inquisitive dogs may also swallow dangerous objects or poisons that are kept around the house. Small objects sometimes get lodged in the back of a dog's throat, obstructing breathing, or may be swallowed and pass down to the digestive tract. If breathing is obstructed, the dog may be very distressed and great care should be taken when handling it (see p. 57).

The signs of poisoning vary depending on the substance ingested (see p. 57), so don't wait for signs to appear if you suspect that your dog has eaten something dangerous. Many common household items, such as bleach, weed killer, antifreeze, insecticide and disinfectant, can be fatal to dogs if ingested.

HEATSTROKE

One emergency that can usually be prevented is heatstroke. This may occur after excessive exercise on a hot day, but is more commonly caused by careless owners who leave their pet in a car. Never leave a dog in a parked car on a hot day, even if you leave the windows open, as temperatures can soar in minutes. If quick action is not taken (see p. 57), permanent brain damage or death may follow. Dogs that are obese, have a heart condition or have short faces (such as Pugs) are at the greatest risk from heatstroke.

TOO MUCH OF A GOOD THING Exercise is essential for a dog, but don't overdo it on a hot day. Heatstroke is a potentially life-threatening situation.

APPLYING A MUZZLE

A dog that is injured or in pain from any cause should be approached cautiously, calmly and slowly. Pain and fright may make any animal dangerous. Never put your face close to the animal. Applying a muzzle with a cord, gauze or cloth will allow you to handle a dog without being bitten.

Step 1 Using the cloth, cord or gauze, gently wrap it around the dog's muzzle to make a loop.

Step 2 Take the ends and wrap them around the muzzle again.

Step 3 Tie the ends behind the head. If the animal is having problems breathing, apply the muzzle loosely.

A READY-REFERENCE EMERGENCY CHART

EMERGENCY	SIGNS	TREATMENT
Unconscious dog	Dog is motionless but has pulse and heartbeat.	• Clear airway and pull tongue forward (see p. 58). • Check for heartbeat (see p. 38). • If you think that the dog may have any broken bones handle extremely carefully (see Suspected fractures). • Take dog to veterinarian immediately.
Suspected fractures	Severe pain, dog not putting weight on leg.	• Handle carefully to cause minimum disturbance. • A small, calm dog can be lifted with both hands to support body. Keep back straight. If a limb is broken, let it dangle while supporting body (see p. 59). • Place larger dog on stretcher without twisting body (see p. 59). • Do not apply splint yourself. • Take dog to veterinarian immediately.
Shock	Dog is weak, cold to touch, has pale or grayish gums and is breathing rapidly.	• Let dog lie in comfortable position. • Keep dog warm by loosely wrapping in blanket or towel. • Take dog to veterinarian immediately.
Minor wound	Shallow with only slight bleeding.	• Clip wound area free of hair. • Clean with antiseptic. • See your veterinarian soon after to prevent infection.
Deep wound	Gaping so underlying tissue or internal organs are visible. Severe bleeding.	• Control bleeding with pressure bandage made of gauze sponge or piece of cloth. • If wound bleeds through wrap, add layers. • If area can't be bandaged, apply direct pressure. DO NOT APPLY TORNIQUET. • Rush dog to veterinarian; maintain pressure on wound.
Drowning	Dog is motionless in water.	• Clean any discharge from the nose and mouth and pull tongue forward (see p. 58). • Hold dog by hind legs and gently swing to drain lungs of water (see p. 59). • If dog does not start breathing, start CPR (see p. 58). • Take dog to veterinarian immediately.

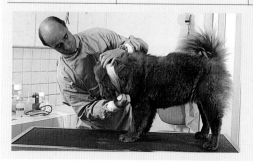

EXPERT TREATMENT

Your veterinarian is a qualified expert. If your dog is in obvious distress, take it to a veterinarian as soon as possible. Do what you can to alleviate pain, but don't waste valuable time with complicated first-aid procedures.

OUT OF ACTION

A serious injury, such as a broken leg, will make your dog's life quite uncomfortable for a while. Do what you can to make this time as pleasant as possible and make sure that your dog is not put in a situation that might aggravate the injury.

EMERGENCY	SIGNS	TREATMENT
Burns	Flame or hot oil comes into contact with fur or skin.	• Cool affected area with cold water. • Apply a cold compress while contacting veterinarian.
Electric shock	Chewing electrical cords can lead to collapse, loss of consciousness, inability to breath, cardiac arrest, shock and burns to mouth.	• Turn off appliance and disconnect cord before touching dog. • Administer CPR if necessary (see p. 58) and take dog to veterinarian immediately.
Heatstroke	Heavy panting, red gums, weakness, collapse. Brain damage or death may follow if immediate help is not sought.	• Lower body temperature gradually with cool water to 103°F (39.5°C). • If ice packs are available, apply them to head and neck. • Take dog to veterinarian immediately.
Choking	Dog is in obvious discomfort, shaking head, salivating, gagging, putting paw to mouth. Gums may turn blue or pale gray and dog may collapse.	• Try to look in dog's mouth. • If you can see and grab object, remove it but be careful that dog doesn't bite. • With a small or medium-sized dog, hold upside down and shake. • If you can't dislodge the object, rush dog to your veterinarian. If your dog has swallowed the object, X-rays and surgery may be required to remove it. • Fish hooks can be removed from dog's mouth or tongue by cutting off barbed tip with pliers. This usually requires tranquilization and the help of a veterinarian.
Poisoning	Twitching, excessive salivation, vomiting, nervousness, diarrhea, difficult breathing, change in pupil size.	• Take dog to veterinarian immediately. • If you know what the dog ate, take the container to the hospital to show the veterinarian.
Seizure	Can be caused by epilepsy, brain injury, poisoning, brain tumor. Causes twitching, crying out, salivation, vomiting, emptying bladder or bowels.	• Don't put hands in or near dog's mouth—a convulsing dog has no control of its actions and may bite you involuntarily. A dog won't swallow its tongue. • It is best not to handle a dog during a seizure, but if you must move it, use a towel or blanket for protection. • Seizures usually end after a short while, but if they continue take your dog to an animal hospital that can handle emergencies.

KEEP YOUR VETERINARIAN'S EMERGENCY NUMBER BY YOUR PHONE AT ALL TIMES

EMERGENCY PROCEDURES

Most health problems are best treated by a veterinarian, but in the event of a sudden accident, immediate action may be required. Knowing what to do in an emergency could be the difference between life and death.

If your dog is unconscious and is not breathing and/or has no heartbeat, administer cardio-pulmonary resuscitation (CPR) and call your veterinarian as soon as possible. CPR is a combination of mouth-to-nose resuscitation and cardiac massage.

MOUTH-TO-NOSE RESUSCITATION

Step 1 Remove any mucus or foreign material from mouth. Pull tongue forward.

Step 2 If dog is unconscious, place your mouth over the nostrils and blow a steady stream of air for 2 to 3 seconds. If dog is small, place your mouth over the dog's mouth and nose. Watch for the chest to rise.

Step 3 Pause for 2 to 3 seconds to allow air to exit lungs. Continue until normal breathing resumes, which may take as long as an hour. Feel for heartbeat and apply cardiac massage if needed.

🐾 CARDIAC MASSAGE

If dog is unconscious and has no heartbeat, apply cardiac massage.

Step 1 Place hand on chest behind elbow and press down gently but firmly (right). Do this five or six times at one-second intervals.

Step 2 Alternate massage with breath from your artificial respiration (see p. 58). Try for 10 minutes.

🐾 DRAINING WATER FROM DOG'S LUNGS

Step 1 If dog is motionless, first clear any discharge from nose and mouth and pull tongue forward (see p. 58, step 1).

Step 2 To drain water from dog's lungs, hold the animal by its hind legs and gently swing it back and forth (left).

ACCIDENTS CAN HAPPEN
Most dogs are good swimmers, but occasionally an unfortunate dog will fall into a swimming pool and could drown.

MOVING AN INJURED DOG

If you suspect that a dog has a fracture, handle the dog so as to cause minimum disturbance. This is especially important if there has been a fracture of the spine, as sudden movement can lead to paralysis.

Check that the airway is not blocked before moving the dog. Do not attempt to apply a splint yourself as this may cause unnecessary stress and waste valuable time. Get the dog to a veterinarian immediately.

Moving a large dog
Carefully place dog on a board or stretcher, without twisting the body.

Moving a small dog
Carefully lift dog with both hands to support the whole body. Try to let the fractured limb dangle.

TRAINING YOUR DOG

*Humans have externalized their
wisdom—stored it in museums, libraries,
the expertise of the learned. Dog wisdom
is inside the blood and bones.*

DONALD McCAIG (b. 1940),
American author

HOW DOGS LEARN

Whether you are bringing home a new puppy or an older dog, it's important to get off to a good start. Remember, your new pet doesn't know the rules of the house. It is your job to show your dog the correct behavior and teach "canine manners."

PUNISHMENT AND REWARD
The best form of punishment is a reprimand, firm but never harsh (below). Once the bad behavior has ceased, reward your pet with praise or a food treat (bottom).

To teach your new dog effectively, it is helpful to understand how animals learn. One of the primary ways learning occurs is through the relationship between a behavior and its consequence. An animal performs a certain behavior and this results in something in return. The relationship between a behavior and its consequence can be either positive or negative, and with repetition, a dog will soon learn the connection.

Reward and punishment both involve a positive relationship between a behavior and its consequence. In other words, the more you do, the more you get, although this consequence may be good or bad.

REWARD
Positive reinforcement (or reward) is the state or event that increases the likelihood a behavior will be repeated. Good behavior, therefore, will increase if immediately followed by a reward. This may be food or simply praise—anything that sends the dog a clear message of approval. The reward need not be the same thing each time. In fact, by varying the reward, you can make learning more fun for you and your dog. When done properly, positive reinforcement is an excellent way to shape a dog's behavior.

PUNISHMENT
Punishment also involves a positive relationship between behavior and consequence. In this case, however, the more you do, the more you get, but what you get is bad. Each time your dog performs an unwanted behavior, the consequences are unpleasant and this should make the behavior decrease. In order for punishment to be effective, however, you must see evidence that the behavior has decreased or ceased. If it has not, then you are probably not punishing the correct behavior.

Punishment is a very difficult tool to use correctly. Excessive punishment can result in fear and aggression, which are counterproductive to learning. On the other hand, punishment that is too mild will not stop the behavior. Either way, it is always easier to teach what you want, rather than punish what you do not want.

NEGATIVE REINFORCEMENT

Negative reinforcement means that there is a negative relationship between a behavior and its consequences. The more you do, the less you get, but what you get is bad. In other words, good behavior prevents something bad and as a result the behavior will increase. A human example would be driving within the speed limit to avoid a ticket. As with punishment, this is a difficult tool to use correctly.

TIMING & FREQUENCY

Of vital importance for learning is the timing and frequency of reward or punishment. As far as timing is concerned, reward or punishment must occur within 5 to 15 seconds of the performance of the target behavior. Remember, behavior is something that occurs all the time, so the last thing the animal does before receiving the reward or punishment is what you affect. A delay of 30 seconds may mean the animal is doing something else when the reward or punishment occurs.

Behavior can be rewarded or punished continuously or intermittently, with differing results. Continuous reward means that every time the animal performs the behavior it receives a reward. A problem with this rate of reinforcement is that when there are no longer rewards, the animal often ceases performing the behavior.

Intermittent reward, on the other hand, means that not every performance of a behavior is rewarded. Instead, the reward may come after two times or five times, or after performing for a certain period of time—the key is that the reward is not always given. This tends to increase the rate and persistence of behavior. Why? Because the animal never knows if this is the time it will be rewarded. In fact, this is often the way bad behaviors are inadvertently reinforced and maintained.

For example, perhaps your dog is barking to come inside. He barks for five minutes and you open the door to let him in. What happened here? Well, you probably let the dog in to avoid bothering the neighbors; however, the dog learned that five minutes of barking opens the door. In the future, the dog will be willing to bark even longer to get inside. See how bad behaviors can be reinforced without trying?

FIRM BUT GENTLE

Playful, active dogs, such as these adorable Löwchens, are naturally willful creatures. However, with firm but gentle training, they will quickly learn what is and isn't acceptable behavior.

"GOOD DOG"

A good rule of thumb is to praise your dog five times more than you punish. Here, a quick pat lets this Golden Retriever know that it is behaving well.

THE WELL-BEHAVED DOG

It is never too early to start teaching your new dog or puppy how to behave around the house. Set the rules and stick to them and before long your dog will know exactly what is and isn't acceptable.

WALK ON THE WILD SIDE
Puppies, such as these Cavalier King Charles Spaniels, love to nip and fight with each other in play. This sort of behavior, however, can be harmful to people, especially young children. You should teach your pups to play with people gently from the outset.

A good rule of thumb in early training is to think about the things you will expect of your pet when he is grown. Will he have to climb stairs? Then teach him. Will you want to put a leash on him, keep him off furniture and out of certain rooms? Then teach your puppy these rules and tasks early on. Start off on the road to good behavior from the outset.

PLAYTIME
Dogs like to play; this is one of their endearing qualities. With proper play, you and your pet can bond, have fun and stay healthy. However, you must teach your pup what is and isn't acceptable behavior when he plays with people.

Young puppies like to chase and nip, but this should be discouraged. One of the things that puppies are learning when they bite other puppies, is how much pressure causes pain. If you watch puppies at play, when one puppy bites too hard, the other puppy will yelp. This usually results in puppy number one being more gentle. We, as owners, need to send the message that those puppy bites hurt. When your puppy puts its teeth on you, yelp and say "ouch" or "no." Let the puppy know in a verbal way that it hurts.

Hitting the puppy, holding its mouth closed and pushing it away may be ineffective. You may only get the puppy more excited and result in increased biting as he takes your harsh methods to mean you wish to play harder. If all else fails, leave. Social isolation is a powerful tool for puppies. They do not like to be alone, and if you leave they lose their playmate. Each and every family member must follow these rules. Never encourage your puppy to jump and bite at any family members, even in play.

64

BED TIME

A puppy should have a small, quiet, safe area to rest in. A crate can work nicely if you allow the puppy some time to get used to it. Try offering treats and keeping the initial times in the crate brief. Never let your puppy out if he is whining or barking, as this sends the message that making noise opens the door.

For an older dog, a small room with a dog bed works well. You might also think about letting your puppy or older dog sleep in your room, either in a crate or dog bed. This is a good bonding experience. You should try to incorporate your pet into the home, not isolate it in the kitchen or in a crate while people are elsewhere.

HANDLING

As your pet grows, you will often need to handle him. You may need to clean out his ears, wipe his feet, bathe or groom him or open his mouth to give medication. By teaching your pet to accept these things from an early age, he will soon learn that you mean no harm.

So, every day, when your pet is quiet (perhaps just after a nap), gently and calmly run your hands over his body.

Lift the ears and look inside them, gently open the mouth, roll him over and check his stomach. Touch the paws as you might if you needed to wipe them dry. If your pet will eventually have a long-haired coat, have short grooming sessions at least three times a week.

While you do these things, praise your pet in a quiet, soft voice and occasionally reward him with a food treat. These sessions should be short and pleasant, stopping just short of excitement. Let your puppy know that good things happen when the two of you interact.

The same holds true for your pet's possessions and food. While your puppy eats, gently pet him. Place your hand in the food bowl and perhaps drop in a tasty morsel. Praise your puppy for allowing you to interact with him while he eats.

SWEET DREAMS
By letting your dog sleep inside the house in a dog bed, you will make him feel like part of the family.

A FRIEND FOR LIFE
If you handle your dog regularly from an early age, it will make life a lot easier when you need to groom him or administer medicine. This Siberian Husky loves the attention.

HOUSETRAINING

When a new puppy enters your life, certain training tasks must become a priority if the experience is to be an enjoyable one for both parties. The first of these is housetraining.

A MATTER OF TIMING
It's important that you quickly establish a routine for your puppy. Feed your pup at the same times each day and make sure that someone is home to take him outside afterward. Your pup is most likely to eliminate within 20 minutes of eating.

AVOIDING AN ACCIDENT
Remember, small puppies have a small capacity to hold urine or stool and should be taken outside often.

Housetraining your puppy begins with a good feeding and watering routine. Establish set times for eating from the outset. A young dog needs to eat several times a day so this means that he will also need to eliminate several times daily. Whenever possible, feeding should be scheduled when people will be home to allow your puppy access to the proper elimination location.

Your puppy is most likely to eliminate within 10 to 20 minutes after eating or immediately after waking or playing. Your housetraining will be most successful if you can take your puppy outside at these times. The focus of housetraining should then be teaching your puppy where to go and what kind of surface to go on. With encouragement, your puppy should soon learn that where to go is outside, and what to go on is grass, gravel or concrete (whichever surface is most available).

INSIDE THE HOME
Supervision and confinement are the two most important tools in successful housetraining. When you are home with your puppy, keep an eye on him at all times. Keep him in the room with you, using a leash if necessary to prevent him wandering off and making a mess. You can leash him to you or to a piece of furniture, but just keep him in sight.

When you notice restlessness or whining, or if the puppy is lying still but not sleeping, hustle him outside; he may be telling you that he has a full bladder or bowel.

If you cannot supervise your puppy, confinement may be necessary. Try using child gates or a dog crate if the puppy is used to it and is not left in it too long. A small, puppy-proof room, devoid of dangerous items the puppy could eat and with an easily washable floor, will work well.

Do not confine the puppy so frequently that it feels isolated. A puppy is a sociable animal and needs to be with people or other pets.

GOING OUTSIDE
When you take your pet outside, you need to let him know what he is supposed to do. Taking him out the same door and to the same location

is helpful. Remember to plan the trips outside to coincide with his need to eliminate. Then, allow the puppy some time to move about, sniff and explore. Use a key phrase to encourage him.

When he actually begins to eliminate, praise profusely! You can't overdo the praise at this time. Use your key phrase so that he will begin to associate it with elimination. Once he has eliminated, it is time to play.

TRAINING TROUBLES
What can you do about a puppy that goes outside and does not eliminate? Or worse yet, comes inside and eliminates in the house? Several things could be contributing to these situations. First, the puppy was not outside when he had to eliminate. Second, someone was not supervising the puppy inside. Third, the puppy was allowed to play and wander and did not eliminate while outside. We want to send the message, eliminate first, play second. It may even be necessary to take the puppy outside, have him eliminate and then bring him back in for a few moments before letting him out again to play.

If your puppy does not eliminate when you take him outside, bring him in and either confine him or watch him closely for any signs that he may need to go. When he begins to exhibit any

of these signs, whisk him outside to the correct location. Don't forget to praise him when he eliminates.

What should you do if your new puppy has an accident inside? If you did not see it happen, do not bring the puppy back and punish him. Remember, unless you reward or punish a puppy within 15 seconds or less, the puppy does not know what he is being punished for. Just clean up the mess and vow to supervise him better in the future. However, if you are right there and your puppy begins to squat, this is the time to use a loud, firm voice and shout "outside!" Then swiftly take your puppy outside to the appropriate location for elimination. If elimination then occurs, immediately switch gears and praise him profusely.

A HELPING HAND
Go outside with your puppy for the first few weeks of training to make sure that elimination is taking place.

BETTER SAFE THAN SORRY
You may need to confine your pups in the early stages of housetraining just to be on the safe side.

TRAINING YOUR DOG

There are many ways to train a dog, but positive reinforcement methods are becoming increasingly popular. Positive reinforcement has the advantage of motivating your dog to "want" to learn and obey.

EARLY LEARNERS
The sooner you start training a dog, the easier it will be for all concerned. Even these tiny Papillon pups are not too young. However, if you have adopted an older dog, don't despair. Dogs learn easily, and can be taught "new tricks" at any age.

FOOD REWARDS
Food rewards should be small, but something that the dog likes. For this Schnauzer (right), a small dog biscuit works well. Rewards should be used continuously until the dog knows the command and then in an intermittent and unpredictable pattern.

Domestic dogs have evolved from wolves that live in packs. In such groups, there are rules that establish leadership and control social interactions. When a dog comes into a human home, it expects to follow rules and obey a leader. A critical goal of training is to help your new dog recognize you as its leader. Setting boundaries will make your pet feel more comfortable, while establishing you as the leader of the pack.

Positive reinforcement is an excellent way to change behavior and the key to training your new puppy successfully (see p. 62). While you will need to reprimand your pet from time to time, always look for good behavior and reward it. Never let good behavior go unnoticed.

STARTING EARLY
It is never too early to start training your pet. In fact, from the moment you bring your puppy home, his learning begins. So, why wait until six months of age to teach him other commands and be faced with bad habits to undo? What is most important

with early training is to be patient. Keep training sessions short, and use methods that are easy on both you and your pet.

Training an older dog is not much different from training a puppy. Some will already know the basic commands, and practice and positive reinforcement may be all that are needed. Others may have developed bad habits that will take time to change, but don't get discouraged. If you cannot make progress on your own, an obedience class may be helpful. With persistence, any dog can be taught new tricks.

TRAINING TIPS
Dog training can be done without using leashes or forced manipulations of the pet's body. However, a leash does have its

advantages. Even if you are not holding onto the end, it signals to your pet that you are its leader. It will also help your puppy get used to wearing a leash when walking.

Dogs watch our movements carefully and hand signals are very effective when training—especially if you are holding food. Hand signals and food that guide the dog into the proper positions can be used to train many traditional commands, such as sit, down, stand, heel, stay and come.

For dogs that love food, a great way to teach new tasks is to use food as the reinforcer, coupled with praise. Other dogs may respond better to a toy, playtime or praise alone.

It is very important that food rewards are only used intermittently, although they should not be eliminated altogether. The goal is to make these food rewards unpredictable. Verbal praise, on the other hand, should be used every time your pet performs correctly.

When teaching the basic commands, say the command one time and wait for your pet to perform the task. Always try to end the session on a high note, with lots of praise.

WHERE & WHEN

A quiet area, with few distractions, is a good place to start training. Any number of family members can participate, but only one person should train the pet at a time. Training sessions need not be long—10 to 15 minutes is long enough for a puppy. Judge the length of time by your puppy's response. If your puppy initially performs well but then loses interest, it may be time to stop.

Do not confine training to regulated sessions. Simple exercises can be incorporated into the daily routine, such as asking your pet to sit prior to feeding or going outside. When food is used as a reinforcer, it is best to train before mealtime when your puppy is hungry. If your pet "wants" something it is more likely to comply.

FINISH ON A HIGH NOTE
Keep training sessions short and interesting. Always try to end on a high note, immediately after the dog has successfully performed a task.

"WATCH ME!"

One task that should be taught to any dog you train is a "watch me" command. This serves to get your dog's attention so that you can then give further commands.

1 With your dog facing you, point to your eyes, and say "watch me." Try to maintain eye contact for about 10 seconds.

2 Release your pet and say "good dog." Repeat frequently at various locations.

TEACHING "SIT"

The fact that a dog has an inflexible spine means that if they tip their heads up far enough, they will sit. You can use this to your advantage when teaching a dog to sit in response to a spoken command. Remember, your puppy already knows how to sit; what you want to do is to produce the response on command.

By using a food treat, you can easily get your pup to sit (see below). Repeat this six to eight times, praising him every time he performs the task.

Only say the word "sit" once as you maneuver the puppy into a sit. Be careful not to hold the food too high above his nose as he might jump up to reach it. Remember to phase out the food reward as soon as your puppy gets used to the command. You want to make sure your puppy will sit even if you do not have food.

1 With your dog facing you, hold a food reward between your fingers and thumb with your palm facing up, in front of the puppy's nose.

2 Then move it up and slightly back over his head. Say "sit" once as you do this. As your puppy follows the treat with his eyes and head, he will sit down!

Praise your dog every time he performs the command correctly.

3 Praise the puppy, saying "good sit," and give him the food reward.

TEACHING "DOWN"

To teach a puppy to lie down, we again look to food to help us guide the puppy into position (right).

You may find that some puppies will not go into the down position when you push the food between their legs. For those pups, it may be necessary to take the food and slowly pull it forward. The puppy should follow it down. Again, once the puppy can associate the word with the action begin to phase out the food, but keep praising.

1 Place your puppy in a sit. Take a food treat, say "down" and quickly bring it from in front of the puppy's nose down to the ground. See how the head follows.

2 Now take the treat and push it between the front legs. As the puppy tries to follow it, the back end will slide into a down position. Say "good down" and give him the food reward.

TEACHING "STAND"

Getting your pup to stand is easy; getting him to do so on command is a little harder.

1 To get your puppy to stand, first place him in a sitting or down position.

2 Take a food treat and pull it forward, away from the puppy, as you say "stand." (If the dog is lying down, pull the treat upward.)

TRAINING TIPS

Try combining these tasks in different combinations. Vary the order, trying to get the puppy to do them with only one food treat or none at all.

Don't confine training to a set session. Employ these tasks throughout the day. Ask your puppy to sit before eating, going out or being petted. Make sure that your puppy will do these tasks whenever you ask and in any location. This will come in handy when you want him to sit for guests at the front door or to wait for a leash before a walk. By controlling your pet's behavior you establish yourself as the "leader."

3 As your puppy gets up, say "good stand" and give him the food reward.

When first teaching a dog to come, using a leash may help.

🐾 TEACHING "COME"

Teaching a dog to come (or "the recall" as it is called in obedience training) is an extremely important and often difficult task. If your dog will reliably come when called, many disasters can be avoided. Yet, often this is not accomplished. Attention to a few details will make this command easier to instill in your dog.

First, never call your dog to you and punish or yell at him. If you call your dog and then punish him, why would he ever want to come in future? Another common pitfall is calling your dog away from something fun. Think about it. So often we call our dogs to take them inside, to take away some object they're happily chewing or to put them in confinement because we are going out. It is important, then, to practice calling your dog under other circumstances. When he comes, give him a pat, or a hug or a food reward and send him back to play. This helps him learn that when he comes to you, it does not always signal the end of something good.

PLAN FOR SUCCESS

At first, keep the distances short, but gradually make your puppy come farther to reach you. You can also practice this task by calling your puppy to you from across the room. If at first he will not come, crouch down, open your arms and make your voice very inviting. Remember to give him a good reason to come to you.

Once your puppy begins to come more reliably, add a "sit" to the end of the come command. Occasionally touch the collar as well. This will get your puppy used to being called and then taken to a new location.

1 Stand close to your puppy with a food reward in your hand.

2 Back up a short distance, wiggle the treat and say "come."

Teaching your dog to come to you on command will make life a lot easier.

3 As your puppy approaches, say "good come" and give him a treat when he gets to you.

In traditional obedience training, the dog is taught to heel on the left of the owner.

🐾 TEACHING "HEEL"
There are two methods you can use to teach "heel" or the follow command.

Method 1 is an extension of the "watch me" command (see p. 69). Repeat this several times and add the command "heel." At first move only short distances but gradually move farther and for longer periods as the puppy learns to stay with you.

1 With your dog in a sit by your side, say "watch me" and make eye contact.

2 Take a couple of steps forward. If your pup is really watching and tries to maintain eye contact, he will move with you.

3 Stop, and when your puppy also stops say "good dog."

Method 2 uses food as a lure to position the pup and lead him forward.

Again, move only a short distance at first so that the puppy is successful. If your puppy lags behind, slap your thigh and use vocal encouragement to keep him with you. To prevent him from forging ahead, you may need to turn or to use a leash.

1 With your puppy sitting at your side, take a food treat in each hand.

2 Place the hand nearest your puppy down at your side and wiggle the treat so that the pup sees it. Say "heel" and move forward a few steps.

3 Raise this hand and bring your other hand in front of the pup (using the upward motion previously used to teach sit) and say "sit."

⚜ TEACHING "STAY"
Teaching "stay" can be another difficult task, so it will be a lot easier if you try for small successes, rather than long stays.

Initially, reward your puppy with food and praise if he does not move for 5 seconds. Then gradually increase the duration of the stay. The same applies to the distance between you and the puppy. Do not go too far at first. This will only result in your puppy breaking the stay and failing the task. Instead, you should always plan for success. If your puppy breaks the stay, the chances are you have gone too far or kept him waiting for too long. If he breaks the stay, promptly fetch him, place him back in position and try again—this time for a shorter distance and less time. When he holds the stay, praise profusely.

1 With your puppy in a sit, place your hand, palm open, in front of his face.

2 Say "stay" in a firm voice as you back away.

Teaching a dog to stay on command may avoid a disaster, especially if you live in a busy urban area.

3 If your puppy does not move for five seconds, reward with food and praise.

 TEACHING "FETCH"
Fetch is a fun game for both you and your puppy, and will provide your pet with much of the exercise it requires. Some dogs will fetch more eagerly than others as certain breeds, such as retrievers, naturally pick things up and carry them around. The hard part is getting them to give them back.

Playing fetch is a great way to stop your dog from getting bored and keep him in shape at the same time.

1 Toss a toy or ball a short distance. When the puppy looks to the toy, say "fetch."

2 As the puppy picks it up, say "good dog" and "come."

3 To get your puppy to drop the toy on command, hold up another toy and say "drop it."

GOLDEN RULES FOR TRAINING

- Keep training sessions short and interesting.
- Say the command one time, and wait for the puppy to perform the task.
- Use food initially to guide the puppy into the correct position. Once the puppy knows the task, give food rewards less frequently.
- Use praise every time your dog performs correctly.
- Try to end every session on a high note, when the dog has completed a task successfully.

4 When your puppy drops the toy, praise him.

5 Now throw the new toy.

COMMON PROBLEMS

*The key to changing unwanted behavior is to recognize what is
motivating and maintaining the behavior. Understanding why
your dog is doing these behaviors is the first step in controlling them.
What follows are some common problems and ways to combat them.*

A REAL HANDFUL
Some people don't mind a dog
jumping on them, but with a large
dog, such as this Newfoundland,
the effect can be overwhelming.
If you want your dog to jump
up, teach it to do so
only on command.

JUMPING UP

Many pet owners complain
about their dog jumping up
on them or their visitors.
However, owners often
inadvertently reinforce this
behavior in their pets. A
common error is to let your
dog jump up in certain
situations and not in others.
It's very difficult for a dog to
understand when jumping is
acceptable and when it is not.

Furthermore, jumping up
usually gets attention—even if
that attention is just pushing
the dog away—and this may
be enough to maintain
the behavior. For young
animals, pushing may
be interpreted as a signal
for play. Crouching down to
greet your pup is a good way
to start training him not
to jump. If you do want
your dog up on you for
petting, then teach
him to jump up
on command.
That way the
behavior is
under your
verbal
control.

To eliminate unwanted
jumping behavior successfully,
you need to identify any
and all reinforcement for the
behavior. If the jumping up
occurs when you come home,
one good strategy is to ignore
your dog until he obeys a
command, such as sit. Do
not give him any attention
until he is sitting calmly.

Another technique that
may work is to anticipate the
jumping behavior and startle
the dog with a very loud
noise. This often gets the dog
to back away so you can then
command the dog to sit before
giving it attention. For some
dogs it may be even more
effective to rush at them
just as they approach you.
Many dogs will back away
to avoid being stepped on,
at which point you can
command them to sit.

What about the dog that
jumps up on visitors? There
are several ways to discourage
this behavior. Keep your dog
on a leash when greeting
people or have your dog
practice "sit" and "stay" in the
doorway of your home. Get
people he knows to approach
him with a food treat and
pet him if he does not jump.
Then practice with people
he is less familiar with. What
is important is practice and
patience. It is not enough to

make your dog sit to be greeted only once in awhile. In order for your dog to learn, he should always sit to be greeted, even if only by members of the family.

For persistent jumpers, headcollars can be a very helpful additional control. These devices encircle both the muzzle and the neck and control the movement of the dog's head. If you control where the head goes, you can control the dog to sit, stay and not jump up on people. These collars do not require strength nor do they choke the dog as training collars do.

🐾 DIGGING

Dogs like to dig and they do it for many reasons. Many breeds, such as terriers, were bred to hunt small animals, and if there are moles or other animals underground they will dig to get to them. The northern breeds, such as Samoyeds or Huskies, will often dig to create a cool spot to lie in. Other dogs dig just because they enjoy it.

Remember, knowing the motivation helps determine how to change the behavior. If your dog is digging because of predatory behavior, this will be extremely difficult to

stop. What you really need to do is get rid of the stimulus.

If a dog is digging to make a cool spot to lie in, then creating a shaded area in the yard might help. If the climate is hot, it may be better to keep the dog inside on certain days.

If your dog digs just because he loves digging, a good option is to set aside an acceptable digging spot in your yard. This spot can be made of a different material, such as sand, or can be surrounded with wood. Then start burying things there that your dog would like to dig up. Begin by burying things close to the surface so your dog can easily smell them. Bury something every day until your dog will reliably go to that spot to dig. Then bury things on a more intermittent basis.

If a dog is digging to expend energy, you might not be providing him with enough exercise and attention. A young puppy is easily bored so don't just leave him in the yard.

FACE TO FACE

Dogs often greet each other face to face, and this may be what they are trying to do when they jump on us. Crouching down to greet a pup may help eliminate jumping behavior.

PROTECTING YOUR GARDEN

Dogs like to dig—it's a fact of life. To keep your pup out of the flower beds, set aside a place in the garden where he is allowed to dig.

NATURAL BEHAVIOR

Barking is a typical canine behavior but it can be annoying for owners and neighbors alike. While you will never stop a dog from barking altogether, you can at least get the behavior under control.

BARKING

Dogs bark for many reasons—to communicate, to indicate excitement and to alert people to intruders. When you have a dog that barks excessively, it is important to determine the motivation.

Some dogs are left outside all day by their owners and drive the neighbors crazy with their barking. This is very difficult to stop and you should instead look at why the dog needs to be left outside in the first place. Is it because you can't trust your dog in the house? If so, then there are other problems that need to be treated first.

If your dog is barking while you are home, and you are not able to make him stop, then you need to teach him a "quiet" command. If you have tried yelling at your pet to be quiet without success, you can assume that he hasn't associated silence with the word you are using. What you need to do is establish a clear association between your command and the desired response (see box).

If you are having difficulty teaching your dog the "quiet" command, you might want to try using a headcollar. When the dog is wearing a headcollar, you can attach a leash to it and use it to close the dog's mouth while you give the command.

A last-resort method to control barking is to use products that administer a correction when the dog barks. Bark collars that use a noise deterrent or those that use a citronella spray are effective. Shock collars are not recommended.

TEACHING "QUIET"

To train a dog to stop barking, you must first get it to start. So, find something that will reliably get the dog to bark, such as the doorbell.

1 Standing in the doorway, ring the doorbell and allow your dog to bark a few times.

2 Hold a treat over the dog's nose while saying "quiet." (It doesn't matter what the word is as long as you use the same one every time.)

3 When the dog stops barking to sniff, praise him. Repeat, each time requiring the dog to be silent for longer periods.

STEALING

Dogs love to pick things up in their mouths, which can be very frustrating to owners, but be careful not to overreact. If you shriek and start chasing the dog, you might frighten him or unwittingly buy into a game. Many dogs love a chase and will flaunt their prize to entice you.

So, when your puppy first begins to take things, never chase him. Instead, try crouching down and gently asking the dog to come. If this doesn't work, try running away. If your pup chases you, you can then stop and praise the puppy for coming to you.

When he comes, try to take the object while saying "drop it." You should teach your puppy a "drop it" command from an early age. Offer him a toy and when he takes it, say "good dog." Then grab the toy lightly, and say "drop it." If the dog lets go, praise him.

If your puppy won't drop the object, try trading with him. Offer him a food treat while saying "drop it." Once the dog drops the object, give the treat to him. Practice taking things from your dog, saying "drop it," throughout the day. Quickly phase out the food reward so that it becomes unpredictable.

Always reward your dog with praise and, if the stolen object is not precious, give it back to him. That way your pet learns that although you take things, you also sometimes give them back.

Food stealing is a more difficult problem to stop. If there is food within reach, it is a rare dog that will not attempt to eat it. Therefore, it is really up to the owner to keep people food out of the dog's way. Sometimes the problem is that your puppy has too much freedom. Supervision is a vital part of early training.

As a last resort, there are a number of products that may help control some stealing behaviors. These include motion sensors that will go off when the dog breaks the field of the alarm. These can be used to alert the owner when the dog has gone into a certain room. For some dogs, the sound of the alarm will be enough of a deterrent. Mats that produce a mild electrical charge will keep dogs out of certain rooms, but these are not recommended.

DOG TOYS

If your pup loves to play tug-of-war with household items, try giving him toys to play with instead. This way, when you teach him to drop it, you can give it back afterward.

A FAIR TRADE

One sure way to get your pet to drop an object is to offer him a favorite treat. This Irish Terrier has just learned that giving up objects has its rewards.

PREVENTING AGGRESSION

Firm, but careful handling from an early age should ensure that your dog is well behaved around people and other animals. Here are some tips:

- Establish yourself as your pet's leader from the outset.
- Always reward calm, subordinate behavior.
- Avoid punishing your dog. If you must reprimand, a firm, verbal rebuke is enough.
- Get your dog used to being handled by all members of the family from an early age.
- Allow frequent socialization with strangers and other pets.
- Avoid tying up your dog outside for long periods.
- Keep your dog on a leash in public places.

KNOW YOUR DOG

Any dog can and will bite in certain situations. It is your responsibility as a pet owner to know your dog and keep it under control or out of situations where it might act aggressively.

Aggression

Aggression in dogs includes many behaviors, including growling, barking, snarling, lunging, snapping and biting. Sometimes a dog will indicate its aggressive intentions by staring and standing tall with its ears and hair erect. Male dogs that have not been neutered (see pp. 32–3) often behave aggressively to other males, resulting in dog fights. Fear and nervousness are also likely to make a dog behave in an aggressive manner.

When aggression is directed toward a person or another animal, it can be dangerous. If your pet is displaying aggression and threatening family members, visitors or strangers, or has bitten people, the intervention of a trained behaviorist is advised.

The best way to deal with aggressive behavior is to prevent it in the first place. If you get a new puppy, establish yourself as his leader from the word go. You can do this by setting rules that are humanely but consistently enforced. Get your new pet used to your handling of his food, toys and body. Do this when he is calm rather than excited by exercise or play. Approach your pet while he is sleeping so that he will not feel threatened by you at this vulnerable time.

Reward good behavior with treats and praise. If you need to take something from your puppy, do so in a firm but gentle manner. If you yell and reach quickly for your pet, you may scare him and prompt aggression in return. Remember, harsh punishment can cause aggression based on either fear or pain.

Some animals will be wary of new people and exhibit aggression when meeting them for the first time. How can this be avoided? Frequent and early socialization with many different people in many locations is a good start. Also, make meeting new people fun by using treats and praise. Keep a treat jar by the front door and have visitors give a treat to the dog on arrival. Your dog will soon learn to associate good things with people coming in the door.

Always reward your dog for calm, subordinate behavior. When people come to visit, teach your dog to sit or lie down for attention. The same applies when meeting people in the park or on a walk. Use a calm, but happy voice to encourage your dog to be friendly with people.

Dogs are very territorial creatures, particularly if they are tied up in the yard a lot. Some dogs will become very protective of that small space and can often become aggressive. Furthermore, when dogs are tied up they have no means of escaping any teasing or other annoyances that

come along. As a result, they may resort to aggressive behavior to stop the intrusion.

If you have adopted an older dog who is aggressive around people or other animals, you may need to use a leash for control, even in the home. This will at least prevent injuries to visitors to your home.

In public, a leash should always be used if you are not sure how your dog will react. If he is obviously anxious and fearful in a situation and won't be calmed, remove him immediately. If this kind of behavior occurs a number of times, you may need to find qualified help. Do not assume that your pet will grow out of the behavior. Aggression is a serious and potentially dangerous problem.

AVOIDING AGGRESSION

Early experiences help determine a dog's behavior, so get your pet used to children from the outset. This American Staffordshire Terrier (above) has made two friends for life. When walking dogs in public, always keep them on a leash (left).

WATCHDOGS

Many owners want a dog that will bark and alert them to intruders. So, how can you create a dog that barks, but does not engage in excessive and annoying displays? The important conditions here are control and early training. Do not let your puppy bark excessively either indoors or outside. Excessive barking can get a dog agitated and increase aggressive behaviors. When excessive displays begin, you must go outside and stop them. You may even need to keep the dog on a leash so you can get him to stop more easily.

GUARD DOGS

Some breeds were developed as guard dogs, so certain traits, such as obedience, loyalty and aggression were actively selected by breeders. While many of these breeds make natural watch-dogs, they must be handled carefully. Training must be firm but never harsh. A good watchdog should learn from the outset to control its aggressive instincts.

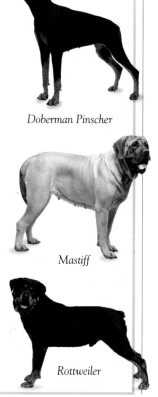

Doberman Pinscher

Mastiff

Rottweiler

German Shepherd Dog

BREEDING AND SHOWING

I am His Highness' dog at Kew:
Pray tell me sir, whose dog are you?

Inscription on the collar of a dog
given to Frederick, Prince of Wales
ALEXANDER POPE (1688–1744),
English poet

BREEDING YOUR DOG

Breeding puppies can be a wonderful experience, but it should be done responsibly. Thousands of dogs are abandoned each year because of unwanted pregnancies. Do not add to this sorry situation.

BEFORE YOU BREED YOUR DOG

- Arrange good homes for all potential puppies.
- Investigate any hereditary disorders that are common in your breed.
- Choose a mate carefully.
- Check that both dogs are registered with a national kennel club.
- Have both dogs examined by a veterinarian, including a check for parasites and brucellosis (a sexually transmitted disease that causes sterility).
- Read up on canine reproduction, pregnancy, birth and postnatal care.

AN AVERAGE LITTER
On average, a bitch will produce five to seven puppies in a litter. Make sure that you arrange for homes in advance for all potential puppies and a few to spare.

If you are going to bring new dogs into the world, aim to improve the standard of the breed. Every dog that is bred should represent an improvement over its parents. In general, it is best to avoid breeding mixed-breed dogs. Dog overpopulation is a huge problem and shelters are already full of unwanted mixed breeds, not to mention purebred dogs. Unless you can guarantee a good home for each and every puppy you breed, you will only be contributing to the problem.

CHOOSING A MATE

To ensure that the pups you breed will be of the best quality, choose a mate from an experienced and reputable dealer. Don't pick a neighborhood dog that will perform for free! Make sure the dog is registered with a national kennel club. However, registration alone does not vouch for the quality of a dog, so check out any potential suitor carefully.

Pay particular attention to the dog's temperament. Although dogs were once bred for specific tasks, most are now kept as companions. Choose a mate who has the qualities of a good companion. Never breed with a dog who is aggressive, overly timid or has hereditary diseases.

THE BREEDING CYCLE

Unlike human beings, dogs breed only during certain times of the year. Although males may attempt to breed at any time, females will only accept them when they are ovulating. At this time the bitch is described as being "in heat" or "in season." The technical term is estrus.

Most bitches come into heat twice a year (wolves and Basenjis have only one heat cycle per year). Depending on a bitch's breed and size she will have her first heat between the age of 6 and 24 months. Smaller dogs come into heat sooner. Wait until your bitch's third or fourth estrus before breeding. This way you can be sure that she is both physically and emotionally mature.

Males go through puberty, begin to produce fertile sperm and are therefore capable of producing puppies generally between seven and nine months of age. They are eager to breed any time afterward.

PHASES OF THE CYCLE

There are four phases of the canine reproductive cycle. The beginning of the heat period is known as proestrus. The most reliable indicator of the beginning of this stage is a bloody vaginal discharge. Other signs are a swollen vulva and frequent urination and licking. Male dogs are attracted to the bitch during this phase, but she will not permit mating. Proestrus lasts for six to eleven days.

Estrus begins when the bitch begins to permit mating. To indicate this, she often crouches, elevates her vulva toward the male and moves her tail to the side. Her vulva becomes soft, tense and hot and the discharge becomes less and less bloody.

Ovulation takes place during estrus, which usually lasts for five to nine days. Great care must be taken at this time to prevent unwanted pregnancies. Any female in season is best confined to the house and taken out only for short, supervised leash walks.

The next stage is called diestrus, characterized by a steady reduction in vulvar swelling and a loss of attractiveness to male dogs. If mating has taken place, this stage is the beginning of

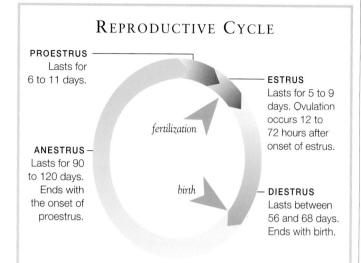

REPRODUCTIVE CYCLE

PROESTRUS
Lasts for 6 to 11 days.

ESTRUS
Lasts for 5 to 9 days. Ovulation occurs 12 to 72 hours after onset of estrus.

fertilization

ANESTRUS
Lasts for 90 to 120 days. Ends with the onset of proestrus.

birth

DIESTRUS
Lasts between 56 and 68 days. Ends with birth.

pregnancy. Even if a bitch is not pregnant, many show signs of pregnancy, a stage known as false pregnancy. Diestrus lasts between 56 and 68 days in pregnant bitches and 60 to 80 days in an unfertilized bitch.

The final stage of the cycle is called anestrus. In the pregnant bitch, it begins with the birth of puppies and ends with proestrus. In a non-pregnant animal its onset is less obvious. Basically, a female dog in anestrus is difficult to tell apart from one who has been spayed.

WHAT TO LOOK FOR IN A MATE

- Choose a good representative of your breed from a reputable and responsible breeder.
- Make sure dog is registered with a national kennel club.
- Make sure he is healthy and doesn't have any hereditary diseases. This may require blood tests, X-rays and eye exams by a specialist.
  - Find out about the dog's temperament. Look for the qualities of a good companion.

MATING AND PREGNANCY

*Once you have found a suitable mate for your dog, you can generally
let nature take its course. When your bitch becomes pregnant, make
the next two months as comfortable for her as you possibly can.*

NOT TONIGHT, DEAR
While mating comes naturally
to most dogs, some dogs may
experience anxiety and be
reluctant to perform the first time.

HINTS FOR NERVOUS COUPLES

- Choose an experienced male.
- Take the bitch to the dog's
  place for mating.
- Arrange for the dogs to meet
  prior to mating.
- Allow them plenty of time to
  get used to each other.
- If it is not possible for the
  dogs to meet prior to mating,
  provide each dog with an
  object that smells of the other.

Once a bitch is in season,
dogs generally have no
problems mating. Some first-
timers, however, do experience
anxiety and may be reluctant
to mate. If you anticipate this
being a problem, there are a
number of ways you can
prepare in advance (see box).

MATING

In dogs, courtship begins
with the male sniffing at the
female's nose, ear, neck, side
and vulva. The bitch sniffs
the male in return and may
want to play as well. When
ready, the bitch typically
presents her hindquarters to
the male and stands still with
her tail to the side. The male
then clasps the sides of the
female with his forelegs,
inserts his penis into the
vagina and begins to thrust.

While inside, the erectile
tissue in his penis swells,
resulting in the so-called
"coital tie." With the penis
firmly in place, ejaculation
begins. Then with their
genitalia still locked, the
dog dismounts and swings to
the side so that the dog and
bitch are facing in opposite
directions. This position is
required for full ejaculation
and may last anywhere from
5 to 60 minutes. Don't try to
separate two dogs in a tie as
injury could result.

THE PREGNANCY

Fertilization occurs about
72 hours after mating and the
gestation period lasts between
56 and 68 days, the average
being 63 days. Pups can be felt
by an experienced person after
about 20 days of pregnancy.

After you have confirmed
that your bitch is pregnant,
go over the basics of prenatal
care, the whelping process
and emergency procedures
with your veterinarian. A
pregnant female requires more
food to support the growth of
the puppies inside her and to
produce the milk that they
will live on after birth. A
good regime to follow is to
feed her the same amount she
normally eats for the first six

weeks. Increase her intake during the final three weeks until she is eating about 50 percent more at the time of whelping than when she was bred. Feed a premium dog food that is specifically designed for all life stages or for pregnancy and lactation.

About a week before the due date, introduce your bitch to her whelping box. The box should be large enough to comfortably accommodate both your dog and her pups. Keep one side low to permit the bitch to easily enter and exit. Place it in a warm, quiet and secluded area. Place soft towels in the bottom and have plenty of fresh ones on hand to replace those soiled during whelping. Try to include a guard rail, about 3 inches (7.5 cm) from the floor and 3 inches from the sides of the box, to prevent the bitch from crushing any puppies against the sides.

Several days before whelping, you will notice a marked enlargement of your bitch's mammary glands. Milk is likely to appear on the nipples at this time. About 24 hours before whelping, she will

begin digging and nesting in her whelping box. At this time, carefully clip the hair around her nipples so that the pups won't have any trouble finding them. Also clip the hair around her vulva if necessary.

At about 12 hours prior to birth, the bitch's rectal body temperature will drop below 100°F (38°C) and she will probably refuse to eat. When she enters the first stage of labor, she will pant, strain, appear restless and sometimes vomit. You may notice a puddle of fluid, indicating that her water bag has broken. Within two hours, her contractions will increase and her first puppy will be produced.

VISIBLY PREGNANT
This pregnant Bull Terrier is almost ready to give birth. A veterinarian can detect a pregnancy after 20 days by feeling a bitch's abdomen, although ultrasound can detect pups from as early as day 16. X-rays can be used safely only during the last three weeks of gestation.

AN IDEAL WHELPING BOX
A whelping box should be large and comfortable with a guard rail around the sides to prevent the newborn pups being accidentally crushed by their mother.

THE BIRTH

Most bitches do not need help to give birth. Interfere only in an emergency. Too much interference may cause a bitch to become nervous and prevent her from adequately caring for her newborns.

MATERNAL INSTINCTS
A mother instinctively knows to lick a newborn pup clean of its placental membranes.

STIFF COMPETITION
Puppies tend to find their own way to their mother's milk. However, if the litter is large, make sure that every puppy gets a chance to feed.

During delivery, your bitch may either stand or lie down. When the first puppy arrives, generally head first, it will be wrapped in placental membranes. The mother usually tears these off and eats them. At this point the pup will take its first breath. The mother then bites off the umbilical cord and eats the placenta, or afterbirth, which normally follows a few minutes later. Make sure that the bitch has expelled an afterbirth for each puppy. If she retains any, she may develop an infection and will need veterinary help.

If she does not remove the placental membranes within the first few minutes of birth or if she neglects to sever an umbilical cord, she needs your help. Remove the sac without delay, as the puppy may suffocate. Start by tearing it away from the face and then the body. Clean any mucus away from the mouth and nose and stimulate the puppy's breathing by rubbing with a towel. Tie off the umbilical cord with unwaxed dental floss and cut it about 2 inches (5 cm) from the pup.

Return the puppy to the mother immediately so she can lick it. A mother will lick each puppy dry to keep it warm and to stimulate it to breathe. This licking will continue for the first few weeks of life to stimulate urination and defecation.

Shortly after being born, the puppy should find its way to the mother's nipples by itself. If it doesn't, you may need to gently point the puppy in the right direction. Suckling soon after birth ensures that each puppy ingests sufficient colostrum (the first milk), which contains antibodies to protect the newborn puppies from disease.

Between each puppy, the bitch may rest for from 10 to 80 minutes. If hours pass and there are still unborn pups inside, call your veterinarian. If the bitch is straining and nothing is produced, it may mean the pup is too large and a Cesarean section may be required.

CARING FOR NEWBORNS

Born blind and deaf, newborn pups are entirely dependent on their mother for food and protection. Make sure that each puppy has access to a nipple and is able to suckle. If a pup is not receiving adequate milk, try holding her up to a nipple several times a day so she does not have to compete with the other puppies.

If the puppy is still not getting enough milk, you may need to supplement her feeding. Your veterinarian can supply puppy formula. Use a small bottle with a hole in the nipple just large enough for a drop of milk to ooze out.

For the first week of life, newborn puppies are unable to shiver or control their own body temperature. They depend on their mother and other pups to keep warm. An external source of heat which keeps the temperature in the whelping box at around 86°F (30°C), such as an electric heating bulb or a hot water bottle covered with a towel, will help keep the pups warm.

Once the pups start to walk, give them a papered bathroom area a short distance from where they sleep. They will naturally urinate and defecate away from their sleeping area.

Handle the puppies daily so that they get used to human contact. Gently clean their eyes, ears and mouth, and trim their nails when necessary. At three or four weeks of age, most puppies will begin to eat food. To make it easier for them, prepare a gruel of puppy weaning diet and water. Offer this in a large bowl to all the puppies three to four times a day. Over the next few weeks, reduce the water in the gruel until it is omitted altogether.

Most bitches wean their puppies after about six or seven weeks. By this time, puppies should be able to eat enough solid food to meet all their nutritional needs. At eight weeks they're ready to leave their mother and littermates, but before you send them off, make sure they have been vaccinated, treated for worms and thoroughly checked by your veterinarian.

BOTTLE FEEDING
If you need to supplement a newborn puppy's feeding, hold the puppy upright in your hand. Gently tilt the puppy's head upward as you insert the nipple in her mouth and invert the bottle.

WHELPING EMERGENCIES

Contact your veterinarian in any of the following cases:

- No signs of birth for over 70 days since mating.
- Evidence of extreme pain, such as crying, licking or biting at vulva.
- No puppy produced within 12 hours of the water bag breaking or within 24 hours of the drop in rectal temperature.
- No puppy produced within 30 minutes of strong contractions.
- More than 2 hours pass between puppies and not all have been delivered.
- Bitch is sick and produces a large amount of bloody or foul-smelling vaginal discharge (a green discharge is normal).

GROWING UP FAST
These 26-day-old puppies are old enough to be eating a weaning diet and to begin exploring the world around them.

SHOWING YOUR DOG

Once the sole domain of the wealthy, dog shows today require only time, commitment and a love of dogs. The variety of shows available makes it easy to find one that both you and your dog can enjoy.

While most people are happy enough for their dog just to be a loving companion, some owners have higher aspirations. If you think your dog is a good enough representative of its breed to be a champion in the show ring, then you might consider conformation shows.

CONFORMATION SHOWS

Conformation simply means conforming to a breed standard (a description of the perfect example of a given breed). At formal conformation dog shows, purebred dogs are judged on how closely they measure up to their breed standard.

Dog shows are either restricted to one breed of dog (known as specialty shows) or are all-breed shows. At either show, the judges first examine and evaluate each dog for overall structure,

fitness, coat color and quality, and temperament. The judges then evaluate each dog's movement, or gait, by watching it move around the ring.

In most countries, dogs of each breed are divided into classes, generally based on age, for the initial round of competition. The winners of each class then compete against each other as well as with dogs that are already champions. The judge then picks the "best of breed." If the competition is an all-breed show, the best of breed winners then compete against all the others in their group (for example, sporting or herding dogs). Finally out of the winners of each group, the "best in show" is picked.

Most dogs at shows are competing for points that will eventually qualify them as champions (designated by the letters Ch. in front of the dog's name). The number of points that a dog can win at a show varies from one to five depending on a variety of factors, including the number of dogs at the show and the dog's breed and sex. For a dog to qualify as a champion it must win 15 points under at least three different judges,

"STACKING"

Stacking a dog means placing it in the correct pose to show off its best features. This West Highland White Terrier has been correctly stacked, with its back straight and its head and tail up.

including at least two scores of three points or more (known as "majors").

Conformation shows are restricted to unneutered, purebred dogs, and for a dog to do well it must be an excellent representative of its breed. Some people choose to handle their dogs themselves at the shows, while others hire professional handlers.

OTHER COMPETITIONS

If formal dog shows sound a little out of your (or your dog's) league, there are other types of competition where both neutered animals and mixed breeds are eligible. These include obedience trials, tracking tests, hunting trials, herding trials and agility competitions.

Obedience trials test both the dog's and handler's ability to perform a specific set of exercises, including such commands as sit, stay, down, heel and retrieve. Tracking tests require a dog to follow a trail by scent. Hunting trials test a dog's hunting ability in the field (to point and retrieve, for example), while herding trials require a dog to control livestock in a variety of difficult situations. In agility competitions, dogs and handlers navigate an obstacle course consisting of tunnels, inclines, seesaws and hurdles, at high speeds.

You may also be able to find a local dog show that gives prizes for the best trick, or even to the dog with the most spots or the biggest ears. Whatever your interest, a dog show can bring out the best in your dog and give you both a chance to show off.

A BOX OF TRICKS

Conformation shows are serious business, and owners have quite an array of implements with which to keep their dogs immaculately groomed. This elaborate grooming kit belongs to the proud owner of a prize-winning Schnauzer.

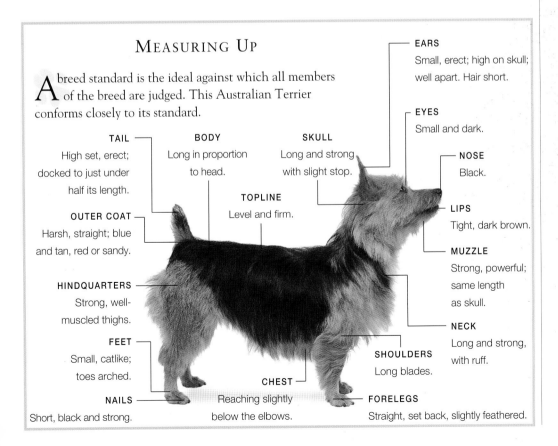

MEASURING UP

A breed standard is the ideal against which all members of the breed are judged. This Australian Terrier conforms closely to its standard.

EARS
Small, erect; high on skull; well apart. Hair short.

EYES
Small and dark.

NOSE
Black.

LIPS
Tight, dark brown.

MUZZLE
Strong, powerful; same length as skull.

NECK
Long and strong, with ruff.

SHOULDERS
Long blades.

FORELEGS
Straight, set back, slightly feathered.

CHEST
Reaching slightly below the elbows.

NAILS
Short, black and strong.

FEET
Small, catlike; toes arched.

HINDQUARTERS
Strong, well-muscled thighs.

OUTER COAT
Harsh, straight; blue and tan, red or sandy.

TAIL
High set, erect; docked to just under half its length.

BODY
Long in proportion to head.

TOPLINE
Level and firm.

SKULL
Long and strong with slight stop.

A GUIDE TO BREEDS

In times of calm or hurricane, in days
of sun or shower,
The dog-paraders, each and all, observe
the canine hour.

And some with pups in single leash,
and some with tugging pairs,
Take out their poodles, pointers, poms and
frisky wire-hairs.

The Dog Parade
ARTHUR GUITERMAN (1871–1943),
American poet

A HISTORY OF THE DOMESTIC DOG

The evolution of the domestic dog is intertwined with the development of human civilization. From scavengers on the outskirts of the first human settlements to the treasured pets of today, dogs have long been with us.

THE MOST LIKELY ANCESTOR
Most experts agree that the domestic dog evolved from the wolf (above). Both have the same number of teeth and display similar hierarchical behavior when in packs.

DOG FIGHTING
This Ancient Greek bas-relief, which dates from about 500 BC, shows an organized dog fight. Such dog fights were only outlawed in relatively recent times.

Domestic dogs, along with coyotes, jackals, wolves and dingoes make up the genus Canis. Although the fossil record is limited, the first members of this genus probably appeared about one million years ago, but the domestic dog developed much later. Due to a number of similarities, both physical and behavioral, it is believed that the domestic dog evolved from the wolf.

By the time humans and wolves began to interact, probably more than 15,000 years ago, there were two distinct types of wolf in the northern hemisphere: those from the north, which were large with long, pale coats; and those from the south, which were slimmer with short, darker coats. These variations were simply natural adaptations to climate, but

EGYPTIAN ARTIFACTS
This sketch of a dog and a hyena (above) is over 3,000 years old. A limestone carving of a dog-headed deity (top left), from 300 BC.

once the bond was established between humans and wolves, the domestic dog evolved as a process of selective breeding.

THE DOMESTICATION OF THE DOG
The domestication of the dog probably began around the time our human ancestors became hunters and gatherers. Wild dogs would have scavenged on the outskirts

of temporary camps and the hunters would have appreciated the warnings they gave of approaching danger. As settlements became more permanent, dogs would have become increasingly useful as guard dogs, and eventually hunting and herding dogs.

From these early times, the evolution of the dog was largely dictated by humans. Dogs were selectively bred to perform specific tasks by breeding together those dogs that exhibited particular traits, such as size, hunting ability and aggression. Gradually, through this process of interbreeding, distinct types of dog were developed and maintained.

Greyhounds and Mastiff-type dogs are the oldest recognizable breeds of which there are historical records. Depictions of Greyhounds have been found on 8,000-year-old fragments of Mesopotamian pottery, and there are records of Mastiffs that are nearly as old as this. In ancient times, Greyhounds were used primarily as hunting dogs, while the large, aggressive Mastiffs were used in battle and as guard dogs.

DIVERSIFICATION

Over many thousands of years, dogs developed and diversified as human needs changed. The evolution of hunting dogs is a good example of this process. The Greyhound was an exemplary hunting dog, swift and powerful, and could chase and kill a variety of prey. However, over the centuries, as hunting methods became more refined and the kinds of prey hunted became more varied, new breeds of hunting dog were developed.

Dogs were now bred not only to chase game but also to sniff it out (scenthounds), to point to it in the field (pointers and setters), to flush it out (spaniels), to retrieve it (retrievers) and to chase it down burrows (terriers).

WALKING THE DOG
This fourteenth-century illustration from Frenchman Gaston Phoebus's *The Book of the Hunt* shows hunting dogs being exercised and groomed by servants.

A GRECIAN URN
A depiction of Cerberus, the three-headed dog of Greek mythology, from about 700 BC.

BREEDING FOR LOOKS

In early times, dogs were bred to perform specific tasks, and how they looked was largely irrelevant. However, even in ancient times this was not always the case.

In the East, there is a long and rich tradition of breeding dogs for appearance. As early as 5,000 years ago, Chinese emperors were breeding tiny "lap dogs" to carry around their palaces. This process of miniaturization led to the development of the toy dogs, many of which became favorites with royalty over the centuries. Toy dogs remain popular pets to this day.

THE INDUSTRIAL REVOLUTION

The greatest influence on the domestication of the dog since wolves and humans first made contact was the Industrial Revolution. During the eighteenth and nineteenth centuries, urbanization and changes in the nature of employment meant that people had more leisure time to devote to hobbies. By the late nineteenth century, breeding and showing of dogs were popular pastimes. As a result, the focus of breeding shifted to the appearance of the dog and the variety of dog breeds grew enormously.

BREED STANDARDS

The basic dog types remained remarkably consistent over thousands of years due to careful breeding. However, no one attempted to define a breed in any official sense until 1867, when *The Dogs of the British Islands* was published, setting out for the first time the defining characteristics of 35 breeds. This introduced the concept of a breed "standard"—an ideal against which a breed could be judged.

Then, in 1873, the world's first kennel club was established in Britain. Known as The Kennel Club, this organization published its own set of standards for 40 breeds. In addition, it stipulated that for a breed to be officially recognized it had to be registered with them. From this point on, kennel club recognition became the defining feature of a breed.

The American Kennel Club (AKC) was set up in 1883 and the Fédération Cynologique Internationale (FCI) followed in 1911, representing European countries. The number of dog breeds grew rapidly, but with each kennel club acting in isolation, recognition of specific breeds varied from country to country.

FIT FOR A KING
A portrait of the young Philippe of France by French painter Pierre Mignard (1612–1695). Small, ornamental dogs have been popular with royalty for centuries.

AN EARLY DOG SHOW
A photograph of a 1895 Kennel Club dog show at the Crystal Palace in London, England.

Today, the AKC recognizes 134 breeds, The Kennel Club recognizes 188 breeds and the FCI recognizes 350. Worldwide, there may be as many as 500 breeds and the number is growing every year.

While any breed must breed true to a consistent set of standards over time, there remains no absolute definition of a dog breed. For example, in Britain the Belgian Shepherd is considered to be one breed consisting of four distinct types, the Malinois, Tervuren, Laekenois and Groenendael. However, in the U.S. the Laekenois is not officially recognized at all while the other three varieties are considered to be distinct breeds. Furthermore, the same breed may differ slightly from one country to another due to local variations in the breed standard.

THE ETHICS OF BREEDING

The proliferation of dog breeds and the constant refining of breed standards over the last hundred or so years have meant that domestic dogs have changed appearance dramatically. While human intervention has always been essential to the evolution of the dog, the performance and health of dogs bred for specific tasks were rarely compromised. However, when dogs are bred for appearance, traits may be selected that actually hinder a dog's performance. The Bulldog, for example, has developed to the point where its large head, wide-set legs, soft palate and sagging facial skin may jeopardize its health and longevity.

Even with hardy working breeds, inbreeding has left a common legacy of genetic diseases, such as hip dysplasia. Today, kennel clubs and responsible breeders go to great lengths to avoid breeding dogs with genetic defects or traits that may compromise their well-being.

AND THE WINNER IS...

The certificate for first prize at the 1895 Norfolk and Norwich Kennel Club dog show (left), held in Norwich, England; and the front cover of the catalog for the 1903 Atlantic City Kennel Club dog show, held in the U.S.

BUILT FOR COMFORT

This illustration from a 1900 French catalog shows a leaner, smaller-headed Bulldog than the one we commonly see today.

CLASSIFYING BREEDS

While some dogs are still bred to perform the same tasks as their ancestors, far more are simply kept as pets. However, dogs remain largely classified by the work for which they were developed.

A HUNTER'S BEST FRIEND
Pointing breeds, such as this Weimaraner, have the uncanny ability to locate a bird in the field and then to literally point it out to a hunter.

A RICH HERITAGE
This illustration from a fourteenth-century hunting treatise by French-man Gaston Phoebus depicts a group of hounds, strikingly similar to today's Greyhounds.

The classification of dogs into groups varies from country to country. This guide to breeds uses the U.S. system.

SPORTING DOGS

Sporting dogs, also known as gundogs, were bred to work with hunters in the field. Pointers were bred to sniff out game birds, and once located, to point toward them with an upraised leg. Setters also located game but would bend down out of the hunter's line of fire. The smaller, faster spaniels were bred to flush out game from the undergrowth for hunters to net or shoot, while retrievers were bred to retrieve game once it was shot.

Today, sporting dogs are popular pets. They retain a liveliness and love of exercise as well as intense loyalty for their owners.

HOUNDS

Dogs from this group are among the most ancient; Greyhounds were the first hunting dogs for which there are historical records. Developed to chase and kill large prey, many are capable of great speed and possess enormous stamina.

Hounds are divided roughly into sighthounds and scent-hounds, depending on how they locate their prey. Some scenthounds are not partic-ularly fast, choosing instead to corner their prey. These days, hounds are often used for racing or in police work. They make good pets but tend to need a lot of exercise.

WORKING DOGS

This is another ancient group, including breeds that date back to times when dogs were used to guard settlements, carry loads and engage in battle. There have been depictions of large Mastiff-type dogs for many thousands of years.

Working dogs are generally large, strong and obedient. Some of them, such as the Doberman Pinscher, still make exemplary guard dogs. Others, such as the Saint Bernard, are used in rescue work.

A HARD-WORKING DOG
This Swiss postcard from the 1930s shows a Saint Bernard pulling a milk cart in a specially made harness. In the past, large dogs often carried out such tasks.

While some dogs within this group can be aggressive, they are unflinchingly loyal to their owners.

TERRIERS

These dogs were developed mainly in the British Isles over the past few hundred years, although there are records of small hunting dogs from earlier times.

Terriers are generally small dogs and were developed to hunt small game, often digging them out of burrows. They are determined and brave, with short legs and powerful jaws. Long-legged terriers, such as the Airedale, were bred to hunt larger game.

Due to their size, terriers are popular pets. While much of their aggression has been bred out of them, they remain playful and exuberant. Many terriers are incorrigible diggers.

TOY DOGS

Miniature dogs were developed by ancient Chinese Emperors as palace companions and lap dogs, and they remained popular with royalty through the ages. These days, they are popular pets, particularly in cities where their size and gentle temperament suit them to apartment living.

NON-SPORTING DOGS

This group contains breeds that don't fit neatly into any of the other categories. Some belong in this group because the task for which they were developed no longer exists. The Bulldog, for example, was bred for bull-baiting and then fighting, pastimes that are now outlawed.

While dogs in this group have little in common, they are some of the most beautiful, intelligent and popular dogs today.

HERDING DOGS

While not as ancient as some of the hounds, herding dogs have been used for thousands of years to protect livestock from predators and to keep them from straying. Herding dogs tend to be very nimble and intelligent and have great stamina.

Today, many of these dogs are still employed in their traditional roles, although they also make wonderful pets if given sufficient exercise and attention.

THE CHASE
This painting by the English artist George Armfield (1840–84) shows a group of terriers chasing a rabbit. Terriers were bred with short legs to enable them to chase rabbits down their burrows.

KEEPING WATCH
Herding dogs are still often used in the jobs for which they were originally bred. This Bearded Collie is keeping a watchful eye over a herd of sheep.

How to Use the Guide

If you are interested in becoming the proud owner of a purebred dog, this is the place to start. This guide provides details of more than 100 of the most popular dog breeds to help you decide which dog is best suited to your needs.

NAME OF BREED

The name of the breed as used by the American Kennel Club. Breeds are arranged in approximate order of height within their respective groups.

INTRODUCTION

This provides a succinct and lively overview of the breed.

MAIN TEXT

The running text provides a detailed description of the breed, including its history, distinguishing characteristics and temperament. It also details the grooming, feeding and exercise requirements for the breed, as well as alerting prospective owners to common health problems that may afflict these dogs.

MAIN IMAGE

A representative of the breed, shown in profile. Some are breed-standard quality, others are pet quality.

SIZE AND WEIGHT

Average size for males and females of the breed. Height is measured from the ground to the withers.

Japanese Chin

The lovely little Japanese Chin is truly a dog to dote on and will gladly return the love that is unfailingly lavished upon it. It is a superlative lapdog with few, if any, flaws or vices.

PET FACTS

- Intelligent, lively, gentle
- Daily brushing
- Regular, gentle
- Ideal for apartment living
- Poor watchdog

BE AWARE
- Matted hair must be clipped off the feet

HISTORY
These gorgeous little dogs have been known in Western countries for only about 150 years. However, they were the pampered pooches of wealthy Japanese, including royalty, for many centuries, having been introduced to Japan from China in ancient times. They are probably distantly related to the Pekingese.

DESCRIPTION
The Japanese Chin looks like a tiny toy. The profuse, straight, longhaired coat comes in white with markings either of black or shades of red. The gait is graceful with the feet lifted high off the ground.

TEMPERAMENT
The engaging little Chin is a lively, happy, sweet-tempered animal, the perfect size for small living spaces. With its gentle ways and charming manners, it is perhaps best suited to homes in which there are no small children.

GROOMING
Although the coat looks as though it might be difficult, a few minutes each day will keep it looking beautiful. Comb out tangles and brush lightly, lifting the hair to leave it standing out a little. A professional dog groomer can show you the correct technique. Dry shampoo occasionally and bathe only when necessary. Clean the eyes every day and check the ears regularly for any signs of infection.

EXERCISE & FEEDING
While they don't require a great deal of exercise, Chins love a daily walk and an opportunity to play in the open. There are no special feeding requirements, but they prefer to "graze" on small meals and tidbits.

HEALTH PROBLEMS
The large and prominent eyes are vulnerable to damage and subject to cataracts and progressive retinal atrophy.

Male: 7–11 in (18–28 cm)
Up to 9 lb (4 kg)
Female: 7–11 in (18–28 cm)
Up to 9 lb (4 kg)

176

TEMPERAMENT
Brief summary of temperament.

GROOMING
Preferred grooming manner and frequency.

EXERCISE
Type and frequency required.

GROUP
Breeds are classified into seven groups according to the U.S. system (see pp. 98–99). Each section has a different page banding for easy reference.

LIVING CONDITIONS
Preferred environment.

WATCHDOG
Brief summary of ability.

PET FACTS

Courageous, alert, affectionate

Daily, extensive

Regular, moderate

Ideal for apartment living, but needs plenty of exercise

Excellent watchdog for its size

BE AWARE
- It is an enthusiastic digger
- Can be jealous and may pick fights with other dogs

BE AWARE
Important information which you should consider before acquiring the breed.

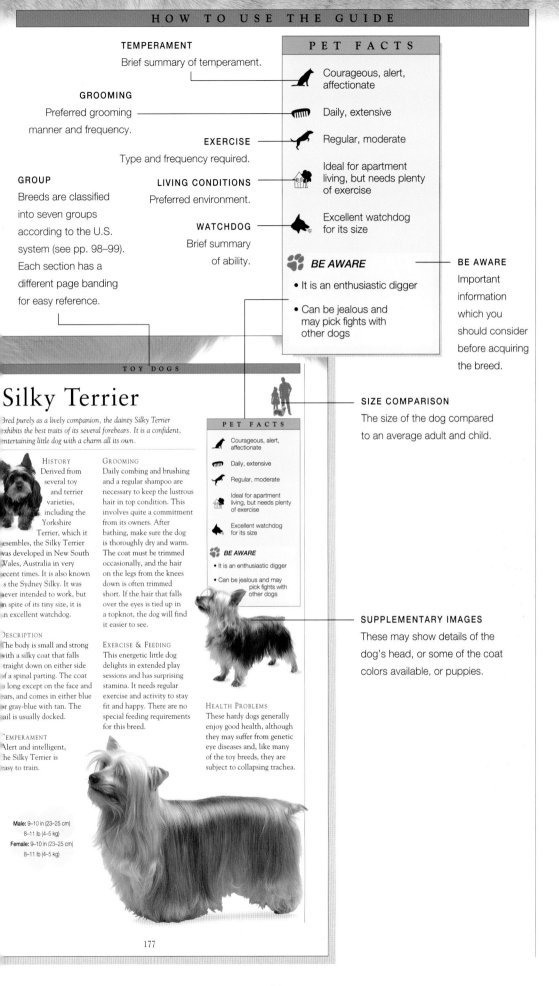

TOY DOGS

Silky Terrier

Bred purely as a lively companion, the dainty Silky Terrier exhibits the best traits of its several forebears. It is a confident, entertaining little dog with a charm all its own.

HISTORY
Derived from several toy and terrier varieties, including the Yorkshire Terrier, which it resembles, the Silky Terrier was developed in New South Wales, Australia in very recent times. It is also known as the Sydney Silky. It was never intended to work, but in spite of its tiny size, it is an excellent watchdog.

DESCRIPTION
The body is small and strong with a silky coat that falls straight down on either side of a spinal parting. The coat is long except on the face and ears, and comes in either blue or gray-blue with tan. The tail is usually docked.

TEMPERAMENT
Alert and intelligent, the Silky Terrier is easy to train.

GROOMING
Daily combing and brushing and a regular shampoo are necessary to keep the lustrous hair in top condition. This involves quite a commitment from its owners. After bathing, make sure the dog is thoroughly dry and warm. The coat must be trimmed occasionally, and the hair on the legs from the knees down is often trimmed short. If the hair that falls over the eyes is tied up in a topknot, the dog will find it easier to see.

EXERCISE & FEEDING
This energetic little dog delights in extended play sessions and has surprising stamina. It needs regular exercise and activity to stay fit and happy. There are no special feeding requirements for this breed.

HEALTH PROBLEMS
These hardy dogs generally enjoy good health, although they may suffer from genetic eye diseases and, like many of the toy breeds, they are subject to collapsing trachea.

PET FACTS

Courageous, alert, affectionate

Daily, extensive

Regular, moderate

Ideal for apartment living, but needs plenty of exercise

Excellent watchdog for its size

BE AWARE
- It is an enthusiastic digger
- Can be jealous and may pick fights with other dogs

SIZE COMPARISON
The size of the dog compared to an average adult and child.

SUPPLEMENTARY IMAGES
These may show details of the dog's head, or some of the coat colors available, or puppies.

Male: 9–10 in (23–25 cm)
8–11 lb (4–5 kg)
Female: 9–10 in (23–25 cm)
8–11 lb (4–5 kg)

177

101

Sporting Dogs

Cocker Spaniel

This attractive dog is smaller than its English cousin but retains the lively, friendly personality for which spaniels are known. The Cocker Spaniel is a most appealing pet.

HISTORY
Although derived from the same stock as the English Cocker Spaniel (see p. 104), the Cocker Spaniel had become so different by the 1930s that it was recognized in the U.S. as a separate breed. British recognition followed about 35 years later.

DESCRIPTION
This is a strong dog with a sturdy, compact body. The fine, silky coat is short on the head and longer on the body—it may even be ground length. It comes in black, black and tan, any solid color, particolors, tricolors and roans. The ears are long and set low on the head and the tail is usually docked.

TEMPERAMENT
Intelligent and responsive, the Cocker Spaniel is generally friendly and good natured. However, some dogs may display aggression toward their owners, a condition similar to Rage Syndrome in English Springer Spaniels (see p. 107).

GROOMING
Some owners prefer to leave the coat long, brushing daily and shampooing frequently. Others clip the coat to medium length to be more functional. Either way, the dog will need regular trimming. When brushing, be careful not to pull out the silky hair.

EXERCISE & FEEDING
These dogs have plenty of stamina and need regular exercise. When walking, avoid brushy thickets that can tangle the coat. There are no special feeding requirements.

HEALTH PROBLEMS
These dogs are subject to ear infections, skin problems (such as seborrhea), inherited eye diseases (such as glaucoma and progressive retinal atrophy) and spinal problems.

PET FACTS

- Lively, happy, friendly
- Daily brushing
- Regular, moderate
- Adapts well to urban living, but needs plenty of space
- Good watchdog

BE AWARE
- Some dogs may display unprovoked aggression

Male: 13–16 in (33–41 cm)
25–35 lb (11–16 kg)
Female: 12–15 in (30–38 cm)
20–30 lb (9–14 kg)

English Cocker Spaniel

An absolute charmer, the joyous English Cocker Spaniel is one of the most popular house pets in its adoptive country. For sheer good looks and personality, it's the leader of the pack.

PET FACTS

- Joyful, affectionate, intelligent
- Regular brushing
- Regular, moderate to vigorous
- Adapts well to urban living, but needs plenty of exercise
- Good watchdog

BE AWARE

- Prone to ear infections so check ears regularly

and occasional roans. The tails are usually docked short.

TEMPERAMENT

Energetic, playful and eager to please, the Cocker performs with unbounded enthusiasm, wagging its stump of a tail and entire hindquarters furiously. It will certainly alert you to the presence of strangers on your property.

HISTORY

The spaniel family originated in Spain—the word may be a corruption of *espaignol*, French for Spanish dog—and various types became popular gundogs all over the world. In Britain, two kinds of spaniel developed along similar lines, the Springer and the Cocker. The Cocker is named for its ability to flush woodcock from the undergrowth.

DESCRIPTION

This strong dog has a sturdy, compact body covered in silky, medium-length, flat-lying hair. The coat comes in solid reds, black, golden and liver, as well as particolors and tricolors with the color being broken up with white,

GROOMING

Regular combing and brushing of the coat is important. Bathe or dry shampoo as necessary. Check the ears for grass seeds and signs of infection. Brush the hair on the feet down over the toes and trim it level with the base of the feet. Trim the hair around the pads, but not that between the toes.

EXERCISE & FEEDING

The English Cocker Spaniel enjoys as much exercise as you can give it. Brush out burrs and tangles after the dog has been playing in grassy fields or woods. There are no special feeding requirements.

HEALTH PROBLEMS

This breed is prone to inherited eye diseases and ear infections due to poor ventilation of the ear canals.

Male: 15–17 in (38–43 cm)
28–34 lb (13–16 kg)
Female: 14–16 in (36–41 cm)
26–32 lb (12–15 kg)

Brittany

An agile and vigorous hunter, the Brittany is admired for its abilities in the field and for its grace and charming personality. Although a companionable pet, it prefers an outdoor life.

HISTORY

The Brittany, or Breton, Spaniel has a long history in its native France, with records of these dogs going back for hundreds of years. Today, it has a growing following in the U.S., where it was officially recognized as the Brittany in 1982. As well as being an excellent tracker and retriever, this dog is also a natural pointer, a trait possibly acquired through interbreeding with setters in the past. In the field, the Brittany tends to work close to its master.

DESCRIPTION

The smallest of the French spaniels, the Brittany is graceful, active and rugged, well muscled and has long-legged, elegant lines. The medium-length coat is dense and feathered on the ears, chest, underbody and upper parts of the legs. It comes in white with orange, black, brown or liver, as well as tricolors and roans. The tail is naturally short, but is still usually docked a little.

TEMPERAMENT

Easy to train and handle, the Brittany is a loving and gentle animal, obedient and always eager to please.

GROOMING

Regular brushing of the medium-length, flat coat is really all that is needed to keep it in good condition. Bathe or dry shampoo when necessary. Check the ears carefully, especially when the dog has been out in rough or brushy terrain.

EXERCISE & FEEDING

These dogs need vigorous activity to stay in peak condition. There are no special feeding requirements.

HEALTH PROBLEMS

While generally a healthy breed, Brittanys are prone to ear infections due to poor ventilation of the ear canals. They also get cataracts and progressive retinal atrophy.

PET FACTS

- Gentle, friendly, energetic
- Regular brushing
- Regular, vigorous
- Adapts well to urban living, but needs plenty of exercise
- Good watchdog

BE AWARE

- These dogs love exercise and have great stamina

Male: 17–21 in (43–53 cm)
35–40 lb (16–18 kg)
Female: 18–20 in (46–51 cm)
30–40 lb (14–18 kg)

Welsh Springer Spaniel

Sociable and very intelligent, the Welsh Springer Spaniel adapts well to any environment but is in its element with space to run and, if you can manage it, access to somewhere it can swim.

HISTORY

Less common than the English Springer Spaniel, to which it is closely related, the Welsh Springer Spaniel is from similar ancient stock. Springer Spaniels were used to "spring" forward at game to flush it out for the net, falcon or hound and, later, the gun. The tail wags faster as the dog nears its quarry.

DESCRIPTION

A hard worker with amazing stamina and endurance, the Welsh Springer is smaller overall than its English cousin, with much smaller and less feathered ears. The thick, silky coat is straight and always pearly white and rich red. The tail is usually docked.

TEMPERAMENT

Its gentle, patient nature and love of children makes the Welsh Springer an easily trained and attractive family pet.

GROOMING

The coat is fairly easy to maintain and regular brushing with a stiff bristle brush will suffice. Extra attention is required, however, when the animal is shedding. Bathe or dry shampoo only when necessary. Check the ears regularly for grass seeds and any signs of infection. Trim the hair between the toes and keep the nails clipped.

EXERCISE & FEEDING

This energetic and lively dog needs plenty of regular exercise, as much of it as possible off the leash. There are no special feeding requirements, but do not overfeed.

PET FACTS

- Sensible, energetic, friendly
- Regular brushing
- Regular, moderate
- Adapts well to urban living, but needs plenty of space
- Good watchdog

BE AWARE

- Without enough exercise, these dogs become bored, fat and lazy

HEALTH PROBLEMS

A generally hardy breed, but like other dogs with large, heavy ears, it is prone to ear infections. Some Welsh Springers also suffer from hip dysplasia and eye problems.

Male: 17–19 in (43–48 cm)
40–45 lb (18–20 kg)
Female: 16–18 in (41–46 cm)
35–45 lb (16–20 kg)

English Spring Spaniel

The handsome robust English Springer Spaniel excels in the field at flushing out game, but also makes a delightful pet in the home. It is a spirited and loyal companion.

HISTORY

One of the largest of the spaniels, the popular English Springer Spaniel descends from the oldest spaniel stock and its blood probably runs in the veins of most modern spaniels. Once known as the Norfolk Spaniel, it is an all-weather retriever and loves the water.

DESCRIPTION

This strong dog has a sturdy, compact body. The soft, medium-length, flat-lying coat comes in all spaniel colors but mainly white with liver or black, with or without tan markings. The tail is usually docked.

TEMPERAMENT

A quick learner, the Springer enjoys company, is patient with the family and makes a good watchdog. Sadly, the breed is prone to an inherited behavioral disorder known as Rage Syndrome, which can cause aggression. Before buying a pup, check whether any of its relatives are afflicted.

GROOMING

The coat is fairly easy to maintain and regular brushing with a stiff bristle brush will keep it looking good. Take extra care when the animal is shedding. Bathe or dry shampoo only when necessary but check the ears regularly for signs of infection.

EXERCISE & FEEDING

The Springer enjoys as much exercise as you can give it. There are no special feeding requirements, but avoid overfeeding these dogs.

HEALTH PROBLEMS

A generally hardy breed, but like other dogs with large, heavy ears, it is susceptible to ear infections. It may also develop allergic skin problems, eye problems and elbow and hip dysplasia.

Male: 19–21 in (48–53 cm)
45–55 lb (20–25 kg)
Female: 18–20 in (46–51 cm)
40–50 lb (18–23 kg)

Golden Retriever

This dog gets the seal of approval from everyone who has ever owned one. Visualize a happy family around a fire—a Golden Retriever asleep on the hearth completes the picture to perfection.

PET FACTS

Calm, affectionate, gentle

Regular brushing

Regular, vigorous

Adapts well to urban living, but needs plenty of space

Good watchdog

BE AWARE

- These dogs shed a fair amount of hair, but regular grooming will help

HISTORY

The ancestry of this breed is difficult to prove, but Golden Retrievers have some of the characteristics of retrievers, Bloodhounds and Water Spaniels, which make them very useful gundogs—they are renowned for their tracking abilities. They are thought to have been developed in the United Kingdom by Lord Tweedmouth, 150 years ago.

DESCRIPTION

This is a graceful and elegant dog. The lustrous coat comes in any shade of gold or cream with the hair lying flat or gently waved around the neck, shoulders and hips. There is abundant feathering.

TEMPERAMENT

These are well-mannered, intelligent dogs with great charm. They are easily trained, always patient and are gentle with children. As a result, they make great companions or family pets. While unlikely to attack, Golden Retrievers make good watchdogs, loudly signaling a stranger's approach.

GROOMING

The smooth, medium-haired double coat is easy to groom. Comb and brush with a firm bristle brush, paying particular attention to the dense undercoat. Dry shampoo regularly, but bathe only when necessary.

EXERCISE & FEEDING

Golden Retrievers like nothing better than to work—if they have regular strenuous duties, so much the better. At the very least they need a long daily walk and preferably an opportunity to run freely. Golden Retrievers love to swim and should be allowed to do so whenever possible. There are no special feeding requirements.

HEALTH PROBLEMS

Skin allergies are common in Golden Retrievers and require immediate veterinary attention. These dogs are also prone to hip dysplasia and genetic eye diseases.

Male: 22–24 in (56–61 cm)
60–80 lb (27–36 kg)
Female: 20–22 in (51–56 cm)
55–70 lb (25–32 kg)

Labrador Retriever

Courageous, loyal and hard working, the Labrador Retriever has earned worldwide respect for its dedication to duty. However, it is also one of the most popular and loving of family pets.

HISTORY
Originally used by fishermen in Newfoundland, rather than Labrador as the name suggests, Labrador Retrievers became indispensable as sled dogs, message-carriers and general working dogs. Once known as St John's Dogs, they were part of every fishing crew. They carry on this tradition of service still, being widely used as guide dogs for the blind and in police work.

DESCRIPTION
This strong, active dog with its solid, powerful frame is a very good swimmer. The tail, described as an "otter" tail, is thick at the base, round and tapered. The coat is dense and waterproof with no feathering, and comes in solid black, yellow, fawn, cream, gold or chocolate, occasionally with white markings on the chest.

TEMPERAMENT
Reliable, obedient and easily trained, Labrador Retrievers are friendly and very good with children. They crave human attention and need to feel as though they are part of the family.

GROOMING
The smooth, shorthaired, double coat is easy to groom. Comb and brush regularly with a firm bristle brush, paying attention to the undercoat. Bathe or dry shampoo only when necessary.

PET FACTS	
	Reliable, loving, loyal
	Regular brushing
	Regular, vigorous
	Adapts well to urban living, but needs plenty of exercise
	Good watchdog

BE AWARE
- If allowed, these dogs quickly become obese

EXERCISE & FEEDING
Labrador Retrievers are energetic dogs, delighted to work and play hard. There are no special feeding requirements, but beware of overfeeding as they easily become obese and lazy.

HEALTH PROBLEMS
Like other large breeds, these dogs are prone to hip and elbow dysplasia. They also suffer from eye diseases, such as cataracts and PRA.

Male: 22–24 in (56–61 cm)
60–75 lb (27–34 kg)
Female: 21–23 in (53–58 cm)
55–70 lb (25–32 kg)

German Pointer

These versatile, athletic dogs are excellent all-rounders, able to track wounded game, point and retrieve. The German Shorthaired Pointer is the older type, but the Wirehaired has the advantage of a durable, hard-wearing coat. Both varieties make good pets.

PET FACTS

Intelligent, reliable, keen; the Wirehaired can be slightly aggressive

Regular brushing; Wire more than Smooth

Regular, vigorous

Adapts to urban living, but needs plenty of space and exercise

Good watchdog

BE AWARE

• With insufficient work, these dogs can become bored and hard to manage

HISTORY

The ancestors of the German Shorthaired Pointer include Spanish and English Pointers, the Bloodhound, French hounds and Scandinavian breeds. The modern dog has such a formidable array of talents that it was, and is, highly prized by hunters. In the search for even greater perfection, they were bred with terriers and Poodles in the late nineteenth century. The result was the German Wirehaired Pointer, which has all of the skills and has gained a tough, rugged coat in the bargain.

DESCRIPTION

These superlative hunting dogs are used for fur and feathered game in all types of terrain and are excellent swimmers. Their lean, muscular bodies and powerful loins give them a useful turn of speed on land, and their strong jaws enable them to carry quite heavy kills. The short, dense, water-resistant coat of the Shorthaired comes in solid black or liver, or these colors with white spots or flecks, or as roans. The Wirehaired has a thick, medium-length, wiry coat, also water-resistant, that comes in solid liver, liver and white, and black and white. The tails of both are usually docked to half the length.

TEMPERAMENT

German Pointers make obedient and affectionate pets and are clean and well behaved in the house, but they are better off and far

Male: 22–26 in (56–66 cm)
55–70 lb (25–32 kg)
Female: 21–25 in (53–63 cm)
45–60 lb (20–27 kg)

happier with an outdoor life and plenty of work to do. Intelligent and reasonably easy to train, the German Pointer has a mind of its own and should never be allowed to get the upper hand. Although both types are generally good with people and reliable with children, the Wirehaired has acquired a slightly aggressive trait along with its wiry coat, probably from its terrier genes, and is inclined to be argumentative with other dogs.

GROOMING

The smooth coat of the Shorthaired is very easy to groom. Just brush regularly with a firm bristle brush, and bathe only when necessary. A rub with a piece of toweling or chamois will leave the coat gleaming.

The Wirehaired's short wiry coat needs a little more attention. You will need to brush it about twice a week with a firm bristle brush and thin it in spring and fall. Bathe only when necessary. Check the ears of both varieties regularly for any discharge or foreign bodies. Check the feet also, especially after the dog has been exercising or working.

EXERCISE & FEEDING

Exercise is of paramount importance for these tireless, energetic animals. They are more than a match for even the most active family and they should not be taken on as family pets unless they can be guaranteed plenty of vigorous exercise. There are no special feeding requirements for these dogs, but always try to measure the amount of food given against the dog's level of activity.

HEALTH PROBLEMS

Generally a hardy and long-lived breed, but like other flop-eared dogs they are prone to ear infections. Some individuals may also suffer from hip dysplasia, genetic eye diseases and skin cancers.

Chesapeake Bay Retriever

A hardy outdoor type, the Chesapeake Bay Retriever is considered a duck dog without peer, with an extraordinary ability to remember where each bird falls and retrieve them all efficiently.

PET FACTS

Keen worker, can be aggressive

Regular brushing

Regular, vigorous; loves to swim

Adapts to urban living, but best with access to the country

Good watchdog

BE AWARE

- These are strong dogs and they have a tendency to be territorial, so they require firm training and good management

HISTORY
The Chesapeake Bay Retriever was developed entirely in the U.S., in the Maryland area, from a pair of shipwrecked puppies that were crossed with various dogs used as retrievers. The result was an intrepid dog, highly valued for its prowess in the field.

DESCRIPTION
Although not universally considered handsome, this medium-sized dog is athletic and strong. The coat is tight, dense, wavy and totally water resistant; the soft undercoat is quite oily and the feet are webbed. It is a strong swimmer and can swim even in heavy, icy seas. Water is shed completely with a quick shake, so the dog stays warm and dry.

The coat color varies from dark tan to dark brown, the colors of dead grass, so it is well camouflaged for its work.

TEMPERAMENT
These dogs are courageous and intelligent, but can be tricky to train. They also have a tendency to be aggressive with other dogs.

GROOMING
The dense, harsh, shorthaired coat is easy to groom. Brush with a firm bristle brush and bathe only if necessary. Bathing destroys the natural waterproofing of the coat.

EXERCISE & FEEDING
These dogs need a great deal of vigorous activity, including swimming, to stay in peak condition. There are no special feeding requirements but measure the quantity of food given against the dog's current level of activity.

HEALTH PROBLEMS
While this breed is generally very healthy, some dogs may suffer from hip dysplasia and hereditary eye diseases.

Male: 23–26 in (58–66 cm)
65–80 lb (29–36 kg)
Female: 21–24 in (53–61 cm)
55–70 lb (25–32 kg)

Vizsla

Hungary's national dog, the agile Vizsla was little known elsewhere until after World War II. This excellent gundog is now becoming increasingly popular outside its country of origin.

HISTORY

Also known as the Hungarian Pointer, the Vizsla was bred for hunting, pointing and retrieving. It is possibly descended from the Turkish Yellow Dog and the Transylvanian Hound, but it is more likely to be the result of crosses with the Weimaraner. A good swimmer, it originally worked the plains, woodlands and marshes, retrieving just as well on land as in water. It is an excellent tracker.

DESCRIPTION

This is a handsome, lean, well-muscled dog that moves gracefully either at a lively trotting gait or in a swift, ground-covering gallop. The coat is short and close, rusty gold to sandy yellow in color and greasy to the touch.

TEMPERAMENT

Although good natured, intelligent and easy to train, the Vizsla is somewhat sensitive and needs to be handled gently. It is reliable with children and quickly adapts to family life.

GROOMING

The smooth, shorthaired coat is easy to keep in peak condition. Brush with a firm bristle brush, and dry shampoo occasionally. Bathe with mild soap only when necessary. The nails should be kept trimmed.

EXERCISE & FEEDING

This is an energetic working dog with enormous stamina. It needs plenty of opportunity to run, preferably off the leash, and a lot of regular exercise. If these dogs are allowed to get bored, they can become destructive. There are no special feeding requirements.

HEALTH PROBLEMS

Vizslas are reasonably healthy dogs, but some suffer from hip dysplasia, epilepsy and genetic eye diseases, such as cataracts and PRA.

Male: 22–26 in (56–66 cm)
45–60 lb (20–27 kg)
Female: 20–24 in (51–61 cm)
40–55 lb (18–25 kg)

Weimaraner

Given firm handling by a strong adult, the confident and assertive Weimaraner makes a wonderful companion and working dog, but you will need boundless energy to keep up with it.

HISTORY

Once widely used in Germany to hunt large prey, such as bears and wild pigs, the Weimaraner became prized in more recent times as a gundog and retriever of small game, such as waterfowl. It is sometimes referred to as the silver ghost.

DESCRIPTION

This superb hunting dog has a well-proportioned, athletic, body. The sleek, close-fitting coat comes in silver-gray to mouse shades, often lighter on the head and ears. The striking eyes are blue-gray or amber. The tail is usually docked.

TEMPERAMENT

Alert, intelligent and strong-willed, the Weimaraner is a versatile breed that is happiest when it is fully occupied with work or tasks that engage its mind. It requires firm and thorough training, makes an excellent watchdog and is good with children.

GROOMING

The smooth, shorthaired coat is easy to keep in peak condition. Brush with a firm bristle brush, and dry shampoo occasionally. Bathe with mild soap only when necessary. A rub over with a chamois will make the coat gleam. Inspect feet and mouth for damage after work or exercise sessions. Keep the nails trimmed.

EXERCISE & FEEDING

These are powerful working dogs with great stamina. They need plenty of opportunities to run free and lots of regular exercise. As they are prone to bloat, it is better to feed them two or three small meals a day rather than one large meal. Do not exercise straight after a meal.

HEALTH PROBLEMS

In general, Weimaraners are a hardy breed of dog. However, like many breeds, they sometimes suffer from bloat and hip dysplasia.

PET FACTS

- Intelligent, obedient, friendly
- Regular brushing
- Regular, vigorous
- Adapts to urban living, but needs plenty of space
- Excellent watchdog

🐾 **BE AWARE**

- This powerful dog requires plenty of exercise to stop it from getting bored
- Prone to sunburn on the nose in summer

Male: 24–27 in (61–69 cm)
55–70 lb (25–32 kg)
Female: 22–25 in (56–63 cm)
50–65 lb (23–29 kg)

Irish Setter

This elegant and graceful dog is much admired for its lustrous chestnut coat with profuse feathering. It is a little lighter and speedier than other setters, having been bred to cope with Ireland's marshy terrain.

HISTORY
The Irish Setter, also known as the Red Setter, evolved in the British Isles over the past 200 years from a variety of setters, spaniels and pointers. Like all setters, these dogs were bred to "set," or locate, game birds and then to remain still while the hunter shot or netted the birds.

DESCRIPTION
The Irish Setter's profusely feathered silky coat comes in rich shades of chestnut to mahogany, sometimes with splashes of white on the chest and feet. The ears are long and low-set and the legs are long and muscular.

TEMPERAMENT
Like most sporting dogs, Irish Setters are full of energy and high spirits. They are also very affectionate, sometimes overwhelmingly so. Although they can be difficult to train, being easily distracted, the effort will be rewarding for both owner and dog. Training must never be strict.

GROOMING
Daily combing and brushing of the soft, flat, medium-length coat is all that is required to keep it in excellent condition.

Keep it free of burrs and tangles, and give a little extra care when the dog is molting. Bathe or dry shampoo only when necessary.

EXERCISE & FEEDING
All setters need plenty of exercise, if possible, running free. If they don't get a long, brisk walk at least daily, they will be restless and difficult to manage. Feed two or three small meals a day rather than one large meal.

HEALTH PROBLEMS
The breed is particularly prone to epilepsy and severe skin allergies. They also suffer from bloat, eye problems and elbow and hip dysplasia.

PET FACTS

- Lively and affectionate
- Daily combing
- Regular, extensive and vigorous
- Needs plenty of space to run free. Unsuited to apartment living
- Not a good watchdog

BE AWARE

- Lack of exercise can make this dog restless and difficult to train
- Prone to skin problems

Male: 26–28 in (66–71 cm)
65–75 lb (29–34 kg)
Female: 24–26 in (61–66 cm)
55–65 lb (25–29 kg)

Gordon Setter

Larger, heavier and more powerful than its cousins, the Gordon Setter was once known as the Black and Tan Setter of Scotland. A natural pointer and retriever, it also makes a delightful pet.

HISTORY

Bred in Scotland as a gundog by the fourth Duke of Gordon in the late eighteenth century, this dog has setter, Collie and possibly Bloodhound genes. It easily handles tough terrain.

DESCRIPTION

This breed has great stamina. The silky coat is generously feathered and is always a gleaming black with tan to reddish mahogany markings. On the face, the markings are clearly defined and include a spot over each eye.

TEMPERAMENT

Calmer than other setters and more reserved with strangers, the Gordon Setter is an excellent, affectionate companion. It is reliable with children and fairly easily trained, but training must never be harsh or heavy-handed, because it is important not to break the dog's spirit.

GROOMING

Regular combing and brushing of the soft, flat, medium-length coat is all that is required to keep it in excellent condition. It is important to check for burrs and tangles, and to give extra care when the dog is shedding. Bathe or dry shampoo only when necessary. Trim the hair on the bottom of the feet and clip the nails.

PET FACTS

- Intelligent, friendly, loyal
- Regular combing and brushing
- Regular, vigorous
- Needs plenty of space to run free; unsuited to apartment living
- Adequate watchdog

BE AWARE

- Lack of exercise can make these dogs restless

EXERCISE & FEEDING

All setters need plenty of exercise, if possible, running free. If they don't get a long, brisk, daily walk, they will be difficult to manage. As these dogs are prone to bloat, it is a good idea to feed them two or three small meals a day.

HEALTH PROBLEMS

The breed is prone to bloat, hip dysplasia and eye diseases, such as progressive retinal atrophy and cataracts.

Male: 24–27 in (61–69 cm)
55–80 lb (25–36 kg)
Female: 23–26 in (58–66 cm)
45–70 lb (20–32 kg)

English Setter

Reliable and hard-working, this beautiful dog has strength, stamina and grace. It also seems to have an innate sense of what is expected of a gundog, responding intelligently to each new situation.

HISTORY
Descended from a variety of Spanish spaniels, this breed was also known as the Laverack Setter, after Edward Laverack, who played a major role in its development.

DESCRIPTION
This elegant dog has a finely chiselled head and large nostrils. Its flat, straight coat is of medium length and comes in white, flecked with combinations of black, lemon, liver, and black and tan. There is feathering along the underbody and on the ears.

TEMPERAMENT
Gentle and high-spirited, these dogs take their duties seriously, and when one becomes part of a family, it is quiet and very loyal. They are friendly, intelligent and adept at anticipating their owner's wishes.

GROOMING
Daily combing and brushing of the medium-length, silky coat is important, with extra care when the dog is shedding. Bathe or dry shampoo only when necessary. Trim the hair on the feet and tail and check the long ears for any signs of infection.

EXERCISE & FEEDING
Like all setters, these dogs require a long daily walk. As they are prone to bloat, feed two or three small meals a day instead of one large one.

HEALTH PROBLEMS
While generally healthy, these dogs may suffer from hip dysplasia, bloat and progressive retinal atrophy.

PET FACTS

Intelligent, friendly

Daily combing and brushing

Regular, vigorous

Needs plenty of space to run free; unsuited to apartment living

Adequate watchdog

BE AWARE
- Will become restless if not given sufficient exercise
- Likely to roam if its yard is not securely enclosed

Male: 24–26 in (61–66 cm)
60–75 lb (27–34 kg)
Female: 23–25 in (58–63 cm)
55–65 lb (25–29 kg)

HOUNDS

Beagle

It's not only its manageable size that makes the Beagle so popular. It is an endearing and engaging creature, eager to romp and play and demanding little of an owner's time for grooming or exercise.

PET FACTS

Alert, joyful, even-tempered

Regular brushing

Regular, moderate

Adapts well to urban living

Not a good watchdog

BE AWARE

• Beagles bay when they bark, which can be irritating

• They are prone to wander

HISTORY

Packs of Beagles were traditionally used to hunt hares by scent, which they did enthusiastically. The name may come from the Celtic word for small, *beag*, or the French for gape throat, *begueule*. The modern dog is considerably larger than those of earlier times, which were often carried about in pockets or saddlebags.

DESCRIPTION

This muscular little dog is the smallest of the pack hounds. Its dense waterproof coat comes in combinations of white, black, tan, red, lemon and blue mottle.

TEMPERAMENT

Beagles need firm handling as they are strong willed and not always easy to train. When they pick up an interesting smell, it is sometimes hard to get their attention. Alert and good tempered, they are rarely aggressive and love children. Indeed, they crave companionship.

GROOMING

The Beagle's smooth, shorthaired coat is easy to look after. Brush with a firm bristle brush, and dry shampoo occasionally. Bathe with mild soap only when necessary. Be sure to check the ears carefully for signs of infection and keep the nails trimmed.

EXERCISE & FEEDING

Energetic and possessing great stamina, the Beagle needs plenty of exercise, but a yard of reasonable size will take care of most of its requirements. A brisk daily walk will cover the rest. There are no special feeding requirements, but if you use food as a motivator when training, be careful that the dog does not become obese and lazy.

HEALTH PROBLEMS

Beagles may suffer from spinal problems, epilepsy, skin conditions and genetic eye diseases, such as glaucoma and cataracts. They also have a tendency to become obese.

Male: 14–16 in (36–41 cm)
22–25 lb (10–11 kg)
Female: 13–15 in (33–38 cm)
20–23 lb (9–10 kg)

Dachshund

These extraordinary "sausage" dogs come in a range of colors, sizes and coat types—it seems there's a sturdy little Dachshund for every taste, although most owners have decided preferences.

PET FACTS

Brave, curious, lively

Regular brushing

Regular, moderate

Ideal for apartment living

Good watchdog

BE AWARE

- It is important to prevent these dogs from becoming obese as they are prone to spinal damage

- They are enthusiastic diggers and will wreak havoc in a garden

HISTORY
The Dachshund (pronounced dak sund) originated in Germany many hundreds of years ago—*Dachs* is the German word for badger. The Dachshund was bred to hunt and follow these animals to earth, gradually becoming highly evolved, with short-ened legs to dig the prey out and go down inside the burrows. Smaller Dachshunds were bred to hunt hare and stoat. Dachshunds have many "terrier" characteristics. They are versatile and courageous dogs and have been known to take on foxes and otters as well as badgers.

DESCRIPTION
Dachshunds come in two sizes—Standard and Miniature. All Dachshunds have a low-slung, muscular, elongated body with very short legs and strong forequarters developed for digging. The skin is loose and the coat comes in three distinct types: smooth, short and dense; longhaired, soft, flat and straight with feathering; and wirehaired with a short double coat, a beard and bushy eyebrows. The wirehaired is the least common and was developed to hunt in brushy thickets. The three coat types come in a range of solid colors, two-colored, brindled, tiger-marked or dappled. These dogs have a big bark for their size, which might be enough to intimidate intruders.

TEMPERAMENT
Alert, lively and affectionate, Dachshunds are great little characters, good company and reasonably obedient when carefully trained.

They can be slightly aggressive to strangers but make wonderful house pets. Miniatures are perhaps less suited to households with young children, as they are vulnerable to injury from rough handling.

Standard
Male: About 8 in (20 cm)
16–32 lb (7–15 kg)
Female: About 8 in (20 cm)
16–32 lb (7–15 kg)

Miniature
Male: About 6 in (15 cm)
Up to 11 lb (5 kg)
Female: About 6 in (15 cm)
Up to 11 lb (5 kg)

GROOMING

Regular brushing with a bristle brush is appropriate for all coat types. Dry shampoo or bathe when necessary, but always make sure the dog is thoroughly dry and warm after a bath. The smooth variety will come up gleaming if you rub it with a piece of toweling or a chamois. Check the ears regularly.

EXERCISE & FEEDING

These are active dogs with surprising stamina and they love a regular walk or session of play in the park. Be careful, however, when pedestrians are about as Dachshunds are more likely to be stepped on than more visible dogs. They should be discouraged from jumping as they are prone to spinal damage. There are no special feeding requirements, but Dachshunds have a tendency to become overweight and lazy. This is a serious health risk, putting added strain on the back.

HEALTH PROBLEMS

Herniated disks in the back can cause severe pain and paralysis of the hind legs. As they are a rather long-lived breed, Dachshunds also suffer problems common to aging dogs, such as obesity, diabetes and cardiac disease. They are also subject to genetic eye diseases and skin problems, including pattern baldness on the ears.

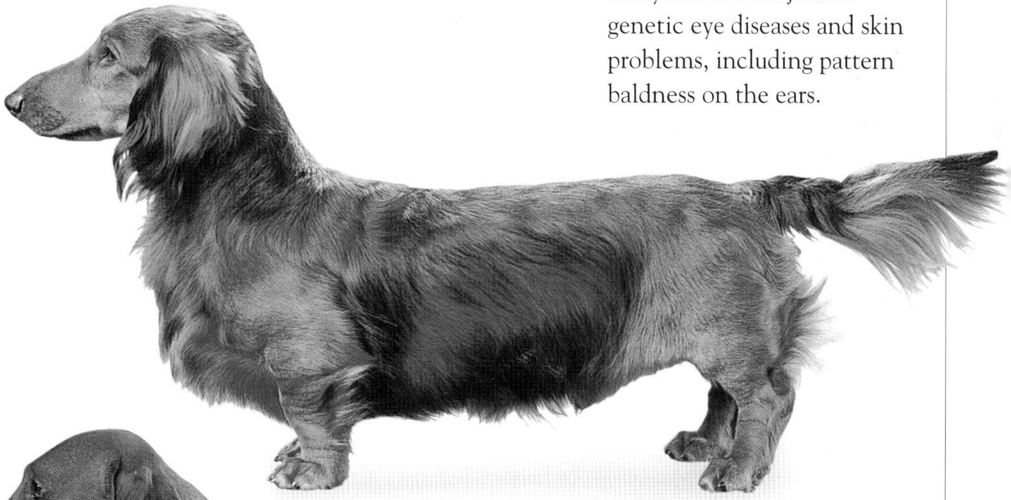

Basset Hound

The mournful face of this gentle, lovable hound belies its lively nature. When hunting, it is single-minded in following a scent, but it also makes a delightful pet in homes where there are young children.

PET FACTS

Gentle and loyal

Weekly brushing, paying attention to ears and feet

Regular, moderate

Well suited to urban living

Not a good watchdog

BE AWARE

- These dogs may smell due to skin and ear infections

- Prone to overeating and becoming fat, if given the opportunity

of white with tan, black and, occasionally, lemon. The ears are long and velvety.

TEMPERAMENT

Good-natured, sociable and gentle with children, Basset Hounds fit into family life well. With proper training, they are obedient, but when they pick up an interesting smell, it is sometimes hard to get their attention.

GROOMING

The smooth, shorthaired coat is easy to groom. Comb and brush with a firm bristle brush, and shampoo only when necessary. Wipe under the ears every week and trim toenails regularly.

EXERCISE & FEEDING

Plenty of moderate exercise will help to keep the Basset Hound healthy and happy but discourage it from jumping and stressing the front legs. Do not overfeed because extra weight places too great a load on the legs and spine. As

HISTORY

While most Basset breeds originated in France (*bas* means "low" in French), the Basset Hound was developed in Britain only about 100 years ago. Its ability to concentrate on a particular scent quickly earned it respect as a hunting partner.

DESCRIPTION

This sturdy dog has short, stocky legs on which the skin is loose and folded. Much of the dog's weight is concentrated at the front of the long, barrel-shaped body. The shorthaired coat sheds only moderately and comes in combinations

they are prone to bloat, it is also wise to feed them two or three small meals a day instead of one large meal.

HEALTH PROBLEMS

Because the ears are long and heavy, they are susceptible to infection. These dogs also suffer from bloat and skin infections, such as seborrhea.

Male: 12–15 in (30–38 cm)
50–65 lb (23–29 kg)
Female: 11–14 in (28–36 cm)
45–60 lb (20–27 kg)

Basenji

A handsome, muscular dog, the Basenji is as fastidious as a cat about its personal grooming, even washing itself with its paws. Although the breed is well known for being barkless, it is not silent, and "yodels" when happy.

HISTORY
These ancient dogs originated in Africa, where they were used for hunting and valued for their great stamina. They were introduced into Europe and then North America in the twentieth century.

DESCRIPTION
The Basenji is a compact, muscular, medium-sized dog, with a distinctive trotting gait. Their loose, silky, shorthaired coats come in combinations of white, tan, chestnut, brindle and black. When alert, the forehead is creased with wrinkles, giving the dog a worried look. The tail is tightly curled over the back. The breeding pattern is unusual, the bitch coming into season only once a year.

TEMPERAMENT
Alert, affectionate, energetic and curious, the Basenji loves to play and makes a good pet, as long as it is handled regularly from an early age. It is very intelligent and responds well to training.

GROOMING
The smooth, shorthaired, silky coat is easy to groom. Comb and brush with a firm bristle brush, and shampoo only when necessary.

EXERCISE & FEEDING
Vigorous daily exercise will keep the Basenji trim and fit—they have a tendency to become fat and lazy unless the owner is conscientious about their exercise regimen.

HEALTH PROBLEMS
This breed may suffer from kidney problems, which must be treated the moment any symptoms are noticed. They are also susceptible to progressive retinal atrophy and intestinal problems.

PET FACTS

Intelligent, playful but very independent

Weekly brushing

Regular, vigorous

Well suited to urban living

Poor watchdog

BE AWARE

- Basenjis like to chew, so provide them with plenty of toys that they can destroy

- They also like to climb, and can easily negotiate chain-wire fences

Male: 16–17 in (41–43 cm)
22–26 lb (10–12 kg)
Female: 15–16 in (38–41 cm)
20–25 lb (9–11 kg)

Whippet

Gentle, affectionate and adaptable, the Whippet makes a delightful companion and jogging partner. Clean and well behaved in the house, it settles happily into family routine.

TEMPERAMENT

Gentle and sensitive, the Whippet makes a surprisingly docile and obedient pet, although it is inclined to be nervous when lively children are around. While it is easily trained, owners must take great care not to break its spirit by being harsh or overbearing.

HISTORY

This descendant of the Greyhound, perhaps with some terrier blood, was used for hunting rabbits in northern England. It was also pitted against its peers in a pastime known as rag racing, in which the dogs, when signaled with a handkerchief, streaked from a standing start towards their owners.

DESCRIPTION

The Whippet's lean, delicate appearance belies its strength and speed—it can accelerate rapidly to about 35 mph (55 km/h). The fine, dense coat comes in many colors or in mixes. The muzzle is long and slender and the overall impression is one of streamlined elegance.

GROOMING

The smooth, fine, shorthaired coat is easy to groom. Brush with a firm bristle brush, and bathe only when necessary. A regular rub all over with a damp chamois will keep the coat gleaming. Keep the nails clipped.

EXERCISE & FEEDING

Whippets kept as pets should have regular opportunities to run free on open ground as well as have long, brisk, daily walks on the leash. There are no special feeding requirements.

HEALTH PROBLEMS

Because of their fine coats, Whippets are sensitive to cold and may get sunburned. Their bones are delicate and easily broken. They are also subject to genetic eye diseases such as cataracts and progressive retinal atrophy.

Male: 19–22 in (48–56 cm)
20–22 lb (9–10 kg)
Female: 18–21 in (46–53 cm)
19–21 lb (9–10 kg)

Norwegian Elkhound

Surprisingly, the handsome Norwegian Elkhound can adapt to warmer climates than its homeland as the thick coat insulates it from both heat and cold. It makes a fine pet.

HISTORY
Dogs of this kind have been used to hunt bears, elk and moose since Viking times. They would chase and hold the prey until hunters arrived for the kill. They were also used to pull sleds.

DESCRIPTION
Although it is totally silent while tracking, the Elkhound is perhaps the most "talkative" dog of all. It has a whole vocabulary of sounds, each with a different meaning, and you will soon learn to recognize its way of telling you there are strangers about.
A member of the Spitz family, the Elkhound has a shortish, thickset body with the tail tightly curled over the back. The coat comes in various shades of gray, with black tips on the outer coat, and lighter hair on the chest, underbody, legs and underside of the tail. There is a thick ruff around the neck.

TEMPERAMENT
While gentle and devoted to its owner, the Elkhound needs consistent training that is firm but never harsh. Although adaptable, it likes a set routine.

GROOMING
Regular brushing of the hard, coarse, weatherproof coat is important, with extra care when the dog is shedding its dense undercoat. At this time, the dead hair clings to the new hair and must be removed with a rubber brush designed for the task. Bathing is largely unnecessary.

EXERCISE & FEEDING
An agile, energetic dog, the Elkhound revels in strenuous activity. The more space it has to move around the better. There are no special feeding requirements.

HEALTH PROBLEMS
This hardy breed is used to a rugged life and suffers from few genetic diseases other than hip dysplasia and the common eye diseases.

Male: 19–21 in (48–53 cm)
50–60 lb (23–27 kg)
Female: 18–20 in (46–51 cm)
40–55 lb (18–25 kg)

Saluki

This ancient breed was used in Arabia, in association with falcons, for hunting gazelle and other game. While the falcons swooped over the quarry, the Salukis gave chase and held the prey for a mounted hunter to kill.

HISTORY

Related to the Greyhound, this fast and agile breed originated in Arabia—the name comes from the now-vanished city of Saluk. They are also known as Gazelle Hounds, although they hunted small animals other than gazelle. In Muslim society, they were thought of as "the sacred gift of Allah" and, traditionally, they were never sold, but could be presented as a gift to a friend or someone of importance.

DESCRIPTION

The athletic appearance is one of total grace and symmetry. Slim and fine-boned, Salukis are built for speed and capable of bursts of 40 mph (65 km/h) or more, but they also have exceptional endurance.

The galloping gait is unusual, and unique to sighthounds, with all four feet being off the ground at the same time when the animal is in full chase. This gives the impression that the dog is flying. There are two types of coat, smooth-haired and feathered. Both have feathering on the ears and on the long, curved tail, but the smooth variety has none on the legs. The soft, smooth, silky coat comes in black and tan, white, cream, fawn, gold and red, as well as various combinations of these. A dog with a small patch of white in the middle of its forehead is thought by Bedouin tribes to have "the kiss of Allah" and is regarded as special.

PET FACTS

- Gentle, loyal and sensitive
- Brush twice weekly
- Regular, moderate
- Adapts well to urban living if given adequate exercise
- Not a good watchdog

BE AWARE

- These dogs are able to jump very high fences
- Cancer is a growing problem for this breed

The aristocratic head is narrow and well proportioned and the feathered ears are long and hanging.

TEMPERAMENT

Gentle, affectionate and intensely loyal, Salukis quickly become part of the family, although they may remain aloof with strangers. They are not at all aggressive but can be rather sensitive and, while easy to train, they become nervous and timid if the trainer's manner is over-bearing or harsh.

GROOMING

The soft, smooth, silky coat is easy to groom and there is little shedding. Comb and brush with a firm bristle brush, and shampoo only when necessary. Be careful not to overbrush as this may break the coat. Trim the hair between the toes or it will matt and make the feet sore.

EXERCISE & FEEDING

Salukis should have regular opportunities to run free on open ground in addition to long daily walks—they make excellent jogging companions. There are no special feeding requirements, but they tend to be light eaters. They also drink less than other dogs, as you might expect, given their region of origin.

HEALTH PROBLEMS

These dogs are prone to cancer and genetic eye diseases, such as cataracts and PRA. Dogs with pale or mottled noses should have sunscreen applied regularly to such sensitive areas during the summer months.

Male: 23–28 in (58–71 cm)
50–60 lb (23–27 kg)
Female: 20–27 in (51–69 cm)
35–55 lb (16–25 kg)

Bloodhound

Brought to England by William the Conqueror, the solemn-looking Bloodhound has entered literature and legend as the archetypal sleuth dog, but it never kills its prey.

PET FACTS

Gentle, sensitive affectionate

Minimal

Regular, vigorous

Adapts to urban living, but needs plenty of space and exercise

Too shy to be a very good watchdog

BE AWARE

• A bored Bloodhound's mournful howl may not be enjoyed by neighbors

• Prone to ear infections because of the long, heavy ears

sometimes a little white on the chest, feet and the tip of the tail.

TEMPERAMENT
Sensitive, gentle and shy, a Bloodhound becomes devoted to its master, and gets along well with people and other dogs; it is rarely vicious.

HISTORY
The Bloodhound's ancestry can be traced directly to eighth-century Belgium, and it is also known as the Flemish Hound. It is able to follow any scent, even a human's, a rare ability in a dog.

DESCRIPTION
Large and powerful, the Bloodhound looks tougher than it is. The skin is loose and seems several sizes too large for the body. The coat is short and dense, fine on the head and ears, and comes in tan with black or liver, tawny, or solid red. There is

GROOMING
The smooth, shorthaired coat is easy to groom. Brush with a firm bristle brush, and bathe only when necessary. A rub with a rough towel or chamois will leave the coat gleaming. Clean the long, floppy ears regularly.

EXERCISE & FEEDING
Bloodhounds love a good run and need a lot of exercise. However, if it picks up an interesting scent you may find it difficult to get its attention. As this breed

is prone to bloat you should feed two or three small meals a day instead of one large one. Avoid exercise after meals.

HEALTH PROBLEMS
These dogs are susceptible to bloat and hip dysplasia. A well-padded bed is recommended to avoid calluses on the joints.

Male: 25–27 in (63–69 cm)
90–110 lb (41–50 kg)
Female: 23–25 in (58–63 cm)
80–100 lb (36–45 kg)

Rhodesian Ridgeback

An all-weather, low-maintenance, dedicated watchdog, the Rhodesian Ridgeback bonds closely with its adoptive family in the early years of its life and makes a devoted, fun-loving pet.

HISTORY

The breed gets its name from a peculiarity of the coat—a well-defined dagger-shaped ridge of hair that lies along the spine in the opposite direction to the rest of the coat. Although they originated in South Africa, it was in what is now known as Zimbabwe that these dogs became prized for their ability to hunt lion and other large game.

DESCRIPTION

This is a strong, active dog with a dense, glossy coat that comes in solid shades of red to light wheaten with a dark muzzle and sometimes a little white on the chest. When alert, the brow is wrinkled.

TEMPERAMENT

Like many powerful dogs, the Rhodesian Ridgeback is a gentle, friendly animal, although it can be a tenacious fighter when aroused. It makes an outstanding watchdog and a devoted family pet. Intelligent and good natured, it is easy to train, but should be treated gently so as not to break its spirit or make it aggressive.

GROOMING

The smooth, shorthaired coat is easy to groom. Brush with a firm bristle brush, and shampoo only when necessary.

EXERCISE & FEEDING

These dogs have great stamina and you will tire long before they do, but they will adapt to your exercise regimen. They love to swim. There are no special feeding requirements, but beware of overfeeding—they will eat all they can get and still act hungry.

HEALTH PROBLEMS

Rhodesian Ridgebacks are a hardy breed, able to withstand dramatic changes of temperature. They are, however, susceptible to hip dysplasia.

PET FACTS

- Brave, gentle, loyal
- Daily brushing
- Regular, moderate
- Adapts well to urban living, but needs plenty of space
- Outstanding watchdog

BE AWARE

- Training should be gentle and start young while the dog is still small enough to manage

Male: 25–27 in (63–69 cm)
80–90 lb (36–41 kg)
Female: 24–26 in (61–66 cm)
65–75 lb (29–34 kg)

Afghan Hound

While undeniably elegant and, when in peak condition, a thing of beauty, the Afghan Hound is not an easy-care pet. Choose one only if you are prepared to make a big commitment in time.

HISTORY

A hardy breed, agile and with great stamina, the Afghan Hound has been used for many centuries in its native land to hunt gazelle and other large prey, including snow leopards. It was especially favored by royalty.

DESCRIPTION

The coat is very long, straight and silky, except on the face and along the spine, and comes in all colors and some combinations. White markings are not liked by breed fanciers. Thick falls of hair on the legs protect the animal from cold.

The end of the tail should curl in a complete ring. The gait is free and springy.

TEMPERAMENT

The enormous popularity of these dogs during the seventies meant that many were acquired for the wrong reasons. Although they are intelligent, Afghan Hounds are not easy to train and, being quite large, they are not easy to handle either. They are definitely not a fashion accessory, and owners need to establish a genuine relationship with them. Too many of these dogs have been abandoned due to unrealistic expectations of owners.

GROOMING

The long, thick coat demands a great deal of attention and must be brushed every day. Dry shampoo when necessary and bathe once a month.

PET FACTS

Independent, lively, loving

Extensive

Regular, vigorous

Adapts well to urban living, but needs plenty of space

Not a good watchdog

BE AWARE

• These dogs require a great deal of attention

EXERCISE & FEEDING

Afghan Hounds love open spaces and must be allowed to run free in a safe area as well as having long daily walks. There are no special feeding requirements.

HEALTH PROBLEMS

While the Afghan is generally a robust breed, some dogs may suffer from hip dysplasia and eye problems, such as cataracts and progressive retinal atrophy.

Male: 26–29 in (66–74 cm)
55–65 lb (25–29 kg)
Female: 24–26 in (61–66 cm)
45–55 lb (20–25 kg)

Borzoi

The well-mannered Borzoi is a dog of grace and beauty, dignified and gentle. If you want a constant companion and can give it the exercise and love it craves, this may be the dog for you.

HISTORY

Also known as the Russian Wolfhound, Borzois were used in pairs by members of the Russian aristocracy to chase wolves. The prey was caught and held by the dogs until the mounted hunter arrived for the kill. They are probably descended from the "gaze hounds" of the Middle East, which they resemble.

DESCRIPTION

A tall, elegant dog, the Borzoi has a lean, muscular body designed for speed. The long, silky, often wavy coat is profusely feathered, and comes in all colors, usually white with colored markings. The small ears are pointed and well feathered.

TEMPERAMENT

Gentle, reserved and some- times nervy around children, Borzois are affectionate with their owners and tolerant of other dogs, but they need plenty of attention.

GROOMING

The long, silky coat is easy to groom. Brush regularly with a firm bristle brush, and dry shampoo when necessary. Bathing presents problems with such a tall dog but shouldn't be required very often. Clip the hair between the toes to keep the feet comfortable and to stop them from spreading.

EXERCISE & FEEDING

To maintain their fitness these dogs need plenty of exercise, including regular opportunities to run off the leash. As they are susceptible to bloat it is a good idea to feed small meals two or three times a day and avoid exercise after meals.

HEALTH PROBLEMS

These large, deep-chested dogs are particularly prone to bloat. As they age, they may also be susceptible to progessive retinal atrophy and cataracts.

Male: At least 28 in (71 cm)
75–105 lb (34–48 kg)
Female: At least 26 in (66 cm)
60–90 lb (27–41 kg)

Greyhound

Agile and fleet of foot, this breed is one of the oldest known, long valued for its hunting prowess. The Greyhound's lean, elegant lines are often emblazoned on the coats of arms of royalty.

HISTORY
Greyhounds probably originated in the Middle East but also have a long history in Europe. They were much sought after as hunting dogs.

DESCRIPTION
Lean and powerful, these dogs are built for speed. Their long, muscular legs can propel them at up to 45 mph (70 km/h). At full stretch, their streamlined movement is a joy to watch. The close, short, fine coat comes in black, gray, white, red, blue, fawn, fallow, brindle or any of theses colors broken with white.

TEMPERAMENT
Gentle and sensitive, the Greyhound makes a surprisingly docile and obedient pet, given its hunting background. It does, however, retain a highly developed chase instinct and should always be kept on a leash in public. Greyhounds are good with children and settle happily into the family routine. While these dogs are easily trained, owners must be careful not to break their spirit by being harsh or overbearing.

GROOMING
The smooth, shorthaired coat is very easy to groom. Simply comb and brush with a firm bristle brush, and shampoo only when necessary. A rub with a chamois will ensure that the coat gleams.

EXERCISE & FEEDING
Greyhounds that are kept as pets should have regular opportunities to run free on open ground as well as have long, brisk walks, preferably at the same time every day. Greyhounds love a regular routine. There are no special feeding requirements, but it is better to give them two small meals a day rather than a single large one.

HEALTH PROBLEMS
Greyhounds are one of the few breeds that do not suffer from hip dysplasia. They have very thin skin that tears easily and are unsuited to cold climates.

PET FACTS

- Docile, loving and sensitive
- Occasional grooming
- Regular, moderate
- Adapts well to urban living if given plenty of exercise
- Good watchdog

BE AWARE
- Should be leashed in public
- May be sensitive to some common anesthetics and flea-killing products

Male: 28–30 in (71–76 cm)
65–70 lb (29–32 kg)
Female: 27–28 in (68–71 cm)
60–65 lb (27–29 kg)

Irish Wolfhound

A true gentle giant, the Irish Wolfhound is affectionate and wonderful around children. It was once used to hunt wolves—so successfully that wolves have disappeared from the British Isles.

HISTORY
After working its way out of a job, the breed was brought back from the brink of extinction about 140 years ago by a British Army officer, Captain George Graham, who saw its potential for rescue work.

DESCRIPTION
A massive, muscular dog, the Irish Wolfhound is the tallest breed in the world. Its rough, wiry coat comes in gray, brindle, red, black, fawn and white. The paws are large and round, with markedly arched toes and strong, curved nails.

TEMPERAMENT
In spite of being a killer of wolves, this dog is gentle, loyal and very affectionate. It is trustworthy around children, although it might knock them over with its large tail. While disinclined to bark, its size alone should be daunting to intruders.

GROOMING
Unless the hard, wiry coat is combed often, it will become matted. Clip out any knots. Trim around the eyes and ears with blunt-nosed scissors.

EXERCISE & FEEDING
Irish Wolfhounds are inclined to be lazy and need a reasonable amount of exercise, but no more than smaller breeds. There are no special feeding requirements.

PET FACTS

Calm and gentle

Daily combing

Regular, moderate

Needs plenty of space. Unsuited to apartments

Adequate watchdog

BE AWARE
- To avoid joint damage, do not take young dogs for long walks
- Can be rather difficult and expensive to look after

HEALTH PROBLEMS
Like many of the giant breeds, these dogs may suffer from heart disease. They are also subject to hip dysplasia and cataracts.

Male: 32–38 in (81–95 cm)
115–125 lb (52–57 kg)
Female: 28–32 in (71–81 cm)
100–110 lb (45–50 kg)

WORKING DOGS

Boxer

If your best friend is a Boxer, you can rely on it absolutely to take care of your property and to be waiting with the most enthusiastic welcome whenever you return home.

HISTORY

Developed in Germany from Mastiff-type dogs, the Boxer was originally used in bull-baiting and eventually crossed with the Bulldog to improve this ability. It was little known outside its country of origin until after World War II, when returning soldiers took some home.

DESCRIPTION

The body is compact and powerful and the shiny, close-fitting coat comes in fawn, brindle and various shades of red, with white markings. The tail is usually docked; ear-cropping is optional.

GROOMING

The Boxer's smooth, shorthaired coat is easy to groom. Brush with a firm bristle brush, and bathe only when necessary.

EXERCISE & FEEDING

An active, athletic breed, Boxers need daily work or exercise. As well as a long, brisk, daily walk, they enjoy a session of play, fetching a ball. There are no special feeding requirements.

PET FACTS

- Lively, loving, loyal
- Occasional brushing
- Regular, vigorous
- Adapts well to urban living, but needs space
- Excellent watchdog

BE AWARE

- These dogs need a strong, energetic owner to play with
- May be aggressive with other dogs

HEALTH PROBLEMS

The shape of the nose can lead to sinus infections and breathing difficulties. They are prone to skin cancer, so any skin lumps discovered during grooming sessions should be investigated as they may be malignant tumors. Boxers can also have serious hereditary heart problems.

TEMPERAMENT

Intelligent and easily trained, Boxers have been widely used in military and police work. Training should start young and be firm and consistent—these exuberant animals need to be handled by a strong adult. They are reliable and protective with children and intensely loyal to their family. Excellent watchdogs, they will restrain an intruder in the same way a Bulldog does.

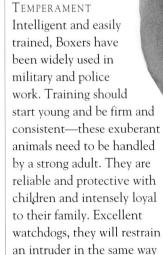

Male: 22–24 in (56–61 cm)
60–70 lb (27–32 kg)
Female: 21–23 in (53–58 cm)
55–65 lb (25–29 kg)

Schnauzer

Although known outside its native Germany for less than a century, the unusual-looking Schnauzer now has admirers worldwide, who are attracted by its high spirits, stamina and loyalty.

HISTORY

The Schnauzer is an ancient German breed, or more correctly, three breeds, since the three sizes, Giant, Standard and Miniature (see p. 162), are considered separate breeds. In the U.S., the Giant and Standard are classified as working dogs while the Miniature is considered to be a terrier. Many countries class all three together in a group known as utility dogs. The name comes from the German word for muzzle, Schnauze, a reference to the distinctive mustache of this breed, but these dogs were once also known as Wirehaired Pinschers. The Giant was originally used for herding cattle and as a guard dog. It was later harnessed to pull small traps. The Standard was prized as a ratter and often accompanied stage coaches and wagons.

DESCRIPTION

An angular, square-looking dog, strong and vigorous, the Schnauzer has a hard, wiry double coat that comes in pure black or salt and pepper colors, sometimes with white on the chest. The thick, prominent eyebrows and long mustache are often trimmed to accentuate the dog's overall square-cut shape. The feet are neat, round and compact, like a cat's paws, with well-arched toes and thick black pads. The tail is usually docked at the third joint.

TEMPERAMENT

These dogs are noted for their reliability and affectionate nature and they make excellent watchdogs. They are intelligent and independent but need firm, consistent training because they are inclined to be headstrong.

PET FACTS

- Spirited, lively, affectionate
- Daily brushing
- Regular, moderate
- Adapts well to urban living, but needs plenty of exercise
- Excellent watchdog

BE AWARE

- The ears are nearly always cropped in the US, but this practice is illegal in Britain
- These dogs may be aggressive with strangers

Standard
Male: 18–20 in (46–51 cm)
30–45 lb (14–20 kg)
Female: 17–19 in (43–48 cm)
30–40 lb (14–18 kg)

GROOMING

The wiry coat is reasonably easy to look after, but unless it is combed or brushed daily with a short wire brush, it will become matted. The undercoat is dense. Clip out knots and brush first with the grain, then against the grain to lift the coat. The animal should be clipped all over to an even length twice a year, in spring and fall, but this is a job best left to an expert. Trim around the eyes and ears with blunt-nosed scissors. Clean the whiskers after meals.

EXERCISE & FEEDING

These energetic dogs will take as much exercise as they can get, and relish play sessions during which they can run off the leash. At very least, they should be given a long, brisk daily walk. Don't overdo it with a very young pup, though, until the frame is strong and mature. There are no special feeding requirements.

HEALTH PROBLEMS

Schnauzers are reasonably healthy dogs, although the Giant may suffer from hip dysplasia and orthopedic problems. Both the Giant and Standard are subject to genetic eye diseases, such as cataracts and progressive retinal atrophy.

Giant
Male: 26–28 in (66–71 cm)
60–80 lb (27–36 kg)
Female: 23–26 in (58–66 cm)
55–75 lb (25–34 kg)

Note: Cropped ears are common in this breed. See p. 31 for more information

Samoyed

The Samoyed is almost always good-humored and ready for any challenge. With its pale, luxurious fur coat and thick, perky tail curled over the back to one side, it makes a spectacular pet.

HISTORY
Samoyeds are members of the Spitz family of dogs, which range throughout Arctic regions. They evolved as pack animals and sled dogs and were used by the nomadic Samoyed tribe of Siberia.

DESCRIPTION
The compact muscular body of this hard-working breed indicates its strength. The thick, silver-tipped coat comes in white, biscuit and cream.

TEMPERAMENT
The Samoyed is too friendly to be of much use as a watch-dog, although its bark will alert you to the presence of strangers. It willingly adapts to family life and gets on well with children. Start training at an early age

GROOMING
Brushing two or three times a week is usually all that is needed, but extra care will be necessary when the dog is shedding. The long coat does not shed, but the woolly undercoat comes out in clumps twice a year. Bathing is difficult and mostly unnecessary, as the coat sheds dirt readily. Dry shampoo from time to time by brushing unscented talcum powder through the coat.

EXERCISE & FEEDING
Samoyeds need a reasonable amount of exercise, but take it easy during warm weather because the woolly undercoat inhibits loss of the heat built up during exercise. There are no special feeding requirements, but Samoyeds are particularly partial to fish.

HEALTH PROBLEMS
Samoyeds are particularly prone to hip dysplasia and also suffer from diabetes. The heavy coat makes these dogs unsuited to life in very hot climates.

Male: 21–24 in (53–61 cm)
45–60 lb (20–27 kg)
Female: 19–21 in (48–53 cm)
45–60 lb (20–27 kg)

Siberian Husky

A member of the Spitz family, the Siberian Husky is able to haul heavy loads over vast distances in impossible terrain. Noted for its speed and stamina, it is often chosen for polar expeditions.

HISTORY
These dogs originated in Siberia and were developed to pull sleds and herd reindeer by the nomadic Chukchi people.

DESCRIPTION
Siberian Huskies are strong, compact working dogs. The face mask and underbody are usually white, and the remaining coat any color. Mismatched eyes are common. The large "snow-shoe" feet have hair between the toes for grip on ice.

TEMPERAMENT
Because they are friendly and bark little, they are ineffective watchdogs, but their wolf-like appearance may deter intruders. Docile and affectionate, they enjoy family life and are dependable around children.

GROOMING
Brush the coarse, medium-length coat twice a week. The woolly undercoat comes out in clumps twice a year and requires extra care. Bathing is difficult and mostly unnecessary, as the coat sheds dirt. An occasional dry shampoo should be enough to keep the coat looking clean. Clip the nails regularly.

EXERCISE & FEEDING
Siberian Huskies need a fair amount of exercise, but don't overdo it in warm weather. They need a large yard with a high fence, but bury the wire at the base of the fence because they are likely to dig their way out and go off hunting. Huskies are thrifty feeders and need less food than you might expect.

HEALTH PROBLEMS
The breed is comparatively free of breed-specific problems, apart from hip dysplasia and occasional eye problems, such as cataracts. Because of their heavy coats, these dogs are unsuited to life in hot climates and should not be excessively exercised in warm weather.

PET FACTS

Playful, friendly, good-natured

Brush twice weekly; more when molting

Regular, vigorous

Adapts well to urban living, but needs plenty of space

Ineffective watchdog

BE AWARE
- Lack of exercise will make these dogs restless; if not securely enclosed, they will go off hunting by themselves

Male: 21–23 in (53–58 cm)
45–60 lb (20–27 kg)
Female: 20–22 in (51–56 cm)
35–50 lb (16–23 kg)

Alaskan Malamute

Despite its wolf-like appearance, this handsome and friendly breed makes a loyal and affectionate family pet. With its strong, powerful body and enormous stamina, it is ideal for work in the Arctic.

HISTORY
These sledding dogs of the Spitz family were named after a nomadic Inuit tribe from Alaska, the Malhemut.

DESCRIPTION
These are powerful, compact working dogs. Their under-body and face masking is always white, while the remaining coat may be light gray to black, gold to red and liver. The plumed tail is carried over the back.

TEMPERAMENT
Malamutes are very active and exceptionally friendly to people but not to other dogs. They look intimidating, but are not good watchdogs.

GROOMING
Brush the dense, coarse coat twice a week, with extra care during shedding—the under-coat comes out in clumps twice a year. Bathing is mostly unnecessary, as the coat sheds dirt readily. Dry shampoo occasionally.

EXERCISE & FEEDING
Malamutes need a reasonable amount of exercise, but don't overdo it in warm weather. They need a large yard with a high fence, but bury the base, because they are likely to dig their way out. They are thrifty feeders and need less food than you might expect. However, they tend to wolf down whatever is offered, which can lead to obesity and bloat.

PET FACTS

- Gentle, friendly, good-natured
- Brush twice weekly; more often when the undercoat is molting
- Regular, vigorous
- Adapts well to urban living, but needs plenty of space
- Ineffective watchdog

BE AWARE
- May be aggressive with other dogs

HEALTH PROBLEMS
The breed is subject to hip dysplasia and eye problems. Malamutes are unsuited to life in hot climates.

Male: 24–26 in (61–66 cm)
80–95 lb (36–43 kg)
Female: 22–24 in (56–61 cm)
70–85 lb (32–38 kg)

Rottweiler

Strong and substantial, the Rottweiler is not a dog for the average home nor for inexperienced owners. It makes an imposing and effective guard dog but needs firm handling and proper training.

HISTORY

The forebears of this breed were left behind throughout Europe many centuries ago by the withdrawing Roman army. In the area around Rottweil, southern Germany, these mastiff-type animals were crossed with sheepdogs to produce "butchers' dogs" capable of herding and guarding livestock.

DESCRIPTION

Compact, muscular dogs, Rottweilers have surprising speed and agility. The thick, medium-length coat conceals a fine undercoat and is always black with rich tan to mahogany markings. The tail is usually docked at the first joint.

TEMPERAMENT

Rottweilers are prized for their aggression and guarding abilities, yet they can, with proper handling, also be loyal, loving and very rewarding companions. They are highly intelligent and have proved their worth beyond question in police, military and customs work over many centuries. Training must begin young, while the dog is still small,

and great care should be taken to ensure that the dog is not made vicious.

GROOMING

The smooth, glossy coat is easy to groom. Brush with a firm bristle brush, and bathe only when necessary.

EXERCISE & FEEDING

You can't give these robust dogs too much work or exercise—they thrive on it. There are no special feeding requirements, but avoid overfeeding.

HEALTH PROBLEMS

Rottweilers are fairly robust and adapt to any climate. However, they may suffer from elbow and hip dysplasia, and eye problems such as cataracts and progressive retinal atrophy.

PET FACTS

- Courageous, intelligent, reliable
- Daily brushing
- Regular, vigorous
- Adapts well to urban living, but needs plenty of exercise
- Excellent watchdog

BE AWARE

- These formidable animals need kind and consistent training from a strong adult to be kept under control
- Rottweilers may be aggressive with other dogs and should be kept on leashes in public places.

Male: 24–27 in (61–69 cm)
95–130 lb (43–59 kg)
Female: 22–25 in (56–63 cm)
85–115 lb (38–52 kg)

Akita

The national dog of Japan, many champions of this breed are considered national treasures. The handsome and much-loved Akita is renowned for its strength, courage and loyalty.

HISTORY

Displaying typical characteristics of the Spitz family, to which it belongs, the Akita has only recently become known outside of its native Japan, where it was used for hunting deer, wild boar and black bears. In feudal times, it was pitted in savage dog-fighting spectacles, but these are now outlawed and the dog has found work with the police and is a reliable guard dog.

DESCRIPTION

The largest of the Japanese Spitz-type breeds, the well-proportioned Akita has a muscular body and a waterproof double coat that comes in all colors with clear, dark markings. The tail is thick and carried in a curl or double curl over the back. Akitas have webbed feet and are very strong swimmers.

TEMPERAMENT

Despite the ferocity of many of its past activities, with diligent training the Akita can make an excellent pet. Care should always be taken, however, around other dogs. This dog likes to dominate and needs a strong, experienced adult to control it.

GROOMING

The coarse, stiff, shorthaired coat requires significant grooming and sheds twice a year. Brush with a firm bristle brush, and bathe only when absolutely necessary as bathing removes the natural waterproofing of the coat.

EXERCISE & FEEDING

The Akita needs moderate but regular exercise to stay in shape. There are no special feeding requirements.

HEALTH PROBLEMS

Illness is rare in this robust breed and Akitas don't need to be pampered. As with most purebred dogs, there is some tendency to hip dysplasia and eye problems.

Male: 26–28 in (66–71 cm)
75–120 lb (34–54 kg)
Female: 24–26 in (61–66 cm)
75–110 lb (34–50 kg)

Bernese Mountain Dog

Once used as an all-around working dog in its native Switzerland, the Bernese Mountain Dog adapts easily to domestic life as long as it is given plenty of loving attention from the whole family.

HISTORY

The Bernese Mountain Dog, also known as the Bernese Sennenhund, made itself useful herding cattle, guarding farms and pulling carts in a specially made harness. It also shares the Saint Bernard's skill at finding people lost in snow. It is one of four Swiss breeds that are probably descended from Roman times.

DESCRIPTION

A large, powerful dog, the handsome Bernese is vigorous and agile. It has a gleaming, soft, wavy black coat with white and chestnut markings.

TEMPERAMENT

These gentle, cheerful dogs love children. They are very intelligent, easy to train and are natural watchdogs. They are very loyal and may have trouble adjusting to a new owner after they are 18 months old.

GROOMING

Daily brushing of the long, thick, silky coat is important, with extra care needed when the dog is shedding. Bathe or dry shampoo as necessary.

EXERCISE & FEEDING

Large, active dogs such as these need a regular exercise regimen. There are no special feeding requirements.

HEALTH PROBLEMS

Bernese Mountain Dogs are particularly prone to hip and elbow dysplasia. They also suffer from hereditary eye diseases and cancer.

PET FACTS

- Placid, cheerful, loving
- Daily brushing
- Regular, moderate
- Adapts well to urban living, but needs plenty of exercise
- Excellent watchdog

BE AWARE

- These are one-owner dogs and may find it difficult to adjust to a new owner

Male: 24–28 in (61–71 cm)
85–110 lb (38–50 kg)
Female: 23–27 in (58–69 cm)
80–105 lb (36–48 kg)

Saint Bernard

Universally admired for its feats of rescue in the snows of the Swiss Alps, the Saint Bernard needs no introduction. For more than 200 years, its courage and skill have been the stuff of legends, and for some, the sight of this dog has signaled the end of an ordeal.

PET FACTS

Placid, affectionate, loyal

Daily brushing

Regular, moderate

Well-suited to urban living if given plenty of exercise

Good watchdog

BE AWARE

• These dogs drool a lot and require regular exercise

• Prone to have problems with eyelids that don't meet properly

HISTORY

Saint Bernards are named after Bernard de Menthon, the founder of a famous hospice built in a remote alpine pass in Switzerland nearly 1,000 years ago to shelter mountain travelers. Exactly when the dogs started to be used at the hospice for rescue work is not known, however it is most likely to have been some time during the seventeenth century.

DESCRIPTION

These are very large, strong dogs. As long as the weight is in proportion to the height, the taller the dog is the better. There are two types of coat, rough and smooth, but both are very dense and come in white with markings in tan, mahogany, red, brindle and black in various combinations. The face and ears are usually shaded with black and the expression is intelligent and gentle.

In rough-coated animals, the hair is slightly longer and there is feathering on the thighs and legs. The rough coat is a modern development, but since it ices up in extreme weather, it makes the dogs less suited to their original environment. The feet are large, with strong, well-arched toes, making Saint Bernards sure-footed in snow and on ice. They have a highly developed sense of smell and also seem to have a sixth sense about impending danger from storms and avalanches.

TEMPERAMENT

Dignified and reliable, the Saint Bernard is generally good with children, in spite of its size. It makes a good watchdog, its size alone an effective deterrent. It is highly intelligent and easy to train, however training should begin early, while the dog is still a manageable size. Bear in mind that an unruly dog of this size presents a problem for even a strong adult if it is to be exercised in public areas on a leash, so take control from the outset.

Male: 27 in (69 cm) or more
110–180 lb (50–81 kg)
Female: 25 in (63 cm) or more
110–180 lb (50–81 kg)

GROOMING

Both types of coat are easy to groom. Comb and brush with a firm bristle brush, and bathe only when necessary with mild soap—shampoo may strip the coat of its oily, water-resistant properties.

During spring and fall, there is considerable shedding. The eyes, which may be inclined to water, need special attention to keep them clean and free of irritants.

EXERCISE & FEEDING

A long walk each day will keep these dogs in good condition, although, of course, a great deal more was expected of them in the past. It is best not to allow puppies too much activity at one time until the bones are well-formed and strong. Short walks and brief play sessions are best until the dog is about two years old. As these dogs are prone to bloat, it is best to feed them two or three small meals a day instead of one large one.

HEALTH PROBLEMS

Like many of the giant breeds, Saint Bernards are particularly susceptible to hip dysplasia. They are also subject to epilepsy and bloat. They sometimes develop skin problems and the thick, warm coat makes them unsuited to life in very hot climates. There may be problems with out-turned eyelids, a condition called ectropion that causes irritation and weeping because the eyelids don't close completely.

145

Bullmastiff

Despite its size and aggressive looks, the Bullmastiff is a devoted family pet and a watchdog par excellence. The strong, silent type, it rarely barks, never loses its temper and is easy to train and control.

PET FACTS

Placid, gentle, loyal

Daily brushing

Regular, moderate

Adapts well to urban living, but needs plenty of space

Excellent watchdog

BE AWARE

• In public places, these dogs should always be kept on a leash by a strong adult

• They crave human attention

HISTORY
This powerful and intimidating dog was developed in Britain by crossing the fast and ferocious Bulldog with the Mastiff—an excellent tracker, large and very strong. The Bullmastiff was widely used by gamekeepers on large estates to deter poachers.

DESCRIPTION
Smaller and more compact than the Mastiff, the Bullmastiff is, nevertheless, a reliable and daunting watchdog. The dense, coarse coat is water-resistant and comes in dark brindle, fawn and red shades. The face and neck are darker and deeply folded. There are sometimes white marks on the chest.

TEMPERAMENT
Although the Bullmastiff is unlikely to attack, it will catch an intruder, knock him down and hold him. At the same time, it is tolerant of children, intelligent, even-tempered, calm and loyal.

GROOMING
The shorthaired, slightly rough coat is easy to groom. Comb and brush with a firm bristle brush, and shampoo only when necessary. There is little shedding with this breed. Check the feet regularly because they carry a lot of weight, and trim the nails.

EXERCISE & FEEDING
These dogs tend to be lazy so provide regular, moderate exercise. They are prone to bloat, so feed them two or three small meals a day instead of one large meal.

HEALTH PROBLEMS
While fairly robust, these dogs are susceptible to bloat, hip dysplasia and some eye problems. They do not tolerate extremes of temperature well.

Male: 25–27 in (63–69 cm)
110–133 lb (50–60 kg)
Female: 24–26 in (61–66 cm)
100–120 lb (45–54 kg)

Doberman Pinscher

Originally developed to deter thieves, the Doberman Pinscher is prized as an obedient and powerful watchdog, but with proper training from puppyhood, it can also become a devoted family pet.

PET FACTS

Intelligent, loyal and fearless, but may be aggressive

Occasional grooming

Regular, vigorous

Adapts to urban living if given enough exercise

Superb watchdog

BE AWARE

- Can become aggressive if not trained from an early age
- Prone to heart problems

HISTORY
These fearless and intimidating dogs were developed late in the nineteenth century by a German tax collector, Louis Dobermann. He drew on a number of breeds, including Rottweilers, German Pinschers, German Shepherd Dogs and Manchester Terriers to produce the ultimate guard dog—obedient and courageous.

DESCRIPTION
The Doberman Pinscher is an elegant, muscular and very powerful dog. It has a well-proportioned chest, a short back and a lean, muscular neck. Its hard, shorthaired, close-fitting coat generally comes in black, or black and tan, although blue-gray, red and fawn also occur.

TEMPERAMENT
This breed's reputation for aggression is generally undeserved, but firm and determined training from puppyhood is essential. Fortunately, they are easy to school and make loyal and obedient watchdogs. As well as being fearless, they are alert, agile and energetic. However, being powerful animals, they should always be watched around young children.

GROOMING
The smooth, shorthaired coat is easy to groom. Comb and brush with a firm bristle brush, and shampoo only when necessary.

EXERCISE & FEEDING
These dogs are very active, requiring plenty of daily exercise. They are not suitable for apartments or houses with small yards. Feed these dogs two or three small meals a day.

HEALTH PROBLEMS
Unfortunately, this breed is subject to a number of health problems. In addition to such common diseases as bloat, hip dysplasia and eye problems, it is also prone to heart disease. Its short coat means that it should never be exposed to extreme cold.

Male: 26–28 in (66–71 cm)
66–88 lb (30–40 kg)
Female: 24–26 in (61–66 cm)
66–88 lb (30–40 kg)

Note: Cropped ears are common in this breed. See p. 31 for more information

Great Pyrenees

The Great Pyrenees is a truly majestic animal that always impresses, but consider the commitment carefully—you must have the space, patience and, most important, time to meet all its needs.

HISTORY

Also known as the Pyrenean Mountain Dog, the Great Pyrenees has a long history in its native France as a guard dog of sheep and châteaux. It is also thought to have been used as a dog of war in ancient times when its temperament was less gentle than it is now.

PET FACTS

Gentle, obedient, loyal

Regular brushing

Regular, extensive

Adapts well to urban living, but needs plenty of space and exercise

Very good watchdog

BE AWARE

- These dogs don't reach maturity until about two years of age

DESCRIPTION

Fully grown, this is a very large animal with a solid, muscular body. The long, coarse outer coat is either straight or slightly wavy; the fine undercoat is soft and thick. The coat is waterproof and solid white or white with patches of tan, wolf-gray or pale yellow.

TEMPERAMENT

Although it is gentle and has a natural instinct for guarding, the Great Pyrenees must be well trained while young and small.

GROOMING

Regular brushing of the long double coat will keep it in good condition, but extra care is needed when the dog is shedding its dense undercoat. The outer coat doesn't mat, so care is relatively easy. Bathe or dry shampoo only when necessary.

EXERCISE & FEEDING

This dog needs plenty of exercise to stay in shape. It need not be vigorous, but it must be regular. There are no special feeding requirements.

HEALTH PROBLEMS

As with many large dogs, there may be problems with hip dysplasia and other orthopedic diseases. They are also prone to hereditary eye diseases and deafness.

Male: 27–32 in (69–81 cm)
From 100 lb (45 kg)
Female: 25–29 in (63–74 cm)
From 85 lb (38 kg)

Mastiff

Few intruders would venture onto a property guarded by a Mastiff, but this magnificent animal also has a gentle side and, if properly handled, is utterly devoted to its own people.

PET FACTS

- Reliable, courageous, but can be aggressive
- Regular brushing
- Regular, moderate
- Adapts well to urban living, but needs plenty of space
- Outstanding watchdog

BE AWARE

- Firm but gentle training is essential to keep this dog under control

HISTORY

There are references to large Mastiff-type dogs going back to antiquity. They were ferocious and formidable fighters and were often used for military work as well as hunting. Today's animals are more correctly called Old English Mastiffs as they all trace their lineage to two surviving English strains.

DESCRIPTION

This large and powerful dog is an imposing sight. The shorthaired coat is dense, coarse and flat-lying and comes in shades of apricot, silver, fawn or darker fawn brindle. The muzzle, ears and nose are black and the wide-set eyes are hazel to brown.

Male: From 30 in (76 cm)
From about 160 lb (72 kg)
Female: From 27 in (69 cm)
From about 150 lb (68 kg)

TEMPERAMENT

An exceptional guard dog, the Mastiff must be handled firmly and trained with kindness if it is to be kept under control. Properly handled, it is docile, good natured and loyal, but it can become a big problem if it gets the upper hand.

GROOMING

The smooth, shorthaired coat is easy to groom. Brush with a firm bristle brush and wipe over with a piece of toweling or chamois for a gleaming finish. Bathe or dry shampoo when necessary.

EXERCISE & FEEDING

Mastiffs are inclined to be lazy but they will keep fitter and happier if given regular exercise. They should always be leashed in public. As these dogs are prone to bloat, feed two or three small meals a day, instead of one large one.

HEALTH PROBLEMS

Mastiffs may suffer from hip dysplasia, bloat and hereditary eye diseases.

Newfoundland

A naturally powerful swimmer, the Newfoundland has an outstanding record of sea rescues to its credit. It was prized by fishermen in its region of origin, along the east coast of Canada.

PET FACTS

Intelligent, gentle, loyal

Daily brushing

Regular, moderate

Adapts well to urban living, but needs plenty of space

Good watchdog

BE AWARE

• Teach pups to be gentle before they grow large

HISTORY

The Newfoundland is one of the few dogs native to North America and did invaluable work for early settlers pulling sleds, hunting and guarding.

DESCRIPTION

This massive dog comes in black, browns, or black with white markings—this variant being known as the Landseer after its depiction in a painting by Sir Edwin Landseer. Like some other water-loving breeds, it has webbing between the toes.

TEMPERAMENT

Famous as the "Nana" dog in *Peter Pan*, these dogs are renowned for being gentle with children. They are adaptable, loyal and courageous, with great strength and endurance.

GROOMING

Daily brushing of the thick, coarse, double coat with a hard brush is important. The undercoat is shed once or twice a year and extra care is required at these times. Avoid bathing unless absolutely necessary, as this strips away the coat's natural oils. Instead, dry shampoo from time to time.

EXERCISE & FEEDING

This gentle giant is quite content to laze around the house, but it will benefit from regular moderate exercise. It should have frequent opportunities to swim and frolic. There are no special feeding requirements, but don't overfeed.

HEALTH PROBLEMS

Being large, heavy dogs, hip dysplasia and other orthopedic problems are common, as are genetic heart conditions. The thick coat makes the breed unsuited to hot climates.

Male: 27–29 in (69–74 cm)
130–150 lb (59–68 kg)
Female: 25–27 in (63–69 cm)
100–120 lb (45–54 kg)

Great Dane

Ancestors of this aristocratic breed have been known in Germany, where they probably originated, for more than 2,000 years. They are surprisingly gentle for their size.

DESCRIPTION
Large, tall, muscular dogs, Great Danes come in fawn, striped brindle, black, blue and harlequin.

TEMPERAMENT
Gentle, loyal, affectionate, playful and patient with children, the Great Dane is well behaved and makes a good watchdog—its size alone is daunting. Start training before it gets too large.

HISTORY
Among the tallest of dog breeds, the powerful, fast and agile Great Dane was originally favored by the German aristocracy for hunting boar and stags.

GROOMING
The smooth, shorthaired coat is easy to groom. Comb and brush with a firm bristle brush, and dry shampoo when necessary. Bathing this giant is a major chore, so it pays to avoid the need by daily grooming. The nails must be kept trimmed.

PET FACTS

- Gentle, loyal, affectionate
- Daily brushing
- Regular, moderate
- Adapts well to urban living, but needs plenty of space
- Very good watchdog

BE AWARE
- Prone to bloat, so avoid exercise after meals

EXERCISE & FEEDING
Great Danes need plenty of exercise, at the very least a long daily walk. They are prone to bloat so feed small helpings and avoid exercise after meals. Ideally, the food dish should be raised so that the dog can eat without splaying its legs.

HEALTH PROBLEMS
Being very large and heavy, Great Danes are prone to hip dysplasia and some genetic heart problems.

Male: 30–34 in (76–86 cm)
120–160 lb (54–72 kg)
Female: 28–32 in (71–81 cm)
100–130 lb (45–59 kg)

TERRIERS

Cairn Terrier

The vivacious little Cairn Terrier will delight you with its antics and steal your heart with its courage and fun-loving ways. It makes an ideal pet, adaptable, friendly and alert.

PET FACTS

- Alert, frisky, friendly
- Regular brushing
- Regular, moderate
- Ideal for apartment living
- Good watchdog

BE AWARE

- Prone to skin allergies

HISTORY

All terriers have much in common, being natural hunters bred to dig their prey out of burrows. They have powerful jaws with large teeth to hold the prey once caught. The Cairn Terrier is one of the oldest of the terriers and has contributed attributes to many varieties through cross-breeding. It originated in the Scottish Highlands, where it hunted among the many cairns that dot the landscape there.

DESCRIPTION

This compact little animal has a hard, shaggy, weather-resistant outer coat that comes in cream, wheaten, red, sandy, gray, brindle, black, solid white or black and tan, with ears and mask often darker. The thick undercoat is soft and furry.

TEMPERAMENT

A strong, fearless and companionable dog, the Cairn Terrier is always ready to play or be petted. Energetic and always on watch, it will alert you to the presence of strangers by its growling and on-guard stance. Cairn Terriers are intelligent and easily trained.

GROOMING

That shaggy "natural" look actually takes quite a bit of maintenance and a neglected coat soon becomes a sorry, matted mess. Brush several times a week, being gentle with the soft undercoat. Once a month, bathe the dog and brush the coat while it dries. Trim around the eyes and ears with blunt-nosed scissors and clip the nails regularly.

EXERCISE & FEEDING

This dog will get enough exercise running around a small garden, but if you live in an apartment, it will need a daily walk or a romp in the park. There are no special feeding requirements.

HEALTH PROBLEMS

While generally healthy, these dogs are prone to allergy problems and subject to dislocating kneecaps and hereditary eye diseases.

Male: 10–13 in (25–33 cm)
14–18 lb (6–8 kg)
Female: 9–12 in (23–30 cm)
13–17 lb (6–8 kg)

Norwich Terrier

A feisty, short-legged little dog, the Norwich Terrier has a big heart and is happiest when looking after its human family. It makes a very good watchdog and devoted companion.

PET FACTS

Fearless, lively, loyal

Daily combing and brushing

Regular, moderate

Ideal for apartment living, but needs plenty of exercise

Very good watchdog

BE AWARE

- To avoid fights, always keep on the leash when other dogs are around

TEMPERAMENT

Although good natured and friendly with people, including children, the Norwich Terrier can be scrappy with other dogs and often bears the scars of brief encounters. It is alert, smart and easy to train.

HISTORY

Until 1964, this breed comprised what later became two groups, those with prick ears and those with ears that fell forward. After that date, drop-eared Norwich Terriers became known as Norfolk Terriers in Britain, and, despite being virtually identical, they are now officially recognized as different breeds. U.S. recognition followed in 1979. The original Norwich Terriers came from East Anglia in Britain.

DESCRIPTION

These lovable dogs are among the smallest of the working terriers. Both breeds have short, sturdy bodies and short legs. Their coats are wiry and straight and come in red, tan, wheaten, black and tan, and grizzle, occasionally with white marks. The faces sport jaunty whiskers and eyebrows. The tails are usually docked.

GROOMING

Care of the shaggy, medium-length, waterproof coat is relatively easy, but daily combing and brushing is important. Take extra care when the dog is shedding. Little clipping is required and bathe or dry shampoo only when necessary.

EXERCISE & FEEDING

These energetic little dogs were bred to work and they thrive on an active life, but they won't sulk if you miss a day now and then. There are no special feeding requirements.

HEALTH PROBLEMS

The breed is hardy and long-lived, although some dogs may suffer from back problems and genetic eye diseases.

Male: About 10 in (25 cm)
10–13 lb (5–6 kg)
Female: About 10 in (25 cm)
10–13 lb (5–6 kg)

Jack Russell Terrier

Admired for its courage and tenacity, the Jack Russell Terrier will take on all challengers. An excellent watchdog, this little dog will also keep your property free of small interlopers, such as snakes.

HISTORY

Although still not universally recognized as an official breed, the Jack Russell Terrier has been around for about 100 years. It takes its name from the English "hunting parson" who developed the dog. It was specially bred with the speed, stamina and agility to hunt foxes.

DESCRIPTION

This tough little dog is clean and a convenient size for a house companion. The coat may be smooth and short, broken (very short wire) or rough and a little longer. Its comes in white, or white with black, tan or lemon markings.

TEMPERAMENT

Jack Russell Terriers are happy, excitable dogs that love to hunt. In fact, they'll chase just about anything that moves. They make vigilant watchdogs, but are sometimes scrappy with other dogs. Smart and quick witted, they must be firmly trained from an early age, but settle well into family life and make devoted pets.

GROOMING

Both smooth and rough coats are easy to groom. Comb and brush regularly with a firm bristle brush, and bathe only when necessary.

EXERCISE & FEEDING

The Jack Russell Terrier is very adaptable and will exercise itself in a small garden, but it is in its element with space to run, hunt and play. There are no special feeding requirements.

HEALTH PROBLEMS

This robust breed has few genetic problems, but may suffer from dislocating kneecaps and some hereditary eye diseases.

PET FACTS

- Curious, vigilant, energetic
- Regular brushing
- Regular, moderate
- Ideal for apartment living
- Excellent watchdog for its size

BE AWARE

- To avoid fights, always keep on the leash when other dogs are around

Male: 10–15 in (25–38 cm)
15–18 lb (7–8 kg)
Female: 9–14 in (23–36 cm)
14–17 lb (6–8 kg)

Australian Terrier

Although its talents as a rat and snake killer are called on less frequently now, the playful little Australian Terrier, nevertheless, retains the best characteristics of a working dog.

PET FACTS

Bold, good-natured, friendly

Regular brushing

Regular, gentle

Ideal for apartment living

Too friendly to strangers to be a good watchdog

BE AWARE

• These dogs are avid hunters

• Quiet and affectionate, great with children, elderly or handicapped.

HISTORY

Developed over the past 150 years in Australia as a working terrier, the lively little Australian Terrier combines the attributes of the several British terrier breeds that contributed to its makeup, mainly Cairn, Yorkshire and Norwich Terriers. Its current role is mainly as a pet.

DESCRIPTION

A sturdy, low-set dog, its straight, weather-resistant, double coat comes in blue and rich tan, clear reds or sand shades. The topknot is lighter and there is a thick ruff. The tail is generally docked short.

TEMPERAMENT

Keen and smart, the Australian Terrier responds well to training and makes a delightful pet. It is always eager to please and loves being around children.

GROOMING

The long, stiff, shaggy coat is easy to care for and doesn't need clipping. Simply brush several times a week, being gentle with the soft under-coat. Brushing stimulates the natural oils and will soon bring the coat to a high gloss. Once a month, bathe the dog and brush the coat while it dries. Trim around the eyes and ears, if necessary, with blunt-nosed scissors. Be sure to clip the nails regularly.

EXERCISE & FEEDING

The Australian Terrier is an adaptable little dog and will happily adjust to as much or as little exercise as you are able to provide—it is quite content in a garden of reasonable size. There are no special feeding requirements.

HEALTH PROBLEMS

While Australian Terriers are generally tough and hardy dogs, they may suffer from dislocating kneecaps, deterioration of the hip joint and skin problems.

Male: 9–11 in (23–28 cm)
9–14 lb (4–6 kg)
Female: 9–11 in (23–28 cm)
9–14 lb (4–6 kg)

West Highland White Terrier

A perfect mascot or companion, the West Highland White Terrier has all the terrier charm and vitality, plus brains and beauty in one neat package. It makes a bright and entertaining pet.

Adaptable, bright, companionable

Daily brushing

Regular, gentle

Ideal for apartment living, but needs regular exercise

Good watchdog

BE AWARE

- Many of these dogs suffer from serious allergic skin problems

- Keep an eye on these dogs, as they are avid hunters

HISTORY

With similar ancestry to the other Highland working terriers, especially the Cairn Terrier, the "Westie" was selectively bred for its white coat so as to be highly visible in the field. It was formerly known as both the Poltalloch and Roseneath Terrier.

DESCRIPTION

This is a sturdy little terrier with an all-white coat and bright, dark eyes. The ears are small, pointed and erect, giving the animal an alert, ready-for-anything look. The tail is carried jauntily and should not be docked.

TEMPERAMENT

Friendly, playful, alert and self-confident, this dog just loves companionship. It is bold, strong and brave, and makes a very good watchdog, despite its size.

GROOMING

The harsh, straight, short-haired double coat is fairly easy to groom and sheds very little. Simply brush regularly with a stiff bristle brush. Brushing should keep the coat clean, so bathe only when necessary. Trim around the eyes and ears with blunt-nosed scissors. The whole coat should be trimmed about every four months and stripped twice a year.

EXERCISE & FEEDING

These dogs enjoy a regular walk or sessions of play in the park but won't be too upset if they miss a day. There are no special feeding requirements.

HEALTH PROBLEMS

Westies are a generally hardy breed, although they may be subject to bad allergic skin problems. They are also prone to hereditary jaw problems and deterioration of the hip joint.

Male: 10–12 in (25–30 cm)
15–18 lb (7–8 kg)
Female: 9–11 in (23–28 cm)
13–16 lb (6–7 kg)

Scottish Terrier

The sturdy, active little Scottish Terrier is so distinctive that it has become something of an unofficial emblem of its native Scotland. While a little stubborn, it nevertheless makes a wonderful pet.

HISTORY

Perhaps the best known, if not the oldest, of the Highland terriers, the modern Scottish Terrier hails from Aberdeen and was developed at least 150 years ago. The correct standard for the breed was hotly debated in Britain until it was formalized in 1880.

DESCRIPTION

This sturdy little dog has very short legs and the way it is groomed makes them look even shorter. Even so, it is a strong, active animal and surprisingly agile. The rough-textured, weather-resistant, broken coat comes in black, wheaten, or brindle of any color. The undercoat is short, dense and soft. Sharply pricked ears give the Scottish Terrier a thoughtful look.

TEMPERAMENT

Although somewhat dignified in its behavior, the Scottish Terrier makes a very good watchdog. It is inclined to be stubborn, however, and needs firm handling from an early age or it will dominate the household.

GROOMING

Regular brushing of the harsh wiry coat is important and extra care should be taken when the dog is molting. Bathe or dry shampoo as necessary. The dog should be professionally trimmed twice a year. The hair on the body is left long, like a skirt, while the hair on the face is lightly trimmed and brushed forward.

EXERCISE & FEEDING

Given a yard of reasonable size, the sporty Scottish Terrier will exercise itself, but it will happily accompany you for a walk or play session in the park and delights in fetching sticks and balls.

There are no special feeding requirements, but beware of overfeeding or it will become obese and lazy.

HEALTH PROBLEMS

A generally robust breed, but sensitivity to fleas may cause skin problems.

Male: 10–11 in (25–28 cm)
19–23 lb (9–10 kg)
Female: 9–10 in (23–25 cm)
18–22 lb (8–10 kg)

PET FACTS

- Happy, brave, loyal
- Regular brushing
- Regular, moderate
- Ideal for apartment living
- Very good watchdog

BE AWARE

- Likes to go wandering
- Prone to skin ailments, including flea allergies

Border Terrier

A plain, no-nonsense little working dog, the Border Terrier is game for anything. It loves being part of a family and is unrestrained in its displays of affection, especially in greeting.

HISTORY

Once known as the Reedwater Terrier, the brave little Border Terrier evolved in the rugged border country between England and Scotland, sharing a common ancestry with other terriers. It was used to hunt foxes, otters and vermin and is perhaps the toughest of the terrier breeds.

DESCRIPTION

One of the smallest of the working terriers, the Border Terrier has a wiry little body to go with its wiry double coat. It comes in reds, blue and tan, grizzle and tan, or wheaten. The muzzle and ears are usually dark and the undercoat very short and dense. The loose skin, which feels thick, enables the dog to wriggle into tight burrows. The head is somewhat different from other terriers and is often described as being otter-like.

TEMPERAMENT

Reliable and intelligent, Border Terriers are easily trained, obedient, sensible and bright. They are generally not aggressive with other dogs but may hunt your cat and drive it crazy.

GROOMING

The durable, wiry coat needs little grooming. Clip out any knots and brush occasionally with a bristle brush. The object is a completely natural look with no artifice. Bathe only when necessary.

PET FACTS

- Energetic, affectionate, loyal

- Minimal

- Regular, moderate

- Ideal for urban and apartment living, but needs plenty of exercise

- Good watchdog

🐾 BE AWARE

- A bored Border Terrier can become destructive and chew things

- Start gentle training from a very early age

EXERCISE & FEEDING

Border Terriers need plenty of exercise—they were bred to hunt and have great vitality and stamina. There are no special feeding requirements.

HEALTH PROBLEMS

These are hardy dogs with few genetic problems. They do, however, suffer from dislocating kneecaps.

Male: 13–16 in (33–41 cm)
13–16 lb (6–7 kg)
Female: 11–14 in (28–36 cm)
11–14 lb (5–6 kg)

Fox Terrier

The look and stance of super-alertness and expectation is the hallmark of the Fox Terrier. Wire and Smooth Fox Terriers are remarkably similar in nearly every way, except in their coats.

HISTORY

Fox Terriers are among the oldest of the terrier breeds and were bred to dig down into burrows to flush out foxes or to catch small animals in their powerful jaws. They were also highly prized as ratters, more than earning their keep around the stables. The Wire was bred for use in rough country, its coat being less vulnerable to damage than that of the Smooth. While the two types are sometimes regarded as a single breed, since 1984 they have been classed as separate breeds in the U.S.

DESCRIPTION

These popular, firm-bodied dogs are familiar to most people. The flat coat of the Smooth is mainly white, with tan, or black and tan markings. The coarse, broken coat of the Wire is dense and wiry, with a soft, short under-coat, and comes in the same colors. The feet of both varieties are small and neat and the V-shaped ears fold and fall forward. The tail is usually docked to three-quarters of its length.

TEMPERAMENT

Keen, alert and independent, the Fox Terrier needs to be firmly trained from an early age. It is generally an easy dog to live with, and enjoys being part of the family. Amazing stories are told of the animal's loyalty and devotion. It is quite reliable with children, although it can be argumentative and feisty with other dogs, even large ones. Fox Terriers make good watchdogs, although the

PET FACTS

Keen, alert, independent

Regular brushing; Wire more than Smooth

Regular, moderate

Ideal for urban or apartment living, but needs plenty of exercise

Good watchdog

BE AWARE

- Fox Terriers are enthusiastic diggers

- Prone to allergic skin conditions

Male: 14–16 in (36–41 cm)
15–20 lb (7–9 kg)
Female: 13–15 in (33–38 cm)
13–18 lb (6–8 kg)

ring. However, if the dog is simply a family pet, the same straightforward care as for the Smooth will suffice to keep the dog clean and comfortable and looking neat and smart.

high-pitched barking can be annoying and may cause problems with neighbors. They may be too boisterous for elderly owners.

GROOMING

The shorthaired coat of the Smooth is easy to groom. Brush with a firm bristle brush, and bathe or dry shampoo when necessary. The coat of the more common Wire presents a few more problems if the dog is to look smart and shapely, since the coat must be kept well trimmed. Professional groomers have quite a bag of tricks to keep the Wire looking its best for the show

EXERCISE & FEEDING

Given a small garden, these irrepressible and athletic dogs will get enough exercise running around by themselves, but if you live in an apartment, you will need to take them for regular long walks or romps in the park, off the leash if possible. Keep on the leash, however, if there are small animals about, as the urge to hunt is strong and they are likely to take off after cats or small dogs. There are no special feeding requirements, but measure the amount of food against the level of activity.

HEALTH PROBLEMS

A hardy breed, these dogs are subject to few genetic weaknesses, although they do have trouble with skin allergies. They are also susceptible to genetic eye diseases, such as progressive retinal atrophy and cataracts.

Miniature Schnauzer

A dog of clean habits and neat size, the perky Miniature Schnauzer makes a delightful little companion for an apartment dweller or someone with a small house and yard.

HISTORY

The Miniature Schnauzer is the smallest of the three Schnauzer breeds (see pp. 136–7), all of which originated in Germany. They are only classified as terriers in the U.S.; most countries classify all Schnauzers as utility or working dogs.

DESCRIPTION

A strong, angular, square-looking dog, the Miniature Schnauzer has a harsh, wiry double coat that comes in salt and pepper or any solid color, sometimes with white on the chest. The thick, prominent eyebrows and long mustache are often trimmed to accentuate the dog's square-cut shape and the tail is usually docked.

TEMPERAMENT

These dogs are noted for their reliability and affectionate nature and make excellent watchdogs. They are spirited and brave, and while not aggressive they will take on much larger dogs should the need arise.

GROOMING

The wiry coat is reasonably easy to look after, but unless it is combed or brushed daily with a short wire brush, it will become matted. Clip out any knots. The animal should be clipped all over to an even length twice a year, in spring and fall, but this is a job best left to an expert. Trim around the eyes and ears with blunt-nosed scissors and clean the whiskers after meals.

EXERCISE & FEEDING

These energetic little dogs enjoy long, brisk, daily walks, and relish play sessions off the leash. There are no special feeding requirements.

HEALTH PROBLEMS

Schnauzers are reasonably healthy dogs, although they may suffer from bladder stones, liver disease, skin disorders and cysts.

PET FACTS

- Spirited, lively, affectionate
- Daily brushing
- Regular, moderate
- Ideal for apartment living, but needs plenty of exercise
- Excellent watchdog

BE AWARE

- The ears are sometimes cropped, but this practice is illegal in Britain
- Prone to cysts, known as "Schnauzer bumps"

Male: 12–14 in (30–36 cm)
11–18 lb (5–8 kg)
Female: 11–13 in (28–33 cm)
10–15 lb (5–7 kg)

Bull Terrier

Although surprisingly gentle, the Bull Terrier is a powerful and determined animal and needs firm handling. Even the much smaller Miniature is not a dog for timid or inexperienced owners.

Miniature
Male: Up to 14 in (36 cm)
Up to 20 lb (9 kg)
Female: Up to 14 in (36 cm)
Up to 20 lb (9 kg)

PET FACTS

Determined, fearless, playful

Regular brushing

Regular, moderate

Adapts well to urban living, but needs space to exercise

Excellent watchdog

BE AWARE

• May be aggressive with other dogs

HISTORY

Bull Terriers were developed in Britain by crossing Bulldogs with Whippets and a variety of terriers. They were once used to bait bulls and for dog fighting, and were prized for their courage, tenacity, agility and speed. The Miniature was developed to have the same qualities in a dog of more manageable size.

DESCRIPTION

A thick-set, muscular, well-proportioned animal, the Bull Terrier has a short, dense coat that comes in pure white, black, brindle, red, fawn and tricolor. Its most distinctive feature is its head, which is almost flat at the top, sloping evenly down to the end of the nose. The eyes are small, dark and closely set.

TEMPERAMENT

A tenacious fighter, the Bull Terrier is more of a danger to other dogs than to people. When properly trained it is usually sweet natured, gentle and playful. Some dogs, however, suffer from obsessive compulsive behaviors, such as tail chasing.

GROOMING

The smooth, shorthaired coat is easy to groom. Brush with a firm bristle brush, and bathe or dry shampoo as necessary. The coat will benefit from a rub with a piece of toweling or chamois.

EXERCISE & FEEDING

Bull Terriers need plenty of exercise, but keep them leashed at all times in public. There are no special feeding requirements, but don't over-feed as they are inclined to become overweight and lazy.

HEALTH PROBLEMS

While generally hardy dogs, Bull Terriers may suffer from a hereditary zinc deficiency, which can cause death. Some pups are born deaf.

Standard
Male: 21–22 in (53–56 cm)
52–56 lb (23–25 kg)
Female: 21–22 in (53–56 cm)
45–60 lb (20–27 kg)

Staffordshire Bull Terrier

A trustworthy, all-purpose dog, the Staffordshire Bull Terrier is intelligent and affectionate, very good with children and an excellent watchdog that will intimidate any intruder.

PET FACTS

- Tough, brave, reliable
- Daily brushing
- Regular, moderate
- Adapts well to urban living, but needs plenty of exercise
- Excellent watchdog

BE AWARE

- Can be aggressive to other dogs. Must be leashed in public

HISTORY

A ferocious fighter, the medium-sized Staffordshire Bull Terrier was used in England for bull baiting and dog fighting until both of these pastimes were outlawed. It was also used to hunt badgers. Like the Bull Terrier, it has Bulldog blood in its makeup, giving it that broad-chested look of immovability.

DESCRIPTION

A substantial, muscular, well-proportioned animal, the Staffordshire has a short, dense coat that comes in white or solid reds, fawn, brindle, black or blue, or any of these colors with white.

TEMPERAMENT

Usually adored and adoring within its own family circle, the Staffordshire needs firm and consistent training to curb its instinct to fight with other dogs. As pups, they tend to chew a great deal so make sure you provide them with plenty of chew toys.

GROOMING

The smooth, shorthaired coat is easy to groom. Brush every day with a firm bristle brush, and bathe or dry shampoo as necessary. The coat will gleam if rubbed with a piece of toweling or chamois.

EXERCISE & FEEDING

Staffordshire Bull Terriers must have plenty of regular exercise, but keep them on the leash in public places at all times. There are no special feeding requirements, but don't overfeed.

HEALTH PROBLEMS

Staffordshire Bull Terriers are relatively free of genetic problems, although some dogs may suffer from cataracts. They may also be subject to breathing problems and can become overheated in very hot weather.

Male: 14–16 in (36–41 cm)
25–38 lb (11–17 kg)
Female: 13–15 in (33–38 cm)
23–35 lb (10–16 kg)

American Staffordshire Terrier

Stoic and reliable, the American Staffordshire Terrier is a dog few strangers would mess with, yet with its own family, this powerful, fine-looking animal is devoted, gentle and loving.

PET FACTS

- Tough, reliable, courageous
- Daily brushing
- Regular, moderate
- Adapts well to urban living, but needs plenty of exercise
- Excellent watchdog

BE AWARE
- To avoid dog fights, keep leashed in public

HISTORY

Developed independently after early Staffordshires were taken to the U.S. during the nineteenth century, the American Staffordshire Terrier is now larger and bigger-boned than its British cousin. It has been recognized as a separate breed since 1936, the qualification "American" being added in 1972.

DESCRIPTION

The American Staffordshire looks much like the British, although it is a larger dog overall. It probably bears an even closer resemblance to Bulldogs of about a century ago, from which it is directly descended. The coat comes in all colors.

TEMPERAMENT

The American Staffordshire should never be confused with the notorious Pit Bull Terrier. Although it is a courageous and tenacious fighter if provoked, and needs firm, kind training to control this instinct, its basic temperament toward people is gentle and loving.

GROOMING

The smooth, shorthaired coat is easy to groom. Brush every day with a firm bristle brush, and bathe or dry shampoo as necessary. A rub with a piece of toweling or chamois will make the coat gleam.

EXERCISE & FEEDING

American Staffordshire Terriers must have plenty of regular exercise, but keep them leashed in public to avoid fights with other dogs. There are no special feeding requirements, but don't overfeed these dogs as they are inclined to put on weight and become lazy.

HEALTH PROBLEMS

Although not particularly long-lived, this breed is reasonably free of genetic weaknesses. Some dogs, however, may develop cataracts.

Male: 17–19 in (43–48 cm)
40–50 lb (18–23 kg)
Female: 16–18 in (41–46 cm)
35–45 lb (16–20 kg)

Bedlington Terrier

In full show trim, the Bedlington Terrier looks more like a lamb than a dog, but it has retained its terrier qualities and is a surprisingly fast runner. It makes a devoted companion.

HISTORY

Once known as the Rothbury Terrier, the Bedlington Terrier gets its speed, agility and grace of movement from its Whippet blood. These attributes once made it popular with poachers, and it earned the nickname of Gypsy Dog. Its work also included ratting in the Northumberland mines.

DESCRIPTION

The body is flexible and muscular, covered in a thick and slightly curly coat with a woolly undercoat. It comes in solid blue, liver and sandy beige, or particolored tan with any of these colors. The eyes are dark to light hazel, depending on the coat color.

TEMPERAMENT

Although they can be stubborn, Bedlington Terriers are relatively easy to train and very affectionate. They love to be the center of attention and make very good watchdogs.

GROOMING

The coat does not shed and requires specialized clipping every six weeks, so it is probably best if you learn to do this yourself. The coat is thinned and clipped close to the head and body to accentuate the shape. Shave the ears closely, leaving a tassel on the tips. On the legs, the hair is left slightly longer. Have a professional groomer show you how to do it. Brush the dog regularly and clean and pluck inside the ears.

PET FACTS

Alert, intelligent, curious

Specialized

Regular, moderate

Adapts well to urban and apartment living, but needs plenty of exercise

Very good watchdog

BE AWARE

• It is an enthusiastic digger

• Can be scrappy with other dogs and is a formidable fighter when provoked

EXERCISE & FEEDING

These active dogs need plenty of exercise and, like other terriers, will be bored and mischievous without it. There are no special feeding requirements.

HEALTH PROBLEMS

Bedlington Terriers may have a serious inherited liver problem known as Copper Storage Disease. They are also prone to hereditary kidney disease and eye problems, such as cataracts and retinal disease.

Male: 16–17 in (41–43 cm)
18–23 lb (8–10 kg)
Female: 15–16 in (38–41 cm)
18–23 lb (8–10 kg)

Irish Terrier

Known for its fighting spirit, the game little Irish Terrier is not for everyone, but it is very adaptable and its courage and loyalty are unquestioned. The breed has a growing band of admirers.

PET FACTS

- Intelligent, loyal, brave
- Regular brushing
- Regular, vigorous
- Adapts well to urban living, but needs plenty of exercise
- Excellent watchdog

BE AWARE
- Very argumentative with other dogs

HISTORY

Among the oldest of the terrier breeds, the Irish Terrier is only now regaining some of the immense popularity it once enjoyed. Admired for its pluck and unconquerable spirit, it was widely used as a guard dog and for hunting foxes, badgers and otters. Later, it excelled in the dog-fighting ring. It is closely related to the Wire Fox Terrier (see p. 160–1) but is slightly longer and larger.

DESCRIPTION

The Irish Terrier looks a little like a small version of the Airedale Terrier (see p. 169). Its hard, short and wiry coat comes in solid red, red-wheaten or yellow-red.

TEMPERAMENT

While sociable with people and devoted to its owner, this dog has an often uncontrollable urge to fight with other dogs, which makes it unsuitable for inexperienced owners.

GROOMING

The hard double coat is easy to groom and rarely sheds. Brush regularly with a stiff bristle brush and remove the dead hair with a fine-toothed comb. Bathe only when necessary.

EXERCISE & FEEDING

Being bred for active work, these dogs need plenty of regular exercise. When walking in public, always keep the dog firmly under control on a leash so that it doesn't fight with other dogs. There are no special feeding requirements.

HEALTH PROBLEMS

Irish Terriers are a robust breed but may suffer from a hereditary urinary problem as well as foot and eye diseases.

Male: 16–19 in (41–48 cm)
25–30 lb (11–14 kg)
Female: 15–18 in (38–46 cm)
23–28 lb (10–13 kg)

Soft-coated Wheaten Terrier

A jolly creature, the Soft-coated Wheaten Terrier seems to retain its carefree puppy ways into adulthood. Its enthusiasm and zest for life make it a delightful companion and pet.

HISTORY

The Soft-coated Wheaten Terrier is now rare in Ireland, where it is thought to have originated, as well as most other parts of the world. An exception is the U.S., where it currently enjoys wide popularity. Like the Irish Terrier, it once earned its keep by performing guard duties, herding sheep and hunting badgers, otters, rats and rabbits.

DESCRIPTION

This is a strong, medium-sized dog with good proportions and great stamina. The soft single coat is long and wavy and doesn't shed. It comes in wheaten shades (pale yellow to fawn).

The face is adorned with a beard and mustache, with lots of hair falling over the eyes. The tail is usually docked.

TEMPERAMENT

Friendly and appealing, the Wheaten is intelligent and easy to train. It makes an excellent watchdog.

GROOMING

Frequent, even daily, combing of the long, profuse coat with a medium-toothed comb is recommended to keep it free of tangles, beginning when the dog is a puppy. The object is to achieve a natural look and brushing can make the soft coat fuzzy.

Clean the eyes and check the ears carefully. Bathe or dry shampoo when necessary.

EXERCISE & FEEDING

These dogs can get by with moderate exercise as long as it is regular. There are no special feeding requirements.

HEALTH PROBLEMS

Wheatens are hardy dogs, but may suffer from hip dysplasia, skin allergies and eye problems, such as PRA. They are also subject to hereditary kidney disease.

Male: 18–20 in (46–51 cm)
35–45 lb (16–20 kg)
Female: 17–19 in (43–48 cm)
30–40 lb (14–18 kg)

Airedale Terrier

A lively, water-loving dog, the Airedale Terrier is very adaptable and fits in well with family life as long as it has plenty of exercise and is not allowed to rule the roost.

PET FACTS

Reliable, loyal, lively

Regular brushing

Regular, moderate

Adapts well to urban living, but needs plenty of exercise

Good watchdog

BE AWARE

- These dogs are incorrigible diggers and are easily bored, so keep them occupied

HISTORY

Largest of the terriers, the Airedale was developed in Yorkshire to hunt otters, badgers and wolves, becoming particularly popular in the Aire Valley. It has since been used extensively in police and military work.

DESCRIPTION

A medium-sized dog with a strong, straight back, the Airedale has a jaunty, alert stance. The stiff, wiry, waterproof coat comes in a combination of dark grizzle or black with red and tan markings, and the face is adorned with beard, mustache and bushy eyebrows. The straight tail, usually docked to the same height as the head, is carried erect. The small, V-shaped ears fold forward to the sides.

TEMPERAMENT

Airedales are intelligent, reliable and loyal. They are not difficult to train, but they don't respond to harsh or overbearing training methods. They are naturally lively and love children.

GROOMING

The Airedale's hard, short-haired, double coat is easy to groom and sheds very little. Brush regularly with a stiff bristle brush to remove the dead hair and bathe only when necessary.

EXERCISE & FEEDING

Being bred for active work, these dogs need plenty of exercise. An adjusted omega-6: omega-3 fatty acid ratio in the diet is recommended if the dog suffers from dry, itchy skin.

HEALTH PROBLEMS

While a generally robust breed, the Airedale may suffer from eye problems, hip dysplasia and skin infections.

Male: 23–24 in (58–61 cm)
40–50 lb (18–23 kg)
Female: 22–23 in (56–58 cm)
40–45 lb (18–20 kg)

TOY DOGS

Chihuahua

Adored by its owners, the intriguing Chihuahua is prized for its tiny size. Although not the best dog for young children, this bright-eyed, dainty creature is perfect for apartment dwellers.

HISTORY

Little is known about the Chihuahua (pronounced chu-wah-wah) before its discovery in Mexico about 100 years ago, although the breed is believed to date back to at least the ninth century.

DESCRIPTION

This is the smallest breed of dog in the world and there are two distinct coat types: smooth and short, or long. The dogs are otherwise identical and can occur in the same litter, although, in Britain, the two are considered separate and never interbred. Every coat color and color combination occurs.

TEMPERAMENT

The Chihuahua is intensely loyal and becomes very attached to its owner, even to the point of jealousy. When strangers are present, it follows its owner's every move, keeping as close as possible. It learns quickly and responds well to training.

GROOMING

The smooth, shorthaired coat should be gently brushed occasionally or simply wiped over with a damp cloth. The long coat should be brushed daily with a soft bristle brush. Bathe both types about once a month, taking care not to get water in the ears. Check the ears regularly and keep the nails trimmed.

EXERCISE & FEEDING

Although it is tempting to carry these dainty creatures about, they will keep fitter if taken for walks. A body harness is safer than a collar. There are no special feeding requirements, but feed small amounts twice a day.

PET FACTS

Affectionate, alert, playful

Regular brushing

Regular, gentle

Ideal for apartment living

Poor watchdog

BE AWARE

• These dogs tend to snap out of fear, so be especially careful when handling

HEALTH PROBLEMS

Although reasonably healthy, Chihuahuas do suffer from eye problems, collapsing trachea, dislocating kneecaps and heart disease.

Male: 6–9 in (15–23 cm)
2–6 lb (1–3 kg)
Female: 6–8 in (15–20 cm)
2–6 lb (1–3 kg)

Pekingese

Venerated since ancient times by the Chinese, the tiny Pekingese is, perhaps, the ultimate lapdog, a devoted companion quite content to loll on a cushion or a lap for as long as one is available.

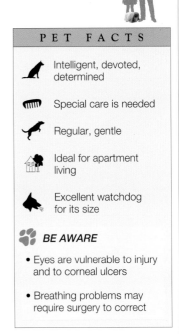

PET FACTS

🐕 Intelligent, devoted, determined

🪮 Special care is needed

🐕 Regular, gentle

🏠 Ideal for apartment living

🐕 Excellent watchdog for its size

🐾 **BE AWARE**

- Eyes are vulnerable to injury and to corneal ulcers

- Breathing problems may require surgery to correct

HISTORY

These fabled dogs once led a pampered life in the Imperial Court of Peking, where the smallest specimens were sometimes carried around in the sleeves of royalty.

DESCRIPTION

This is one of the few breeds in which the female is heavier than the male. The extravagant, long, straight, flowing coat has profuse feathering and comes in all colors, except albino and liver. The face is flat with a dark, wrinkled muzzle and drooping heart-shaped ears. These tiny, heavy-boned dogs have a characteristic rolling gait.

TEMPERAMENT

Although small, Pekingese are excellent watchdogs. They are loyal, alert, courageous and good tempered, and fit in well with the family routine.

GROOMING

Daily combing and brushing of the very long, double coat is essential. Take extra care around the hindquarters, which can become soiled and matted. Females shed the undercoat when in season. Dry shampoo regularly. Clean face and eyes daily and check the hairy feet for burrs and objects that stick there.

EXERCISE & FEEDING

Pekingese are disinclined to take walks and, although they don't need much exercise, they will stay in better health if given regular sessions of play activity. There are no special feeding requirements, but Pekingese will quickly become obese if overfed.

HEALTH PROBLEMS

Pekingese often encounter difficulty when giving birth and should be under the care of a veterinarian at this time. Like other short-nosed breeds, they are subject to breathing problems. The prominent eyes are very sensitive, and prone to corneal ulcers and injury.

Male: 6–9 in (15–23 cm)
10–14 lb (5–6 kg)
Female: 6–9 in (15–23 cm)
10–14 lb (5–6 kg)

Papillon

A real charmer, the Papillon steals hearts with its dainty elegance and amusing antics. It loves to be the center of attention and enjoys being fussed over, so it makes a delightful companion or family pet.

HISTORY
The origin of the Papillon (French for "butterfly" and pronounced pah-pee-yon) is uncertain, but by the sixteenth century it had become a breed cherished among the European nobility.

DESCRIPTION
Because of the tail, which is long and plumed and carried curled over the back, the Papillon was once called a Squirrel Spaniel. Its long, lustrous coat is white with patches of any color, except liver. The "butterfly" ears are heavily fringed and there is a well-defined white noseband.

TEMPERAMENT
Intelligent and adaptable, these animated little dogs have perky, friendly natures, but tend to become quite possessive of their owners. As watchdogs, their usefullness

is limited by their tiny size, but at least they will alert you to unusual noises or the arrival of strangers.

GROOMING
Daily combing and brushing of the long, silky, single coat is important and fairly straightforward. These dogs are usually clean and odorless. Bathe or dry shampoo when necessary. Keep the nails clipped and have the teeth cleaned regularly because they tend to accumulate tartar.

EXERCISE & FEEDING
These playful little dogs love to go for a run but won't fret too much if confined to the house for days at a time. Like any dog, they benefit from a regular exercise regimen. There are no special feeding requirements for this breed.

PET FACTS

Animated, friendly, alert

Daily brushing

Regular, gentle

Ideal for apartment living

Not a good watchdog

BE AWARE

- Sensitive to some commonly used anesthetics

- Papillons are small enough to wriggle through fences that might appear to be secure

HEALTH PROBLEMS
In general, Papillons are a fairly robust breed although they do suffer from some eye and knee problems.

Male: 8–11 in (20–28 cm)
8–10 lb (4–5 kg)
Female: 8–11 in (20–28 cm)
7–9 lb (3–4 kg)

Pomeranian

While the Pomeranian adores pampering and petting, it also loves to play and be active. In other words, it is a most accommodating creature, ready to fit in with the needs of any type of owner.

HISTORY

The Pomeranian resembles the much larger sled-pulling Spitz-type dogs from which it is descended. It was deliberately bred down in size during the nineteenth century, when toys and miniatures were very popular.

DESCRIPTION

This little dog looks like a walking powderpuff of black, gray, blue, orange, cream, shaded sable or particolored hair. Its small, cheeky, fox-like face peers out from an outsize ruff. The spectacular tail is carried over the back.

TEMPERAMENT

Easy to train, the happy little Pomeranian makes a good watchdog, despite its tiny size. It will alert you to anything unusual by setting up a commotion of barking. Although excitable, it is obedient and easily calmed.

GROOMING

Frequent brushing of the very long, double coat is recommended. If you work from the head, parting the coat and brushing it forward, it will fall neatly back in place, so the task, although time-consuming, is relatively easy. The cottony undercoat is shed once or twice a year. Dry shampoo when necessary. Clean the eyes and ears daily and take the dog for regular dental checkups.

EXERCISE & FEEDING

There is no need to make special provision for exercise if there is a small area for the dog to play in. Otherwise, a session of play in the park from time to time will suffice. There are no special feeding requirements for this breed.

HEALTH PROBLEMS

The breed is subject to eye problems and the knees are susceptible to dislocation. Some animals lose their teeth as they get older.

Male: 7–12 in (18–30 cm)
3–7 lb (1–3 kg)
Female: 7–12 in (18–30 cm)
3–7 lb (1–3 kg)

Yorkshire Terrier

Originally, Yorkshire Terriers were pressed into service as ratters, a job they did very well. Later, they claimed the spotlight with their unusual appearance and quickly became a favored breed as pets.

HISTORY

Developed only a little more than a century ago, the Yorkshire Terrier is a mysterious blend of various terriers, English, Scottish and Maltese. The toys we see today are much smaller than their forebears and the breed enjoys great popularity.

DESCRIPTION

The ultra-long, fine, silky coat parts along the spine and falls straight down on either side. It is steel-blue on the body and tail, and tan elsewhere. Puppies are usually black and tan. The tail is usually docked to half its length. If the dogs are not for showing, many owners opt for a natural shaggy look.

TEMPERAMENT

Alert, indomitable and spirited, the Yorkshire Terrier is also admired for its loyalty. Despite its diminutive size, it makes an excellent watchdog, defending its territory in no uncertain manner.

GROOMING

For show purposes, there are many tricks to caring for the Yorkshire Terrier's long, single coat, and strict guidelines must be adhered to. For the ordinary pet owner, daily combing and brushing and regular shampooing are necessary to keep the lustrous hair in top condition. This involves quite a commitment in time and effort.

EXERCISE & FEEDING

Although it doesn't need a lot of exercise, this lively little warrior will benefit from regular opportunities to run and play. There are no special feeding requirements.

HEALTH PROBLEMS

Yorkshire Terriers are subject to eye problems, including cataracts, progressive retinal atrophy and dry eye. They also suffer from deterioration of the hip joint, dislocation of the knee and collapsing trachea. Their teeth should be scaled regularly.

PET FACTS

Brave, feisty

Daily, extensive

Regular, gentle

Ideal for apartment living

Good watchdog despite its size

BE AWARE

- Barking can cause problems with neighbors

- These dogs are not good with children

Male: 7–9 in (18–23 cm)
4–7 lb (2–3 kg)
Female: 7–9 in (18–23 cm)
3–7 lb (1–3 kg)

Japanese Chin

The lovely little Japanese Chin is truly a dog to dote on and will gladly return the love that is unfailingly lavished upon it. It is a superlative lapdog with few, if any, flaws or vices.

HISTORY

These gorgeous little dogs have been known in Western countries for only about 150 years. However, they were the pampered pooches of wealthy Japanese, including royalty, for many centuries, having been introduced to Japan from China in ancient times. They are probably distantly related to the Pekingese.

DESCRIPTION

The Japanese Chin looks like a tiny toy. The profuse, straight, longhaired coat comes in white with markings either of black or shades of red. The gait is graceful with the feet lifted high off the ground.

TEMPERAMENT

The engaging little Chin is a lively, happy, sweet-tempered animal, the perfect size for small living spaces. With its gentle ways and charming manners, it is perhaps best suited to homes in which there are no small children.

GROOMING

Although the coat looks as though it might be difficult, a few minutes each day will keep it looking beautiful. Comb out tangles and brush lightly, lifting the hair to leave it standing out a little. A professional dog groomer can show you the correct technique. Dry shampoo occasionally and bathe only when necessary. Clean the eyes every day and check the ears regularly for any signs of infection.

EXERCISE & FEEDING

While they don't require a great deal of exercise, Chins love a daily walk and an opportunity to play in the open. There are no special feeding requirements, but they prefer to "graze" on small meals and tidbits.

HEALTH PROBLEMS

The large and prominent eyes are vulnerable to damage and subject to cataracts and progressive retinal atrophy.

Male: 7–11 in (18–28 cm)
Up to 9 lb (4 kg)
Female: 7–11 in (18–28 cm)
Up to 9 lb (4 kg)

Silky Terrier

Bred purely as a lively companion, the dainty Silky Terrier exhibits the best traits of its several forebears. It is a confident, entertaining little dog with a charm all its own.

HISTORY
Derived from several toy and terrier varieties, including the Yorkshire Terrier, which it resembles, the Silky Terrier was developed in New South Wales, Australia in very recent times. It is also known as the Sydney Silky. It was never intended to work, but in spite of its tiny size, it is an excellent watchdog.

DESCRIPTION
The body is small and strong with a silky coat that falls straight down on either side of a spinal parting. The coat is long except on the face and ears, and comes in either blue or gray-blue with tan. The tail is usually docked.

TEMPERAMENT
Alert and intelligent, the Silky Terrier is easy to train.

GROOMING
Daily combing and brushing and a regular shampoo are necessary to keep the lustrous hair in top condition. This involves quite a commitment from its owners. After bathing, make sure the dog is thoroughly dry and warm. The coat must be trimmed occasionally, and the hair on the legs from the knees down is often trimmed short. If the hair that falls over the eyes is tied up in a topknot, the dog will find it easier to see.

EXERCISE & FEEDING
This energetic little dog delights in extended play sessions and has surprising stamina. It needs regular exercise and activity to stay fit and happy. There are no special feeding requirements for this breed.

HEALTH PROBLEMS
These hardy dogs generally enjoy good health, although they may suffer from genetic eye diseases and, like many of the toy breeds, they are subject to collapsing trachea.

PET FACTS

- Courageous, alert, affectionate
- Daily, extensive
- Regular, moderate
- Ideal for apartment living, but needs plenty of exercise
- Excellent watchdog for its size

BE AWARE
- It is an enthusiastic digger
- Can be jealous and may pick fights with other dogs

Male: 9–10 in (23–25 cm)
8–11 lb (4–5 kg)
Female: 9–10 in (23–25 cm)
8–11 lb (4–5 kg)

Maltese

Celebrated since Roman times and perhaps even earlier, the main purpose in life of the glamorous little Maltese has always been to lift the spirits of its countless doting owners.

HISTORY

Especially favored by women through the ages, the gentle Maltese is featured in many famous paintings.

DESCRIPTION

With its compact little body, short legs and silky, dazzlingly white coat, this dog is sure to be the center of attention. The oval eyes are large and dark, with black rims. The profuse single coat falls long and straight, parting along the spine and eventually reaching the ground, concealing the legs and feet completely. It is always white, sometimes with lemony or beige markings. The tail arches gracefully over the back.

TEMPERAMENT

Intelligent and easy to train, the Maltese enjoys being groomed, petted and fondled. Lively and alert, it will let you know by barking if strangers are about.

GROOMING

Daily combing and brushing of the long coat is important, but be gentle as the coat is very soft. Clean the eyes daily to prevent staining, and clean the beard after meals for the same reason. Bathe or dry shampoo regularly, making sure the animal is thoroughly dry and warm afterward. Clean the ears and pull out hairs growing inside the ear canal. The eyes should be checked regularly and cleaned if necessary. The hair on the top of the head is often tied up in a topknot to keep it away from the eyes.

EXERCISE & FEEDING

Maltese enjoy a regular walk or session of frolicking in the park and they remain playful well into old age. There are no special feeding requirements for these dogs but avoid overfeeding.

PET FACTS

Even-tempered, affectionate

Regular, extensive. Be gentle with soft coat

Regular, gentle

Ideal for apartment living

Adequate watchdog

BE AWARE

- The eyes are inclined to weep from time to time, staining the face

- Prone to sunburn along the hair parting

HEALTH PROBLEMS

This breed is generally long-lived, hardy and healthy. Like most pure-bred dogs, however, they are subject to genetic eye diseases.

Male: 8–10 in (20–25 cm)
4–6 lb (1.5–3 kg)
Female: 8–10 in (20–25 cm)
4–6 lb (1.5–3 kg)

Shih Tzu

Entertaining little dogs that love company, Shih Tzus like nothing better than to sit on your lap and be groomed—which is just as well, because the magnificent coat demands extensive care.

HISTORY

A number of similarities suggest that the Shih Tzu (pronounced shidzoo) is descended from Tibet's Lhasa Apso, possibly as a result of being crossed with the Pekingese after it was introduced into China. The Shih Tzu is also known as the Chinese Lion Dog or the Chrysanthemum Dog.

DESCRIPTION

This is a proud-looking little dog with a long body and short legs. The thick, long, luxuriant coat can be any color, but a white blaze on the forehead and a white tip on the tail are very desirable.

TEMPERAMENT

Endowed with loads of character, the gentle, loyal Shih Tzu makes friends easily and responds well to training.

GROOMING

Daily combing and brushing of the long, soft, double coat with a steel comb and a bristle brush is essential, with extra care during shedding. The long hair on the top of the head is usually tied in a topknot to keep it out of the dog's eyes. Dry shampoo as necessary and bathe once a month. Check the ears regularly for infection and remove food scraps from the beard after meals. Clip out any matting on the feet.

EXERCISE & FEEDING

These are naturally active little dogs but, if allowed, like to lounge about in their own particular spot. They should be encouraged to get out and about and will keep fitter with a daily walk. There are no special feeding requirements, but don't overfeed or they will quickly become fat.

HEALTH PROBLEMS

The prominent eyes are prone to injury and tend to get dry from exposure, causing them to ulcerate. Shih Tzus are also subject to ear infections and inherited kidney problems, and they may suffer breathing difficulties in hot weather.

Male: Up to 11 in (28 cm)
9–16 lb (4–7 kg)
Female: Up to 11 in (28 cm)
9–16 lb (4–7 kg)

Toy Poodle

The dainty Toy Poodle loves company and is the perfect pet for an older or less active person with time to pamper this diminutive natural clown and be amused by its antics.

HISTORY

The Toy Poodle is the smallest version of the Poodle (see pp. 192–3), originally used in Germany and France as a retriever of waterfowl. Later, it was favored by circus performers for its comic appearance and because it was easy to train.

DESCRIPTION

This active little dog has a dense, woolly coat of springy curls. The hair keeps growing and is not shed and, for this reason, the Toy Poodle is often recommended as a pet for people with allergies. The coat comes in solid red, white, cream, brown, apricot, black, silver and blue.

TEMPERAMENT

Sensitive and remarkably intelligent, the Toy Poodle is highly responsive and very easy to train. It makes a very good watchdog for its size.

GROOMING

Poodles must be bathed regularly and clipped every six to eight weeks. Clean and check the ears frequently for wax or infection and pull out hairs growing inside the ear canal. The traditional clips were developed to lighten the weight of the coat for swimming and protect the joints and major organs from cold, but many pet owners opt for a plain lamb clip, the same length all over. The teeth need regular scaling.

EXERCISE & FEEDING

Although they love to go for a walk, and will keep in better humor and be fitter if given regular opportunities to run free and play, Toy Poodles are not demanding as far as exercise goes. There are no special feeding requirements.

PET FACTS

- Very intelligent, loyal
- Comb and brush daily
- Regular, gentle
- Ideal for apartment living
- Very good watchdog for its size

BE AWARE

- When purchasing a puppy, check carefully for genetic disorders
- These dogs prefer to live indoors

HEALTH PROBLEMS

Toy Poodles are subject to dislocated knees, epilepsy, diabetes and genetic eye diseases, such as progressive retinal atrophy and cataracts.

Male: Up to 11 in (28 cm)
6–9 lb (3–4 kg)
Female: Up to 11 in (28 cm)
6–9 lb (3–4 kg)

Pug

Not at all pugnacious, this lovable softie is even-tempered and good with children. Pugs love company and only want to be your best friend, but they will sulk if left out of family activities.

HISTORY

Although dogs very similar to Pugs appear on ancient Chinese porcelain and paintings, the origin of the breed is shrouded in mystery. They seem always to have been house dogs or pets rather than dogs bred for any particular task.

DESCRIPTION

While not exactly handsome, the Pug, nevertheless, has a certain appeal. It has a square, thickset, stocky body with a sleek, soft coat that comes in fawn, apricot, silver and black, all with black muzzle and velvety ears. Moles on the cheeks are considered beauty spots. The tail lies in a tight curl, or even, in the best specimens, a double curl on the back. The jaunty, rolling gait is quite distinctive.

Male: 12–14 in (30–36 cm)
13–20 lb (6–9 kg)
Female: 10–12 in (25–30 cm)
13–18 lb (6–8 kg)

TEMPERAMENT

Intelligent, easily trained, and with a big bark for its size, the Pug makes a good watchdog. It is playful, loyal and affectionate and makes a captivating companion that will shadow your every move or curl up on your lap.

GROOMING

The smooth, shorthaired coat is easy to groom. Brush and comb with a firm bristle brush, and shampoo only when necessary. Clean the creases on the face regularly.

EXERCISE & FEEDING

Strong dogs with short straight legs, Pugs enjoy energetic games and will keep in better health if given regular exercise. Don't overfeed, as Pugs will eat more than is good for them, quickly becoming obese and living much shorter lives.

HEALTH PROBLEMS

Pugs are stressed by both hot and cold weather and are accustomed to living indoors. They are prone to allergies and the short muzzle contributes to chronic breathing problems.

PET FACTS

- Smart, sociable, mischievous
- Daily brushing
- Regular, moderate
- Ideal for apartment living if given enough exercise
- Good watchdog

BE AWARE

- A Pug's prominent eyes are prone to injury
- Prone to sinus and breathing problems

Miniature Pinscher

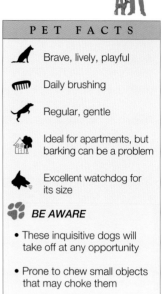

The Min-Pin, as it is often called, is a very active terrier-type of dog. Its courage is undoubted, and it was valued in Germany, where it originated, as a ratting dog of outstanding vigilance and tenacity.

HISTORY
Known only in Germany until about 100 years ago, these dogs are now popular throughout the world.

DESCRIPTION
A small, neat dog with a characteristic high-stepping, "hackney" gait, this breed makes a lively and delightful pet. The coat comes in black, blue and chocolate, all with sharply defined tan markings on the face and matching patches on the chest and above the eyes. Solid reds are also seen. The tail is usually docked short.

TEMPERAMENT
This brave, playful little dog will bark and nip at intruders and, for its size, makes an excellent watchdog. It is not suited to families with small children because, if handled roughly, it is likely to be injured and react aggressively.

GROOMING
The smooth, shorthaired, hard coat is easy to groom. Comb and brush with a firm bristle brush, and shampoo only when necessary. Loose hair can be removed by wiping over with a warm, damp washcloth.

EXERCISE & FEEDING
These dogs don't require a lot of exercise but should be given regular opportunities to run and play. Any yard in which they run loose needs to have a fence high enough to prevent their determined efforts to escape and explore. There are no special feeding requirements.

HEALTH PROBLEMS
Miniature Pinschers are robust animals on the whole, but are subject to eye and joint problems. Bitches often have difficulty giving birth and should be under the care of a veterinarian at this time.

Male: 10–12 in (25–30 cm)
8–10 lb (4–5 kg)
Female: 10–11 in (25–28 cm)
8–9 lb (about 4 kg)

PET FACTS

- Brave, lively, playful
- Daily brushing
- Regular, gentle
- Ideal for apartments, but barking can be a problem
- Excellent watchdog for its size

BE AWARE
- These inquisitive dogs will take off at any opportunity
- Prone to chew small objects that may choke them

Chinese Crested

If you are looking for a novelty, this may be just the pet for you, but choose a Chinese Crested only if you are ready to return the affection this dainty little creature is so eager to give.

HISTORY

It is not known how or even where this breed originated, although it seems to have existed in ancient China. There are many similarities to the Mexican Hairless.

DESCRIPTION

There are two distinct varieties of this unusual dog: one is hairless, except for its head, feet and tail, and called, not surprisingly, the Hairless; the other, the Powderpuff, has a coat of long, soft hair. Both come in numerous colors, either solid or mixed, or all-over spotted. Strangely, the two types often occur in the same litter.

TEMPERAMENT

Chinese Cresteds tend to become very attached to their owners and have difficulty adjusting to new ones. They crave constant companionship.

GROOMING

Daily combing and brushing of the long, fine, double coat of the Powderpuff is important, with extra care required when the dog is shedding. The woolly undercoat becomes matted if neglected. Bathe the Hairless frequently and massage a little oil or cream into the skin to keep it supple.

EXERCISE & FEEDING

Although these dogs enjoy brisk walks, they do just as well with regular sessions of play. There are no special feeding requirements, but do not overfeed these dogs, as they will become obese if given the chance. They should not be given bones to chew as they often have an incomplete set of teeth.

HEALTH PROBLEMS

The skin of the Hairless reacts to contact with wool and must be protected from sunburn. This variety is also unsuited to cold climates.

Male: 9–13 in (23–33 cm)
Up to 12 lb (5 kg)
Female: 9–13 in (23–33 cm)
Up to 12 lb (5 kg)

Cavalier King Charles Spaniel

A fearless, lively little dog with a cheerful disposition, the Cavalier King Charles Spaniel is friendly and sociable with both people and other dogs, and is far more hardy than the average toy breed.

PET FACTS

Lively, friendly, playful

Regular brushing

Regular, gentle

Ideal for apartment living

Adequate watchdog

BE AWARE

• These dogs are highly prone to heart disease

tricolored black, tan and white. The coat is long and silky and free of curls, although it is sometimes wavy. The ears are long, silky and well feathered. The tail is sometimes docked to two-thirds of its length.

HISTORY

Developed from a cross between a King Charles and a Cocker Spaniel (see p. 104), the Cavalier differs greatly from its forebears. Its breeders were trying to reproduce a toy dog similar to those seen in portraits from the time of England's Charles II—he was said to dote on these animals.

DESCRIPTION

Compact and handsome, the Cavalier is slightly larger than the King Charles and has a longer muzzle, but comes in the same colors: solid reds, chestnut and white, black and tan, and

TEMPERAMENT

The Cavalier is easily trained, clean and sensible, and makes a delightful and diverting companion.

GROOMING

The smooth, longhaired coat is easy to groom. Comb or brush with a firm bristle brush, and bathe or dry shampoo as necessary. Always make sure the dog is thoroughly dry and warm after a bath. Check the eyes and ears carefully for any signs of infection.

EXERCISE & FEEDING

Whatever exercise you can provide will be just fine with this adaptable dog, although it does enjoy a good romp in the park. There are no special feeding requirements.

HEALTH PROBLEMS

Although it is classed as a toy, the Cavalier has little of the fragility usually associated with these breeds. However, heart disease is very common. They are also subject to hereditary eye diseases and dislocating kneecaps, and the long, well-feathered ears are prone to infection.

Male: 12–13 in (30–33 cm)
10–18 lb (5–8 kg)
Female: 12–13 in (30–33 cm)
10–18 lb (5–8 kg)

Italian Greyhound

A graceful and delicate-looking dog, the Italian Greyhound is a perfect miniature of its larger forebear. A clean, odorless animal, it will adapt happily to any reasonably quiet, loving home.

PET FACTS

- Obedient, loving, sensitive
- Minimal
- Regular, moderate
- Adapts well to urban living if kept in a quiet household
- Not a good watchdog

BE AWARE
- Prone to broken legs and slipped kneecaps

HISTORY

The Italian Greyhound has been around since ancient Egyptian times. Whatever its original purpose, perhaps flushing birds, chasing small game or killing rats, it has been bred for the past few centuries purely as a pet. In most countries it is classified as a toy breed.

DESCRIPTION

Lithe and streamlined, these dogs are capable of short bursts of speed. The glossy, satiny coat comes in various shades of fawn, cream, white, red, blue, black and fawn, and white splashed with any of these colors.

TEMPERAMENT

As it tends to be timid and must be handled very gently, this is a pet for a quiet household where there are no lively children. In stressful situations it needs constant reassurance by stroking.

GROOMING

This dog is one of the very easiest to groom. All that is needed to keep the fine, silky coat gleaming is a rubdown with a piece of rough toweling or chamois. If absolutely necessary, the animal can be bathed, but make sure it is thoroughly dry and warm afterward.

EXERCISE & FEEDING

Italian Greyhounds are active little dogs and love to run free and play as well as have regular walks. There are no special feeding requirements.

HEALTH PROBLEMS

Italian Greyhounds are prone to broken legs and slipped kneecaps, especially when they are young. They are also susceptible to hereditary eye problems and seizures, and because of their fine coats they should not be exposed to extreme weather conditions.

Male: 12–15 in (30–38 cm)
6–10 lb (3–5 kg)
Female: 12–15 in (30–38 cm)
6–10 lb (3–5 kg)

NON-SPORTING DOGS

Bichon Frise

It's easy to see why people are enchanted by the fluffy Bichon Frise. It loves to be the center of attention and is always eager to please—altogether a delightful and amusing companion.

PET FACTS

- Charming, friendly, alert
- Extensive
- Regular, gentle
- Ideal for apartment living
- Good watchdog

BE AWARE

- If neglected, the coat quickly becomes a sorry, matted mess

HISTORY

Although it first came to notice as the darling of French royalty during the sixteenth century (*bichon* is French for lapdog; *frisé* means curly), the Bichon Frise is thought to have originated in the Canary Islands and was once called the Teneriffe. Its French or Belgian forebears may have been taken there by sailors.

DESCRIPTION

This sturdy, confident little dog has a lively, prancing gait and a puffy white coat, sometimes with cream or apricot markings. The eyes are round and dark and the large, round nose is black.

TEMPERAMENT

A gregarious individual, the Bichon Frise is playful and merry and not aggressive to people or other dogs. It is intelligent and easy to train.

GROOMING

Daily brushing of the long, soft coat with a stiff bristle brush is essential. The fine, silky hair falls naturally in curls and is usually cut with scissors to follow the contours of the body and brushed out to a soft cloud. Dry shampoo as necessary and bathe once a month. Trim around the eyes and ears with blunt-nosed scissors and clean the eyes meticulously to prevent staining.

EXERCISE & FEEDING

These are active little dogs and play will take care of most of their exercise needs, but they do love a walk and especially a romp in the open. There are no special feeding requirements.

HEALTH PROBLEMS

Bichon Frises are a fairly sturdy breed, although some of them may suffer from epilepsy and dislocating kneecaps. They are also subject to eye problems, such as cataracts and blocked tear ducts, the last of which can cause the eyes to run, staining the white coat.

Male: 9–12 in (23–30 cm)
7–12 lb (3–5 kg)
Female: 9–11 in (23–28 cm)
7–12 lb (3–5 kg)

Lhasa Apso

This bewitching creature seems to be composed entirely of hair, but the Lhasa Apso is neither a toy nor a lapdog. It is a rugged little animal that earns its keep as a companion and watchdog.

HISTORY
Rarely seen outside Tibet until fairly recently, the Lhasa Apso was bred in monasteries as a temple and palace sentinel. It takes part of its name from the Tibetan capital, Lhasa.

DESCRIPTION
This shaggy little dog looks like a small version of the Old English Sheepdog. Gold, creams and honey are the most popular colors, but the coat also comes in dark grizzle, smoke, slate and particolors of black, white or brown.

TEMPERAMENT
Adaptable, affectionate and loyal, these hardy little dogs thrive on human companionship and don't like to be left alone. Their hearing is acute and they will alert you to any unusual sounds and to the approach of strangers. They are playful, intelligent, easily trained dogs and make delightful companions.

GROOMING
The long topcoat parts along the spine and falls straight on either side. Daily combing and brushing is important. The thick undercoat will become matted if neglected. Dry shampoo as necessary. Some owners opt for easier care with a short all-over clip. Check the feet for matting and for foreign matter stuck there. Clean eyes and ears meticulously.

EXERCISE & FEEDING
Although they love to walk and scramble about and will be fitter and happier if given regular opportunities to run free and play, Lhasa Apsos don't demand exercise. There are no special feeding requirements, but clean any dribbles of food off the beard after each meal to avoid staining and matting.

HEALTH PROBLEMS
Lhasa Apsos are relatively free of health problems, although they may suffer from genetic kidney problems. Poor ventilation of the ears may cause ear infection.

Male: 10–11 in (25–28 cm)
14–18 lb (6–8 kg)
Female: 9–10 in (23–25 cm)
12–16 lb (5–7 kg)

PET FACTS

- Playful, devoted, alert
- Daily, extensive
- Regular, gentle to moderate
- Ideally suited to apartment living
- Very good watchdog

BE AWARE

- They need a lot of grooming
- Nervous around strangers

Schipperke

While the agile, hardy and independent little Schipperke is remarkably self-sufficient, it is sociable, adapts well to family life and makes a well-behaved, loyal and affectionate pet.

HISTORY

The name possibly derives from the Flemish for "little boatman," because Schipperkes (pronounced skipper-keys) were popular watchdogs on Belgian barges, keeping rats and mice in check. They are probably related to the Groenendael, a Belgian Shepherd Dog.

DESCRIPTION

These small dogs have a harsh double coat, usually black, but gold and some other solid colors do occur. The hair is smooth on the fox-like head, elsewhere more erect, and the male has a standing ruff around the neck. Schipperkes are often born without a tail. If a tail is present, it is closely docked within a few days of birth.

Male: 10–13 in (25–33 cm)
12–16 lb (5–7 kg)
Female: 9–12 in (23–30 cm)
10–14 lb (5–6 kg)

TEMPERAMENT

This plucky little dog backs down for nobody and makes an excellent watchdog. It is alert and very curious, and nothing escapes its attention. Undemanding and devoted to its owner, it looks on itself as part of the family.

GROOMING

The Schipperke is very clean and pretty much takes care of its own grooming, but to keep the medium-length double coat in top condition, comb and brush regularly with a firm bristle brush. Dry shampoo when necessary.

EXERCISE & FEEDING

In general, Schipperkes are an active breed. While some will be content with sessions of free play in a yard or park, others will want at least a long daily walk. There are no special feeding requirements.

PET FACTS

Curious, brave, loyal

Minimal

Regular, moderate

Adapts well to urban living and is ideal for an apartment if given plenty of exercise

Excellent watchdog

BE AWARE

• This dog tends to be very suspicious of strangers

HEALTH PROBLEMS

This breed is remarkably free of genetic problems, apart from the common eye diseases and occasional cases of hip dysplasia. Some dogs get mild skin infections, but these are easily treated.

Boston Terrier

Besides being an excellent watchdog, the Boston Terrier has much to recommend it—easy-care, handy size and a delightful disposition. No wonder it is one of the most popular breeds in the U.S.

PET FACTS

Playful, devoted, fearless

Daily brushing

Regular, moderate

Ideal for apartment living

Excellent watchdog

BE AWARE

• Bitches often experience difficulties giving birth to their large-headed pups

HISTORY

The Boston Terrier's direct forebears are English and French Bulldogs and the White English Terrier. It was developed in the U.S. only about 150 years ago as a fighting dog, a pastime that has since been outlawed. Although it is still always ready to scrap with other dogs, its behavior toward people is not aggressive.

DESCRIPTION

Boston Terriers are compact and well-muscled dogs. Their faces are unmistakeable, with short, wide muzzles, prominent eyes set far apart and short, erect ears. These dogs come in brindle or black, both with white markings.

TEMPERAMENT

Playful and very affectionate, they like to be part of the family. They are reliable with children, intelligent, easy to train and, despite being relatively small, make excellent watchdogs.

GROOMING

The smooth, shorthaired, fine, glossy coat is easy to groom. Comb and brush with a firm bristle brush, and bathe only when necessary. Wipe the face with a damp cloth every day and clean the prominent eyes carefully. Check both the ears and eyes for grass seeds. Ticks may also lurk in the ears. The nails should be clipped from time to time.

EXERCISE & FEEDING

Regular walks or sessions of free play in a fenced yard are all Boston Terriers need to stay in shape. There are no special feeding requirements.

HEALTH PROBLEMS

These short-faced dogs may have breathing difficulties when stressed by exertion and hot or cold weather. Whelping is often difficult as the pelvis is narrow, and the large-headed pups are often delivered by Cesarean section. Heart and skin tumors are common problems in this breed. The prominent eyes are prone to injury.

Male: 11–15 in (28–38 cm)
15–25 lb (7–11 kg)
Female: 11–15 in (28–38 cm)
15–25 lb (7–11 kg)

Bulldog

These stalwarts have come to epitomize determination and the broad-chested stance certainly suggests immovability, if not downright stubbornness. Yet Bulldogs make loving and lovable pets.

HISTORY

In earlier times, Bulldogs were fighting dogs that would take on opponents such as bulls, bears, badgers, or even other dogs in the ring. When such bloodsports became unpopular, breeders concentrated on developing the breed's non-ferocious traits.

DESCRIPTION

The coat comes in reds, fawn, brindle or fallow, or white pied with any of these colors. The muzzle is sometimes dark. With its stocky legs set squarely at each corner of its compact, muscular body, the

Bulldog's deliberate gait has become a waddle.

TEMPERAMENT

Absolutely reliable, and although its appearance can be somewhat intimidating, it is among the gentlest of dogs. Just the same, it will see off any intruder, and few would risk a close encounter with a dog brave enough to bait a bull.

GROOMING

The smooth, fine, shorthaired coat is easy to groom. Comb and brush with a firm bristle brush, and bathe only when necessary. Wipe the face with a damp cloth every day to clean inside the wrinkles.

EXERCISE & FEEDING

Bulldogs would just as soon not take any exercise, but they will stay fitter if given some regular, not overly strenuous activity such as walking. There are no special feeding requirements, but be careful not to overfeed them as they easily become obese. They can also be somewhat possessive of their food.

HEALTH PROBLEMS

Whelping is difficult and the large-headed pups are usually delivered by Cesarean section. Bulldogs are prone to breathing difficulties because of their short muzzles. Some have small windpipes as well. They are also stressed by exertion and hot or cold weather.

PET FACTS

- Reliable, gentle, kind
- Daily brushing
- Regular, moderate
- Adapts well to urban living
- Very good watchdog

BE AWARE

- Bulldogs tend to drool and snore
- Prone to chronic respiratory problems

Male: 14–16 in (36–41 cm)
45–55 lb (20–25 kg)
Female: 12–14 in (30–36 cm)
35–45 lb (16–20 kg)

Poodle

Once a Poodle owner, always a Poodle owner—fanciers of this breed seldom become attached to another. The winning ways of these clever animals captivate almost everyone.

HISTORY

Known since the thirteenth century, the Poodle is a gundog originally used in Germany and France as a retriever of waterfowl. Later, it was favored by circus performers for its comic appearance and because it was very easy to train. Despite the claims of several other countries, France has now been officially recognized as its country of origin, and the breed occupies a special place in the affections of the French. Its ancestors probably include the French Barlut and the Hungarian Water Hound.

DESCRIPTION

Poodles come in three officially recognized sizes, Standard (the largest), Miniature and Toy (the smallest, see p. 180). They are active, sure-footed dogs with excellent balance, moving lightly and easily with a springy, trotting gait. Their dense, woolly coats of springy curls are either brushed out to a soft cloud and clipped in one of several standard styles, or simply combed for a more natural look. The fine, harsh-textured hair keeps growing and is not shed, and for this reason the Poodle is often recommended as a pet for people with allergies. The coat comes in solid white, cream, brown, apricot, black, silver and blue. Puppies' tails are usually docked at birth to half their length in Standard dogs and two-thirds of their length in Miniatures and Toys.

PET FACTS

- Very intelligent, loyal
- Comb and brush daily
- Regular, moderate
- Ideal for apartment living, but needs plenty of exercise
- Very good watchdog, particularly the Standard

BE AWARE

- When purchasing a puppy, check carefully for genetic disorders
- These dogs fret if not given enough human company

TEMPERAMENT

Considered by many the most intelligent of all breeds, the Poodle makes a very good watchdog for its size, seldom becoming aggressive. It has a great sense of fun, loves to play and will feel slighted if left out of family activities. Somewhat sensitive, it may become jealous of children.

Miniature
Male: 11–15 in (28–38 cm)
15–17 lb (7–8 kg)
Female: 11–15 in (28–38 cm)
15–17 lb (7–8 kg)

GROOMING

Poodles must be bathed regularly and clipped every six to eight weeks. Check the ears frequently for mites and pull out hairs if neccesary. The traditional clips were developed to lighten the weight of the coat for swimming and protect the joints and major organs from cold, but many pet owners opt for a plain lamb clip, the same length all over, because it is easier and more economical to maintain. The teeth need regular scaling.

EXERCISE & FEEDING

Although they adore water and love to go for walks, Poodles are not demanding as far as exercise goes. They will, however, keep in better spirits and be fitter if given regular opportunities to run and play off the leash. The Standard retains its sporting instincts, has great stamina and needs more activity than the smaller varieties. To prevent bloat, feed two or three small meals a day instead of one large one, and avoid exercise after meals.

HEALTH PROBLEMS

A long-lived breed, Poodles are, nevertheless, subject to many genetic diseases. Cataracts and progressive retinal atrophy may cause blindness, and allergies and skin conditions are common. Miniatures are subject to diabetes, epilepsy and heart disease, while Standards get hip dysplasia and bloat.

Standard
Male: 15–24 in (38–61 cm)
45–70 lb (20–32 kg)
Female: 15–22 in (38–56 cm)
45–60 lb (20–27 kg)

Tibetan Terrier

While it is treasured in its native Tibet as a symbol of good luck, you will probably cherish your appealing little Tibetan Terrier more for its delightful ways and joyous zest for life.

HISTORY

Still something of a rarity in Western countries, the Tibetan Terrier was little known outside Tibet until about 70 years ago. It is not a true terrier as it does not dig prey out of burrows. In its homeland it is something of an all-purpose farm dog.

PET FACTS

	Loving, alert, playful
	Regular combing
	Regular, gentle
	Ideal for apartment living
	Good watchdog

BE AWARE

- They are very energetic dogs, requiring regular play

- They are good jumpers, so escape-proof your yard

DESCRIPTION

This compact little animal is nimble and sure-footed—it will stand on its hind legs and jump quite high to see what is on a table, especially if senses food. The shaggy coat is fine and long, falling over the face. It comes in white, golden, cream, gray shades, silver, black, particolor and tricolor. The tail is well feathered and carried proudly curled over the back.

TEMPERAMENT

These gentle, engaging animals are easy to train, alert and full of bravado. They will certainly let you know if strangers are around.

GROOMING

Comb the long, double coat every second day with a metal comb to keep it free of tangles. The dense, fine, woolly undercoat is shed twice a year and extra care is needed during shedding. Bathe or dry shampoo as necessary.

Trim around the eyes with blunt-nosed scissors and check the ears regularly.

EXERCISE & FEEDING

Sessions of play and regular walks will keep this lively dog fit and happy. There are no special feeding requirements, but if allowed they can become finicky about their food.

HEALTH PROBLEMS

Tibetan Terriers are generally fairly robust, although they do suffer from some genetic eye diseases.

Male: 14–16 in (36–41 cm)
18–30 lb (8–14 kg)
Female: 13–15 in (33–38 cm)
16–25 lb (7–11 kg)

Keeshond

A natural watchdog, the Keeshond is a great favorite in its native Holland, in spite of not being considered a pure-bred. It is a long-lived dog and becomes deeply attached to its owners.

PET FACTS

- Gentle, intelligent, devoted

- Daily brushing

- Regular, moderate

- Ideal for apartment living, but needs plenty of exercise

- A natural watchdog

BE AWARE

- Ticks are hard to locate in the dense undercoat

HISTORY

Originally used as watchdogs on barges in Holland, the Keeshond (pronounced kays-hond) was sometimes called the "smiling Dutchman" for its perpetual good-natured grin. It is a member of the Spitz group of dogs and has the typical tightly curled tail.

DESCRIPTION

Keeshonden are compact, muscular animals with a cream or pale gray undercoat and a luxurious outer coat that comes in shades of gray with black tips and stands away from the body. The markings are quite definite and there are distinctive pale "spectacles" around the eyes.

TEMPERAMENT

Reliable, adaptable, easy to care for and loyal to its family, the Keeshond is a natural watchdog and easy to train for other tasks.

GROOMING

Grooming is not as onerous as you might expect, but daily brushing of the long coat with a stiff bristle brush is important. Brush with the grain first, then lift the hair with a comb, against the grain, and lay it back in place. Bathe or dry shampoo only when necessary. The dense undercoat is shed twice a year, in spring and fall.

EXERCISE & FEEDING

These dogs will readily adapt to an exercise regimen, whether it be demanding or easy, but they will keep fitter with regular activity. Don't use a choke chain as it will spoil the spectacular ruff. There are no special feeding requirements, but beware of overfeeding as they put on weight quickly.

HEALTH PROBLEMS

While generally robust, some Keeshonden are subject to hip dysplasia, heart defects and genetic eye diseases.

Male: 17–19 in (43–48 cm)
55–65 lb (25–29 kg)
Female: 16–18 in (41–46 cm)
50–60 lb (23–27 kg)

Shiba Inu

Because of its convenient size and vivacious, outgoing personality, the Shiba Inu is now the most commonly owned pet dog in its native Japan, and is gaining in popularity worldwide.

PET FACTS

Energetic, friendly, loyal

Regular brushing

Regular, moderate

Ideal for urban or apartment living, but needs plenty of exercise

Good watchdog

BE AWARE

- Needs firm, consistent training

- Prone to wreak havoc on your house as a puppy, and digs and climbs with ease

HISTORY

The Shiba Inu is the smallest of the Japanese Spitz-type dogs and was originally bred to flush birds and small game from brushwood areas. The name Shiba possibly comes from a Japanese word for brushwood, or it may derive from an old word meaning small (*inu* means dog).

DESCRIPTION

The Shiba looks like a much smaller version of the Akita (see p. 142). Agile and well proportioned, it has a strong body and alert bearing. The double coat usually comes in red tones, sable or black and tan, with pale shadings on the legs, belly, chest, face and tail.

TEMPERAMENT

Lively and good natured, Shibas are smart but somewhat difficult to train. They are very independent and choose which commands to obey. Although extremely sociable, they can be aggressive to unfamiliar dogs.

GROOMING

The coarse, stiff, shorthaired coat is easy to groom. Brush with a firm bristle brush, and bathe only when absolutely necessary as this removes the natural waterproofing of the coat.

EXERCISE & FEEDING

This is an active dog needing lots of exercise. There are no special feeding requirements.

HEALTH PROBLEMS

The breed is generally hardy and healthy with few genetic weaknesses. Its waterproof, all-weather coat protects it in both cold and hot conditions, so it can live outdoors if you have a secure yard of reasonable size. However, it does regard itself as part of the family and doesn't like to be left alone outside.

Male: 14–16 in (36–41 cm)
20–30 lb (9–14 kg)
Female: 13–15 in (33–38 cm)
18–28 lb (8–13 kg)

Chow Chow

An appealing, unusual-looking dog, the Chow Chow is less exuberant than many of its fellows, but nevertheless affectionate and loyal. It has a growing band of devotees around the world.

HISTORY
Physically very similar to fossilized remains of ancient dogs, the Spitz-type Chow Chow probably originated in Siberia or Mongolia. Used as a temple guard, it later became the favored hunting dog of Chinese emperors. It was almost unknown in the West until about 120 years ago.

DESCRIPTION
The two most distinctive features of the Chow Chow are its blue-black tongue and its almost straight hind legs, which make its walk rather stilted. Its dense, furry, double coat is profuse and comes in solid black, red, fawn, cream, blue or white, sometimes with lighter or darker shades, but never particolored. The ears are small and rounded and there is a huge ruff behind the head, which gives it a lion-like appearance.

TEMPERAMENT
Although something of a challenge to train, the strong-willed Chow Chow makes a very good watchdog. It has a reputation for ferocity, probably undeserved, but is a tenacious fighter if provoked.

GROOMING
Regular brushing of the long outer coat is important to maintain the lifted, standing-out look. Extra care is needed when the dog is shedding its dense undercoat. Dry shampoo when necessary.

EXERCISE & FEEDING
Chow Chows can be lazy, but they will keep fitter with regular exercise. There are no special feeding requirements, but don't overfeed.

HEALTH PROBLEMS
These dogs have problems with hip and elbow dysplasia and are prone to genetic eye diseases.

PET FACTS

Reserved, independent: a one-person dog

Regular brushing

Regular, moderate

Adapts well to urban living, but needs space

Very good watchdog

BE AWARE

- Unsuited to hot climates due to very thick coat

- Be careful with strangers

Male: 18–23 in (46–56 cm)
50–65 lb (23–29 kg)
Female: 18–22 in (46–53 cm)
45–60 lb (20–27 kg)

Chinese Shar Pei

The Chinese Shar Pei is thought to be about 2,000 years old. The loose, wrinkled skin gives these animals an appealingly worried, forlorn look.

HISTORY

This ancient breed originated in China but almost became extinct during this century. There was a resurgence of interest in these dogs in the sixties and they are now popular pets.

DESCRIPTION

Both heavily wrinkled dogs with large heads and smaller-headed dogs with tighter-looking skins occur in this breed. The stiff, short, bristly coat feels rough to the touch and comes in black, red, fawn, apricot and cream, often with lighter tones on the backs of the hindquarters and tail. The small ears fall forward and the tail is carried in a curl. Like the Chow Chow, these dogs have a blue-black tongue.

TEMPERAMENT

Once used as fighting dogs, the well-mannered Chinese Shar Pei has a surprisingly friendly, easy-going nature and makes a delightful companion, although it may be aggressive toward other dogs. It needs firm but gentle training and is a good watchdog.

GROOMING

Regular brushing with a bristle brush is enough to keep the unusual coat in good condition. Dry shampoo or bathe when necessary and keep an eye out for mites.

EXERCISE & FEEDING

Chinese Shar Peis need regular exercise, but keep them on a leash in public. There are no special feeding requirements.

PET FACTS

- Amiable, intelligent, independent
- Regular brushing
- Regular, moderate
- Adapts well to urban living, but needs plenty of space
- Good watchdog

BE AWARE

- These are high-maintenance dogs as they require a great deal of medical attention. Many have chronic skin problems and require corrective eye surgery

HEALTH PROBLEMS

There may be problems with in-turned eyelids, a condition known as entropion that can result in blindness and usually requires corrective surgery. Chinese Shar Peis are also prone to chronic skin problems, including allergies, infections and mites.

Male: 18–20 in (46–51 cm)
40–55 lb (18–25 kg)
Female: 18–20 in (46–51 cm)
40–55 lb (18–25 kg)

Dalmatian

Exuberant and fun-loving, the Dalmatian is an excellent choice for anyone with the time to exercise and train it. Although it always turns heads, it is much more than a mere fashion accessory.

HISTORY
The handsome Dalmatian's origins are obscure, but in nineteenth-century Europe, and particularly Britain, its main work was to run beside horse-drawn carriages. This may have been to protect the travelers inside or perhaps merely for appearance. It also kept the stables clear of rats.

DESCRIPTION
A picture of elegance, the Dalmatian is of medium size with the lean, clean lines of the Pointer, to which it may be related. It is well muscled and has a short, hard, dense coat of pure white with well-defined, black or liver-colored spots randomly splashed over it. The feet are round with well-arched toes and the nails are either white or the same color as the spots.

TEMPERAMENT
Spirited and playful, these dogs adore children and can be trusted with them. They are rather sensitive, so training takes patience and gentle but firm handling. They like to spend time with their owners.

GROOMING
The smooth, lustrous, short-haired coat is easy to groom. Comb and brush with a firm bristle brush, and bathe only when necessary.

EXERCISE & FEEDING
A Dalmatian is not an ideal dog for apartment dwellers unless it can be taken out for a brisk walk or run several times a day. It needs plenty of vigorous exercise. There are no special feeding requirements.

HEALTH PROBLEMS
Dalmatians have problems with skin allergies and urinary bladder stones. They are also prone to deafness.

PET FACTS

- Gentle, sensitive, energetic
- Daily brushing
- Regular, vigorous
- Adapts well to urban living, but needs plenty of space
- Good watchdog

BE AWARE
- Newborn pups are spotless; markings develop during the first year
- Make sure a puppy's hearing has been checked before purchasing

Male: 19–23 in (48–58 cm)
50–65 lb (23–29 kg)
Female: 19–23 in (48–58 cm)
45–60 lb (20–27 kg)

HERDING DOGS

Shetland Sheepdog

The Sheltie, as it is affectionately known, is well endowed with both beauty and brains. Intuitive and responsive to its owner's wishes, it makes a charming family pet, becoming deeply attached.

HISTORY

This beautiful dog looks like a small version of the Collie (see p. 209), but it has developed over centuries on the Shetland Islands where it was used for herding sheep. Other Shetland animals, notably ponies and sheep, are also miniaturized.

DESCRIPTION

Strong, nimble and lightly built, the Sheltie is a fast runner and can jump well. The most common colors for the long, shaggy coat are sable, blue merle and tricolor, but it also comes in black with white or tan.

TEMPERAMENT

Alert and remarkably intelligent, the sensitive Sheltie likes to feel like part of the family. It is easy to train, but may be shy with strangers.

GROOMING

The coat is easier to care for than you might expect, but regular brushing is important. Mist the coat lightly with water before you begin and tease out mats before they get bad, but use the comb sparingly. The dense undercoat is shed twice a year, in spring and fall. The coat readily sheds dirt and mud and Shelties are quite fastidious about their cleanliness. Bathe or dry shampoo only when absolutely necessary.

EXERCISE & FEEDING

This active, graceful dog needs lots of exercise, preferably running free. There are no special feeding requirements.

HEALTH PROBLEMS

While Shelties are generally healthy, some dogs may suffer from cataracts and progressive retinal atrophy, as well as liver and skin disease. Blue merles should be checked for any signs of deafness.

PET FACTS

- Obedient, loyal, intelligent
- Regular brushing
- Regular, moderate
- Ideal for apartment living, but needs plenty of exercise
- Good watchdog

BE AWARE

- Excessive barking can be a problem with this breed
- Sensitive to some heartworm preventatives

Male: 13–15 in (33–38 cm)
14–18 lb (6–8 kg)
Female: 12–14 in (30–36 cm)
12–16 lb (5–7 kg)

Pembroke Welsh Corgi

Long associated with royalty, especially the British monarchy, the Pembroke Welsh Corgi is a widely recognized and popular pet. Its neat size and affectionate nature alone recommends it.

HISTORY
The Pembroke and Cardigan Welsh Corgis have been considered separate breeds for only about 70 years. The origins of both are open to conjecture, but the Pembroke is thought to have been taken to Wales from Belgium by weavers about 1,000 years ago. It was greatly valued for herding sheep and cattle in the steep hills.

DESCRIPTION
The long, powerful little body is set on short, well-boned legs. The coat comes in red, sable, fawn, tan and black, all with or without white. The most noticeable difference from the Cardigan is in the tail. The Pembroke's is quite short or docked very close to the body.

TEMPERAMENT
Pembrokes adore children, but because their way of getting sheep or cattle to move is to nip at their heels, they have a tendency to also nip people. This trait should be firmly discouraged from an early age. They are wary of strangers and make very good watchdogs.

GROOMING
The soft, medium-length, water-resistant coat is easy to groom. Comb and brush with a firm bristle brush, and bathe only when necessary. The coat is shed freely twice a year.

EXERCISE & FEEDING
Naturally active little dogs, they should always be encouraged to remain so. There are no special feeding requirements, but don't overfeed or they will become obese and lazy.

HEALTH PROBLEMS
This breed is reasonably healthy. However, the short legs and long back make it prone to slipped disks in the spine. There may also be problems with epilepsy and hereditary eye diseases, such as cataracts and progressive retinal atrophy.

PET FACTS

Affectionate, loyal, independent

Regular brushing

Regular, gentle

Ideal for apartment living, but needs plenty of exercise

Very good watchdog

BE AWARE
- Heavy shedding twice a year and some year-round dropping of hair

Male: 10–12 in (25–30 cm)
25–30 lb (11–14 kg)
Female: 10–12 in (25–30 cm)
24–28 lb (11–13 kg)

Cardigan Welsh Corgi

Although it has not attained the widespread popularity of the Pembroke, the Cardigan Welsh Corgi is a great favorite in Wales, and in fact predominates in many rural communities.

the coat comes in any color, except pure white. Slightly longer in the body than the Pembroke, the Cardigan also differs by having a long, thick tail and larger, more widely spaced ears.

HISTORY
The Cardigan Welsh Corgi may have arrived in Wales from Scandinavia, but whatever its origins, it has become indispensable for the herding of cattle in parts of that country's rugged terrain. The dogs nip at the heels of the large beasts, then duck out of the way of vengeful kicks.

DESCRIPTION
A tough, fearless little animal, it can move very fast on its short, well-boned legs. The face is quite fox-like and

TEMPERAMENT
Intelligent and easy to train, Cardigans make obedient little workers. Like Pembrokes, they should be firmly discouraged from nipping. Because of their tendency to nip, they are not well suited to households with children. Wary of strangers, they make very good watchdogs.

GROOMING
The wiry, medium-length, water-resistant coat is easy to groom. Comb and brush with a firm bristle brush, and bathe only when necessary. The coat is shed twice a year.

EXERCISE & FEEDING
Even more active than the Pembroke, Cardigans must

have regular exercise. There are no special feeding requirements, but don't overfeed or they will become obese and lazy.

HEALTH PROBLEMS
While generally hardy, they share with the Pembroke a susceptiblity to spinal problems and some inherited eye disorders.

PET FACTS

- Obedient, alert, intelligent
- Regular brushing
- Regular, gentle
- Ideal for apartment living, but needs plenty of exercise
- Very good watchdog

BE AWARE
- These dogs may suffer from spinal problems

Male: 10–13 in (25–33 cm)
25–30 lb (11–14 kg)
Female: 10–13 in (25–33 cm)
25–30 lb (11–14 kg)

Puli

The "dreadlocks" worn in such a carefree way by the Puli are a special adaptation to protect the animal from extremes of weather. In mature coat, these dogs are an amazing sight.

PET FACTS

Happy, playful, intelligent

Extensive grooming

Regular, moderate

Adapts well to urban living, but needs plenty of space

Good watchdog

BE AWARE

• A heavy, waterlogged coat may drag the dog down in open water

HISTORY

This fabulous dog is currently enjoying unprecedented popularity in its native Hungary, where it was originally prized as an excellent sheepdog and guard. Before this, it may have lived in Central Asia. Like a few other herding breeds, it jumps on or over the backs of the sheep while moving them along.

DESCRIPTION

The wiry, medium-sized Puli is among the most unusual-looking dogs in the world. Its long, dense, water-resistant double coat falls in naturally matted cords, eventually reaching the ground and hiding its legs completely. The hair is usually black, often reddish or tinged with gray, but it also occurs in white, gray, or apricot. The gait is quick and skipping. The tail, of medium length and curled over the back, is sometimes docked.

TEMPERAMENT

Pulis, or more correctly Pulik, are agile, intelligent creatures that respond well to training—they are used successfully as police dogs in Hungary and make great companions.

GROOMING

This coat does not shed and is often left in its natural state—simply separate the strands with your fingers from time to time. The dog can be bathed when necessary, but disturb the cords as little as possible. Clean around the ears and eyes regularly. Some owners prefer to clip their dog and not allow the coat to cord.

EXERCISE & FEEDING

Pulik are energetic and lively and enjoy plenty of regular activity, but take it easy on hot days. There are no special feeding requirements.

HEALTH PROBLEMS

These dogs are fairly hardy, although they may suffer from hip dysplasia and eye problems. They are not suited to hot climates.

Male: 16–18 in (41–46 cm)
25–35 lb (11–16 kg)
Female: 14–16 in (36–41cm)
20–30 lb (9–14 kg)

Australian Cattle Dog

The Australian Cattle Dog, also known as a Heeler, has in its make-up the best characteristics of its several antecedents. If you need a working dog, this is as good as they get.

DESCRIPTION
Not your average pampered pooch, this tough, medium-sized dog was bred for hard work. There are two coat colors: speckled blue, with tan or black markings, or speckled red, with dark red markings.

HISTORY
A potent cocktail of blood runs in the veins of the Australian Cattle Dog: blue merle Collie, Dalmatian, Old English Sheepdog, Australian Kelpie, the little-known Smithfield and the native Dingo. The result is a working dog with few equals, ready, willing and able to drive cattle across vast distances under harsh, hot, dusty conditions. Both its guarding and herding instincts are very strong and may extend to people and other pets.

TEMPERAMENT
The Australian Cattle Dog is absolutely loyal and obedient to its master, but it is something of a one-person dog. It may also feel compelled to establish dominance over other dogs.

GROOMING
The coarse, shorthaired, weather-resistant coat needs little care and is very easy to groom. Just comb and brush with a firm bristle brush, and bathe only when necessary.

EXERCISE & FEEDING
These animals have incredible stamina and will enjoy all the activity you can give them. Exercise is of paramount importance—without enough they can be bored and destructive. There are no special feeding requirements.

HEALTH PROBLEMS
While Australian Cattle Dogs are extremely hardy, they may suffer from hereditary deafness and occasional eye problems, such as progressive retinal atrophy.

Male: 17–20 in (43–51 cm)
32–35 lb (15–16 kg)
Female: 17–19 in (43–48 cm)
30–35 lb (14–16 kg)

Border Collie

Ready, willing and able sums up the Border Collie asleep at your feet. You might think you've succeeded in tiring him out, but move a muscle and he'll be instantly alert, ready to learn a new trick.

HISTORY

Developed for herding sheep in the rugged Scottish border country, the Border Collie's speed and stamina made it an outstanding worker and now a favorite worldwide.

DESCRIPTION

These athletic little dogs have well-proportioned bodies, lean and well muscled. The medium-length, double coat comes mainly in black with white, sometimes tricolored with tan, and also blue merle with white markings. There is often lavish feathering on the legs, underbody and tail, and a ruff behind the head. It is noted for the way it mesmerizes sheep with its eyes.

TEMPERAMENT

Highly intelligent and eager to please, Border Collies are easily obedience trained, but harsh training can make them submissive. They are wonderful pets, especially in homes with energetic children, but can be scrappy and jealous with other dogs.

GROOMING

Regular combing and brushing will keep the coat gleaming, with extra care needed when the soft, dense undercoat is shedding. Bathe or dry shampoo only when necessary. Check the ears and coat regularly for ticks.

EXERCISE & FEEDING

Fast and agile, these lively little dogs have boundless energy and thrive on hard work and play. They are a delight to see streaking after a ball, or bringing straying sheep back to the fold. They also love to swim. There are no special feeding requirements, but don't allow them to become overweight and lazy.

HEALTH PROBLEMS

Although generally hardy, the breed is subject to some joint problems and genetic eye diseases, such as progressive retinal atrophy.

PET FACTS

	Intelligent, cooperative, joyful
	Regular brushing
	Regular, vigorous
	Adapts well to urban living, but needs plenty of space
	Good watchdog

BE AWARE

- These dogs must have enough exercise—boredom leads to bad habits

- Ticks can be hard to locate in the thick undercoat

Male: 19–22 in (48–56 cm)
30–45 lb (14–20 kg)
Female: 18–21 in (46–53 cm)
27–42 lb (12–19 kg)

Australian Shepherd

Highly regarded in farming circles as an outstanding working dog long before its official recognition as a breed, the Australian Shepherd is not yet widely appreciated beyond this sphere.

HISTORY

Despite the misleading name, the Australian Shepherd is not Australian at all but was developed entirely in the U.S. to work as a herding dog on ranches. It is possible that the name was derived from one of the dog's ancestors. The breed's principal forebears were most likely Spanish dogs that accompanied the Basque shepherds and herds of fine Merino sheep exported to both America and Australia in the early days of the colonies. At some point, it was probably crossed with Collie stock. It has only quite recently gained recognition as a distinct breed.

DESCRIPTION

A medium-sized dog, the Aussie, as it is known, has a lean, muscular body and coarse, medium-to-long coat, which is well feathered on the ears, chest and underbody and the tops of the legs. There is a thick ruff on the chest and neck. The coat color and pattern are remarkably varied. The tail is very short or missing. If present, it is usually docked.

TEMPERAMENT

Extremely intelligent, easily trained, obedient and very responsive, these dogs seem to know exactly what is required of them.

GROOMING

The coat is easy to groom and needs very little attention.

PET FACTS

Keen, obedient, loyal

Minimal

Regular, vigorous

Adapts to urban living, but needs plenty of space and exercise

Good watchdog

BE AWARE

• They are sensitive to some heartworm preventatives

Brush occasionally with a firm bristle brush, and bathe only when necessary.

EXERCISE & FEEDING

This energetic working dog needs plenty of vigorous exercise to stay in shape, or better yet some real work to do. There are no special feeding requirements.

HEALTH PROBLEMS

Australian Shepherds are healthy and hardy, although they can suffer from hip dysplasia and eye problems.

Male: 19–23 in (48–58 cm)
40–70 lb (18–32 kg)
Female: 18–22 in (46–56 cm)
35–65 lb (16–29 kg)

Bearded Collie

The friendly, even-tempered Bearded Collie is an attractive family pet, but as it needs lots of exercise and care and is fairly long-lived, potential owners should consider their commitment carefully.

HISTORY

A working sheepdog for most of its known history, especially in Scotland, these dogs were formerly called Highland Collies. They are thought to have developed from Polish Lowland Sheepdogs taken to Scotland about 500 years ago.

DESCRIPTION

Well proportioned and compact, the Bearded Collie looks a bit like a small Old English Sheepdog with an undocked tail. It has a shorter muzzle than other collies. The harsh, long double coat comes in all shades of gray, slate, black, red, brown and fawn, with or without white markings. There is a long, silky beard and abundant feathering.

TEMPERAMENT

Intelligent, responsive and fearless, Bearded Collies are willing workers with great stamina and endurance. They love children, but due to their size and herding instinct they may frighten a small child.

GROOMING

Daily brushing of the long, shaggy coat is important—mist the coat lightly with water before you begin. Tease out mats before they get bad and give extra attention when the dog is shedding. Use the comb sparingly. If you prefer, the coat can be professionally machine clipped every two months or so. Bathe or dry shampoo when necessary. It is difficult to locate ticks in the thick undercoat, so check regularly.

EXERCISE & FEEDING

This is an active dog that needs lots of exercise, preferably running free. There are no special feeding requirements.

HEALTH PROBLEMS

Bearded Collies are a hardy breed with few genetic weaknesses, although hip dysplasia and eye defects do occasionally occur. Some dogs may react badly to certain heartworm preventatives, so consult your veterinarian before giving medication.

PET FACTS

- Energetic, alert, playful
- Daily brushing
- Regular, vigorous
- Adapts well to urban living, but needs plenty of exercise
- Good watchdog

BE AWARE

- If not discouraged from an early age, Bearded Collies tend to bark a lot

Male: 21–22 in (53–56 cm)
45–55 lb (20–25 kg)
Female: 20–21 in (51–53 cm)
40–50 lb (18–23 kg)

Collie

Instantly recognizable to generations of children who were brought up watching the television series "Lassie," the Collie is now one of the most popular dogs in the world.

The head is long and tapered, and the facial expression is gentle and knowing.

TEMPERAMENT

Very sociable and dependent on human company, Collies can be aloof with strangers. They are family oriented and good with children. Intelligent and easy to train, they make good watchdogs but can be terrible barkers.

HISTORY

The Collie was used in the Scottish Lowlands as a hard-working sheepdog. Its name derives from the term used for the local black sheep, colleys. There are two types, identical except for the length of their coats: the Rough Collie and the less common Smooth Collie. The Rough Collie is by far the most popular variety and is generally referred to simply as the Collie. Its magnificent coat provides protection from the cold.

GROOMING

The spectacular stiff coat sheds dirt readily and a thorough weekly brushing will keep it in good condition. Take extra care when the soft, dense under-coat is being shed. Clip out any mats and bathe or dry shampoo as necessary.

EXERCISE & FEEDING

The Collie needs plenty of exercise, preferably some of it off the leash. There are no special feeding requirements.

HEALTH PROBLEMS

Collies are subject to epilepsy, hip dysplasia, skin infections and eye problems, such as progressive retinal atrophy and a condition known as collie eye anomaly (CEA). They are sensitive to some heartworm preventatives.

DESCRIPTION

A large, strong dog, the Collie often has the typical markings of white collar, chest, feet and tail tip. The main colors of the long, thick double coat are sable, tricolor, white and blue merle.

Male: 24–26 in (61–66 cm)
60–75 lb (27–34 kg)
Female: 22–24 in (56–61 cm)
50–65 lb (23–29 kg)

Belgian Shepherd Dog

The picture of power and grace, the Belgian Shepherd makes its appearance in several guises, but beneath its skin-deep beauty is a reliable, hard-working and very adaptable animal.

HISTORY

The dogs used in Belgium to guard and herd sheep are all closely related but in recent times have evolved into one basic type with four distinct varieties differentiated by appearance. They are the Groenendael, Laekenois, Malinois and Tervuren (or Tervueren). In the U.S., the rare Laekenois has not yet been officially recognized and the other three are classified as separate breeds. The popular Groenendael is known simply as the Belgian Sheepdog.

DESCRIPTION

Similar to German Shepherd Dogs, with well-shaped heads and long muzzles, each variety is distinguished by its coat. The Belgian Sheepdog has an abundant, glossy, longhaired, black coat, sometimes with small white markings. The Tervuren is also longhaired, but comes in fawn, gray and mahogany and any shade in between. The hair is tipped with black and the mask and the tips of the ears are also black. Both of these dogs have a generous ruff around the neck, larger in the male. The Malinois is fawn to mahogany with the same black tips and shaded areas as the Tervuren, but the hair is shorter. Around the neck, the hair thickens to a deep collar. The Laekenois has similar coloring to the Malinois, but the short hair is harsh and wiry.

PET FACTS

- Obedient, willing, intelligent
- Regular brushing for shorthaired coats, more extensive for longhaired coats
- Regular, vigorous
- Adapts well to urban living, but needs plenty of exercise
- Very good watchdog

BE AWARE

- Thorough training is essential

Male: 24–26 in (61–66 cm)
65–75 lb (29–34 kg)
Female: 22–24 in (56–61 cm)
60–70 lb (27–32 kg)

TEMPERAMENT

Essentially working dogs, Belgian Shepherds are easily trained, reliable and obedient. Their training should always be patient, firm and consistent—if you are harsh or overbearing they will become uncooperative. They make excellent police and guard dogs, and this type of work is currently their main occupation. They do, however, make excellent pets, ever-watchful, alert and loyal, and they thrive on loving companionship.

GROOMING

The smooth, shorthaired coat of the Malinois is easy to maintain. Brush regularly with a firm bristle brush, and bathe only if absolutely necessary as bathing removes the waterproofing of the coat. Care of the longer-coated Belgian Sheepdog and Tervuren is more demanding. Their coarse, straight outer coats are heavy and of medium length; the undercoats are very dense.

Daily combing and brushing is important, with extra care when the animals are shedding. Clip out mats that form, particularly in the ruff and on the legs, and clip hair from between the toes and on the outer ears. The rough, wiry coat of the Laekenois needs only an occasional brushing with a firm bristle brush. It should be rough-looking but never curled. Again, bathing is not recommended.

EXERCISE & FEEDING

Remember that these are working dogs, used to an active outdoor life. As such, they need a lot of exercise, preferably off the leash as much as possible. There are no special feeding requirements, but do not overfeed as all varieties tend to become obese and lazy.

HEALTH PROBLEMS

These are hardy, healthy animals with few genetic diseases, although some get hip dysplasia and eye problems.

Old English Sheepdog

If you have endless patience and lots of time to spend exercising and grooming the Old English Sheepdog, your reward will be the love of a faithful and supremely glamorous companion.

PET FACTS

Intelligent, playful, loyal

Daily, extensive

Regular, vigorous

Adapts well to urban living, but needs plenty of space

Good watchdog

BE AWARE

- If bored and lonely, these dogs can be mischievous

- It doesn't take long for the coat to get out of control

HISTORY
Commonly called Bobtails, Old English Sheepdogs were developed for herding livestock, both sheep and cattle, in England's West Country.

DESCRIPTION
A large, hardy, thickset, muscular dog, it has a distinctive low-pitched, loud, ringing bark. The shaggy coat is free of curls and comes in gray, grizzle, blue or blue merle, with or without white markings.

TEMPERAMENT
Playful and intelligent, Old English Sheepdogs learn quickly, but training should be started while the animal is still of a manageable size.

GROOMING
The coarse, longhaired coat needs constant care to keep it in top condition. Unless it is combed and brushed right through to the dense, waterproof undercoat at least three times a week, it will become matted and the dog may develop skin problems or be plagued by parasites. Clip out any tangles carefully so as not to nick the skin. A grooming table will make the whole job easier. If you prefer, the coat can be professionally machine-clipped every two months or so. In former times, these dogs were shorn along with the sheep. Trim around the eyes and rear end with blunt-nosed scissors.

EXERCISE & FEEDING
These dogs were developed for hard work and love a good run. There are no special feeding requirements.

HEALTH PROBLEMS
Being thick coated, this breed is not suited to hot climates. Like many heavy dogs, they are subject to hip dysplasia. They are also susceptible to genetic eye diseases.

Male: 22–24 in (56–61 cm)
From 65 lb (29 kg)
Female: 20–22 in (51 cm)
From 60 lb (27 kg)

German Shepherd Dog

It seems as if the incredibly versatile German Shepherd Dog can be trained to do any job. Admired the world over for its intelligence and excellence as a guard dog, it seems to thrive on a life of service.

PET FACTS

PET FACTS

Fearless, loyal, intelligent

Daily brushing

Regular, vigorous

Adapts well to urban living, but needs plenty of space

Outstanding watchdog

BE AWARE

- These dogs require firm, consistent handling by a strong adult

- This breed suffers from many genetic diseases

HISTORY

Known also as Alsatians, German Shepherd Dogs were originally bred as herding dogs. Nowadays, their tasks include police, rescue, tracking and military work. They also make devoted companions and watchdogs.

DESCRIPTION

Handsome, well proportioned and very strong, they must be firmly trained to obedience from an early age. The coat most often comes in black with tan, sable or all black, but other colors do occur. The nose is always black.

TEMPERAMENT

These dogs seem ever-vigilant and constantly on duty. They are both loved and feared, with good reason. They are inclined to be reserved and you must win their friend ship, but from then on their loyalty is unquestioned.

GROOMING

Daily combing and brushing of the thick, coarse coat is important, and take extra care when the dog is shedding its dense undercoat. At this time, the dead woolly hair clings to the new hair and must be removed with a slicker brush designed for the task. Bathe or dry shampoo only when necessary.

EXERCISE & FEEDING

German Shepherd Dogs revel in strenuous activity, preferably combined with training of some kind. Feed them two or three small meals a day instead of one large meal.

HEALTH PROBLEMS

This breed suffers from many health problems, including skin ailments, hip and elbow dysplasia, bloat, genetic eye diseases, epilepsy and heart defects.

Male: 24–26 in (61–66 cm)
75–95 lb (34–43 kg)
Female: 22–24 in (56–61 cm)
70–90 lb (32–41 kg)

Briard

A gentle giant, the Briard is now becoming better known and appreciated outside its native France, where it is highly regarded as an excellent working dog and devoted pet.

TEMPERAMENT
A long history of working with humans has made Briards sweet natured and gentle. They are intelligent and easy to train, making wonderful family pets and very good watchdogs.

HISTORY
The Briard's lineage goes back more than 1,000 years, although today's dog is more elegant than those of earlier times. In its native France it has long been regarded as a shepherd dog, and during World War I soldiers were impressed by its abilities as a messenger and by the way it pulled supply wagons. It first appeared in the U.S. in the late eighteenth century.

DESCRIPTION
A large, muscular animal, the Briard's gait is smooth and appears almost effortless. The long, shaggy coat comes in solid colors, especially black and fawns, the darker the better. The hind legs have double dewclaws.

GROOMING
If the dog is kept outside, the coat seems to largely take care of itself. If the dog spends a lot of time indoors, you may wish to brush the long coat regularly and bathe or dry shampoo as necessary.

EXERCISE & FEEDING
Briards are working dogs and require plenty of vigorous exercise. There are no special feeding requirements.

PET FACTS

- Gentle, reliable, intelligent
- Regular brushing
- Regular, vigorous
- Adapts well to urban living, but needs plenty of exercise
- Very good watchdog

BE AWARE
- The herding instinct is strong

HEALTH PROBLEMS
This breed is generally healthy, although hip dysplasia, cataracts and PRA do occur.

Male: 23–27 in (58–69 cm)
70–80 lb (32–36 kg)
Female: 21–25 in (53–63 cm)
65–75 lb (29–34 kg)

Bouvier des Flandres

Everything about the Bouvier des Flandres says dependability—from its workmanlike body to its calm, steady manner. Today, its work includes police duties and guiding services for the blind.

HISTORY

The Bouvier des Flandres, or Ox-Drover of Flanders, originated in pastoral regions around the Franco-Belgian border, where it was used for herding and guarding. During World War I, it was used as a messenger and an ambulance dog.

DESCRIPTION

First and foremost a working dog, the Bouvier is powerful and short in the body. The rough, long, shaggy double coat comes in black, gray, brindle, salt and pepper, and fawn, sometimes with a white mark on the chest. A thick beard and mustache adorn the face. The tail is usually docked.

TEMPERAMENT

Adaptable and even tempered, the Bouvier goes about its business quietly and calmly. It is easy to train and is an excellent watchdog.

GROOMING

If the dog is kept outdoors, the harsh, dry coat seems to look after itself, shedding dirt and water easily. If the animal lives in the house, you may wish to brush the long coat regularly and bathe or dry shampoo when necessary. This will certainly enhance the appearance and both dog and owner will enjoy the contact. Trim the coat occasionally, if necessary.

EXERCISE & FEEDING

Energetic and active, the Bouvier needs plenty of exercise. There are no special feeding requirements.

PET FACTS

- Stable, loyal, obedient
- Regular brushing
- Regular, moderate
- Adapts well to urban living, but needs plenty of exercise
- Excellent watchdog

BE AWARE

- These dogs can be suspicious of strangers

HEALTH PROBLEMS

These hardy dogs are used to harsh conditions and are rarely ill. However, some dogs may suffer from hip dysplasia and eye problems, such as cataracts.

Male: 23–28 in (58–71 cm)
75–90 lb (34–41 kg)
Female: 22–27 in (56–69 cm)
60–80 lb (27–36 kg)

FURTHER INFORMATION

Every dog must have his day.

JONATHAN SWIFT (1667–1745),
English writer and satirist

GLOSSARY

belton term used to describe the distinctive coloration of English Setters (white hairs flecked with blue, lemon, orange or liver).

black and tan common combination of black coat with tan markings.

blue pale discoloration of black coat.

blue merle blue-gray streaked with black.

brindle gray or tawny coat streaked with darker color.

chestnut medium-brown color.

chocolate dark fawn to brown color.

cropping the practice of removing part of the ear to make it more erect; illegal in some states and countries.

cross breeding the breeding together of two purebred dogs to create a cross breed.

dewclaws a digit on the inside of a dog's leg; those on back legs are usually removed.

double coat strong, resistant coat covering soft undercoat.

docking the practice of removing part of the tail soon after birth; traditional for many breeds but discouraged in some countries.

drop ear long, floppy ears that hang down.

fallow pale cream to light fawn color.

feathering long hair fringing the ears, legs, tail and body.

gaze hounds another term for sight hounds.

grizzle blue-gray color.

gundog dogs bred to work with hunters in the field (sporting dogs).

hackles hair on neck and back.

harlequin white with blue or black patches.

in season when female is ready for mating (estrus).

liver chocolate or brown color.

mane long hair around the neck.

mask shading on head.

molting the seasonal loss of undercoat; shedding.

muzzle the projecting part of the head, including mouth, nose and jaws.

particolor an even mix of two colors.

prick ear erect, pointed ear.

quarry a hunting term for prey.

roan white mixed evenly with another color.

sable white with black shading.

salt and pepper mix of black and white hairs.

slate dark gray color.

smooth coat short, flat-lying coat.

solid color uniform coat of one color.

stop indentation between the forehead and muzzle.

stripping removal of dead hairs from a dog's coat.

topcoat strong, resistant outer coat.

topknot long hair on top of the head.

topline the outline of the dog between the withers and the tail.

tricolor coat of three distinct colors.

undercoat dense, soft coat for insulation; sometimes water resistant.

wheaten pale yellow or fawn.

whelping giving birth.

wirehaired harsh, dense coat.

withers a point just behind the neck, from which a dog's height is calculated.

INDEX

Bold page numbers indicate the main reference and italics indicate illustrations and photos.

INFORMATION DIRECTORY

*The following organizations will be able to supply you with
information on local bodies to contact for details on registration,
standards, dog shows, shelters and other information required.*

NORTH AMERICA

**American Kennel
Club (AKC)**
51 Madison Avenue,
New York, New York 10010,
USA
Tel: (212) 696 8200
Fax: (212) 696 8299
E-mail: http://www.akc.org

**Humane Society of the
United States (HSUS)**
2100 L Street NW
Washington, DC 20037,
USA
Tel: (202) 452 1100
Fax: (202) 778 6132
E-mail: http://www.hsus.org

**American Society for the
Prevention of Cruelty
to Animals (ASPCA)**
424 East 92nd Street,
New York, New York
10128-6804, USA
Tel: (212) 876 7700
Fax: (212) 348 3031
E-mail: http://www.aspca.org

**American Veterinary
Medical Association**
1931 N. Meacham Road,
Suite 100, Schaumberg,
Illinois 60173-4360, USA
Tel: (847) 925 8070
Fax: (847) 925 1329
E-mail: http://www.avma.org

**Canadian Kennel
Club (CKC)**
Commerce Park
89 Skyway Avenue,
Suite 100, Etobicoke
Ontario M9W 6R4,
Canada
Tel: (416) 675 5511
Fax: (416) 675 6506

EUROPE

The Kennel Club
1–5 Clarges Street,
Piccadilly,
London W1Y 8AB,
England
Tel: (171) 629 5828
E-mail: http://www.the-
kennel-club.org.uk

**British Veterinary
Association**
7 Mansfield Street
London W1M 0AT,
England
Tel: (171) 636 6541
Fax: (171) 436 2970

**Royal Society for the
Prevention of Cruelty
to Animals (RSPCA)**
RSPCA Headquarters
Causeway, Horsham,
West Sussex RH12 1HG,
England
Tel: (1403) 264181
Fax: (1403) 241 048

**Fédération Cynologique
Internationale (FCI)**
Place Albert 1er, No. 13
6530 Thuin,
Belgium
Tel: (32 71) 591238
Fax: (32 71) 592179

AUSTRALIA
Note: The Australian
National Kennel Council
(ANKC) cannot be
contacted directly. Enquiries
should be made through
state and territory bodies.

**Royal New South
Wales Canine Council**
PO Box 632
St Marys, NSW, 2760,
Australia
Tel: (02) 9834 3022
Fax: (02) 9834 3872

**Victorian Canine
Association**
PO Box K9
Ascot Vale, Vic., 3032,
Australia
Tel: (03) 9376 2255
Fax: (03) 9376 1772

RSPCA Australia
PO Box E369
Kingston, ACT, 2604
Tel: (06) 282 8300
Fax: (06) 282 8311
E-mail: rspca@ibm.net

ACKNOWLEDGMENTS AND CREDITS

The publishers would like to thank the following people for kindly allowing their dogs to be photographed for this book:

Airedale Terrier "Solaris," owned by Gish Lesh/Strongfort Kennels
Akita "Bronco," owned by Alan Molan
Australian Shepherd "Tango" "Yankee" "Costner" "Nevada" and "Uppity," owned by Mandy Lees/ Leesway Kennels
Australian Terrier "Zoe," owned by Mr D.J. Freshwater and Mrs R.M. Withers
Basset Hound "Monte," owned by Mrs R. Tissington and "Wilbur," owned by Julie O'Flynn
Bearded Collie "Douglas" and "Cameron," owned by Julie Wardell
Bedlington Terrier "Max," owned by Liz Wells/ Breckland Kennels
Belgian Shepherd Dog "Phebus" "Prince" "Lily" and "Sassy," owned by Ian and Roslyn Keech/ Lanaken Kennels
Bernese Mountain Dog "Oscar," owned by Lynn Brand and handled by Marilyn McLeod-Woodhouse
Bichon Frise "Meaning," owned by Julia Jeffrey
Bloodhound "Belle," owned by Adrian Chapman
Border Collie "Kelby" and "Wiki," owned by Jane Fookes
Border Terrier "Hughie," owned by Carol Maciver
Borzoi "Zin" and "Trezor," owned by Claire O'Reilly
Boston Terrier "Claire," owned by Elaine Bond
Bulldog "Nelson," owned by Elaine Bond
Cairn Terrier "Bella," owned by Margaret Hill; "Scarlet," owned by "Kitch" Robinson; and "Jessie," owned by A. Fielder-Gill
Cavalier King Charles Spaniel "Bernard" "David" "Chips" and "Chintz," owned by Jeanie Montford
Collie "Diane," owned by Mrs S. Jackson/Jodivale Kennels; "Nikki," owned by Samantha Dunn and Gaye Jones
Dalmatian "Chanel" (black-spotted), owned by Dianne Wright and "Presto" (liver-spotted), owned by Carolyn Byrnes-Suchy
Dachshund, Standard Smooth "Peter," owned by Sue Rose and handled by Peter Nordstrom
Doberman Pinscher "Indi" and "Bazza," owned by Janel Sefton
English Setter "Storm" "Chloe" and "Dessie," owned by Gray Lenz
Fox Terrier, Smooth "Radar," owned by Ken Sheppard
Fox Terrier, Wire "Beano," owned by Wendy Brown
German Pointer, Shorthaired "Trekker," owned by Lynn and Carolyn Butler
German Pointer, Wirehaired "Storm," owned by Anne Atkinson/Korskote Kennels
Gordon Setter "Blair" and "Blake," owned by Ann and Andrew Finlaison
Great Pyrenees "Miss Lily" "Star" and "Harley," owned by Chris Burrows/Impyrator Kennels
Irish Setter "Jarrah," owned by Bruce McLean and handled by N. and S. Ryan
Irish Terrier "Roxy," owned by Mike and Sandra Potts/Stormdust Irish Terriers
Irish Wolfhound "Sean" and "Jenna," owned by Stephen and Soile Gendle
Italian Greyhound "Malibu" "Dermott" "Minky" "Jessica" "Anna" and "Gemma," owned by Claire Needham

Jack Russell Terrier "Leda" and "Jessica," owned by Margaret Giles
Japanese Chin "Prince," owned by Maribel Eather
Labrador Retriever "Guy," owned by Hugh and Elizabeth Gent and "Sarah" "Tillie" "Zac" and "Misty," owned by Ann Murray
Lhasa Apso "Sam" and "Tina," owned by Jennifer Longmire
Mastiff "Coady" and "Taylor," owned by Peter Docherty/Mastdoch Kennels
Miniature Pinscher "Tyson" "Nikki" and "Carla," owned by J.V. and D.L. Cardona/ Pindona Kennels
Newfoundland "Joss" and "Tawny," owned by Tracy Shaw
Norwich Terrier "Rambo" and "Georgia," owned by Gordon Todorovitch and Sharon Proud
Old English Sheepdog "Thomas," owned by Rose Dillon
Papillon "Paddington" "Angelique" and "Cassandra," owned by Rebecca Grabham and handled by Dorothy Cooper; "Penny," "Missy" and "Oscar," owned by Dorothy Cooper
Pekingese "Damian," owned by Sylvia O'Cass
Pomeranian "Kazu" "Pepper" and "Mickey," owned by Elizabeth Ann Friedman
Poodle, Miniature "Madison," owned by Gordon and Susan Lasslett
Poodle, Toy "Amber," owned by Nola Westren
Pug "Bertie" "Ernie" and "Herbie," owned by Lois and Felicity Way/Hugapug Kennels
Saint Bernard "Tuffy" "Sparky" "Justine" and "Jackie," owned by Matina Butcher/Stiniyasu Saint Bernard
Saluki "Zhar" "Sam" and "Ebony," owned by Cathy Smith
Samoyed "Alexis" and "Tarnie," owned by Vivienne E. Zavattaro
Schipperke "Rocket," owned by Colin Banks/ Ecebe Kennels
Schnauzer, Giant "Tasman," owned by Craig and Marie Douglas/Reisenhund Kennels
Schnauzer, Standard "Harry," owned by Jenny Larven
Scottish Terrier "Jock Jnr" and "Clair," owned by Mary-Lou Keating
Shar Pei "Minka" and "Tyler," owned by Vicki Pocklington
Shetland Sheepdog "Luck" "Josh" and "Harry," owned by Christine Hatzikiriakos
Shih Tzu "Oliver," owned by E.T and Mrs M. Pickering and handled by J. and L. Sheppard/Erintoi Kennels
Siberian Husky "Earl," owned by Richard and Mara Herba
Silky Terrier "Hannah" "Anne-Marie" "George" and "Penny," owned by Marie Watt/Rydedale Kennels
Springer Spaniel, Welsh "Benjamin" "Sarah" and "Clifford," owned by Peter Jones and Kevin O'Neill
Staffordshire Bull Terrier "Ziggy" and "Zac," owned by Ivan Zalac/Tuxzat Kennels
Vizsla "Drum," owned by Lynn and Carolyn Butler
Welsh Corgi, Cardigan "Star," owned by Jean Georgiou and "Cullen," owned by Kerry Williams
Welsh Corgi, Pembroke "Cindy," owned by Dan Scott and handled by Michelle Vannus
Yorkshire Terrier "Distinction" and "June," owned by Dorothy Cooper

The publishers would like to thank the following people for their assistance in the preparation of this book:

Paul and Nellie Abela/Powerbulmas Kennels; Thomspon Carl Aguma; Arrassmith McHale & Associates; Lyn Britza; Caroline Burch; Wendy van Buuren; Philip and Stephen Cauchi/La Grota Kennels; Brett Chaytor/Ropin' the Wind Kennels; John and Toni Comerford; Miriam Coupe; Carole Doherty/ Everalert Kennels; Kylie Delacourt; Pat Ellis; Christine Farrugia; Michelle Fernando; Karen Francis; Maureen Hanley; John Hugo and Karen Outtrin; Robin Hill; Robyn Hopkins; Dianne Horner; Henny and Ralph Kammer/Stavast Kennels; Colleen Khoury; Linda Lee; Gish Lesh; Mrs B. Lewis; Donald and Christina Mascord; Max and Glenda Mason; Sue McFadden/Glenbriar Kennels; Marilyn McLeod-Woodhouse/Schöhardt Kennels; Rachel Millner; Carol Moeser; Alan Molan; Sara Nightingale; Peter Mortimer; Kylie Mulquin; Peter Nordstrom; Noel David Papworth/Melcathra Kennels; Pets World, Warringah Mall, Sydney; Alan Poulton; Vicki Regner; Joy Schafer; Garry Somerville; Peter and Lydia Sparkowski/Shenan Kennels; Bill and Margot Stevenson/Apocodeodar Kennels; Margaret and Rachelle Thomas; Kristin Wakefield; P. and G.J. Wakefield; Alan Walker; Z. Whitelaw; Michael Wigg; Sylvia and Bob Williamson; Mike and Nina Work; Ivan Zalac/Tuxzat Kennels

Special thanks to Alan Poulton for his invaluable assistance.

PHOTOGRAPH CREDITS:
(t = top; b = bottom; c = center; l = left; r = right; AA/ES = Animals Animals/Earth Scenes; AGI = AGI Photographic Imaging; Auscape = Auscape International; AP = Animal Photography; AU = Animals Unlimited; BCL = Bruce Coleman Limited; Bridgeman = The Bridgeman Art Library; Iams = The Iams Company; ME = Mary Evans Picture Library)

All photographs by Stuart Bowey/AD-LIBITUM except:

2 Jean-Michel Labat/Auscape 4–5 Alan and Sandy Carey/ Oxford Scientific Films 6–7 ME 8–9 Jean-Michel Labat/ Auscape 10–11 The American Museum in Britain, Bath 12b Stan Fellerman/Stock Photos P/L 15t Renee Stockdale/AA/ES; b Jane Burton/BCL 16b Jean-Paul Ferrero/Pho.n.e/Auscape 18bl Jean-Paul Ferrero/Ardea London 19br H Clark/FLPA 20t Danegger/Silvestris 21br Robert Pearcy/AA/ES 22–23 Iams 24bl Lanceau/Cogis/ Auscape 25t Richard Hutchings/TPL 26tl Bill Bachman 27tr Iams 28cr Hermeline/Cogis/Auscape; b J Ardel/Auscape 29t J Bastable/FLPA; br Australian Picture Library 31cr Vidal/ Cogis/Auscape 32t Renee Stockdale/ AA/ES; b RT Willbie/ Animal Photography 33t Bill Bachman; b Rex Features/Austral International 34t Bob Herger/TPL 35tr Stuart Cumings/Stock Photos P/L 36–37 Musee Conde, Chantilly/Giraudon 39t Francais/Cogis/Auscape 42t AU; bl Hermeline/

Cogis/Auscape 44t AU; b Renee Stockdale/ AA/ES 45t AU; b Bill Bachman 46t Labat/Lanceau/Cogis/ Auscape 47c Iams 49t Kerscher/ Silvestris 52t Lanceau/Cogis/Auscape 53b AU 54t Norvia Behling/AA/ES; b Varin/Cogis/Auscape 56b Jean-Paul Ferrero/Auscape 57t Norvia Behling/AA/ES 59cr R Willbie/Animal Photography Ltd 60–61 Scuola di S. Giorgio degli Schiavoni Venezia/Scala 62tl Francais/Cogis/ Auscape 65t Richard Gross/Stock Photos P/L 66t Sally Anne Thompson/Animal Photography 67t Berger Alfons/Silvestris 69 Bill Bachman 71c Jane Burton/BCL 72t Bill Bachman/Stock Photos P/L 77br Gissey/Cogis/Auscape 78tl Labat/Cogis/Auscape 80b Lanceaus/Cogis/ Auscape 82–83 Musee Conde, Chantilly/Giraudon 84–85b John Daniels/Ardea London 87t AU; b Sally Anne Thompson/Animal Photography 88t Liz Bombford/Survival Anglia/ Oxford Scientific Films; b John Daniels/Ardea London 89t Hermeline/Cogis/Auscape; b Jane Burton/BCL 90 AGI/Iams 92–93 Bonhams, London/Bridgeman 94tl Ancient Art and Architecture Collection; cl S Michael Bisceglie/AA/ES; cr Louvre, Paris/ Bridgeman Art Library; b Museo Nationale Athenai/Scala 95t Musee Conde, Chantilly/ Giraudon; b Louvre, Paris/Giraudon 96t Versailles, Chateau/Giraudon; b ME 97tl ME; tr ME; b ME 98t JM Labat/Ardea London; b Musee Conde, Chantilly/Giraudon 99tl ME; tr Bonhams, London/ Bridgeman; b JM Labat/Auscape 103b AGI/Iams, 104b AGI/Iams 105b AGI/Iams 107b AGI/Iams 108b AGI/Iams 112tl Tara Darling; cr Francais/ Cogis/Auscape; b Francais/Cogis/Auscape 114b AGI/Iams 119b AGI/Iams 120b AGI/Iams 121t AGI/Iams; c AGI/Iams; b AGI/Iams 123b AGI/Iams 124b AGI/Iams 125b AGI/Iams 129b AGI/Iams 130b AGI/Iams 132b AGI/Iams 135b AGI/Iams 140b AGI/Iams 141b AGI/Iams 146b AGI/Iams 151b AGI/Iams 154c Sally Anne Thompson/Animal Photography 157b AGI/Iams 162b AGI/Iams 163b AGI/Iams 165b AGI/Iams 168t Tara Darling/Paw Prints; b AGI/Iams 171b AGI/Iams 173cr AU 175br Jane Burton/BCL 178b AGI/Iams 183b AGI/Iams 189br AGI/Iams 193b AGI/Iams 194b AGI/Iams 195b AGI/Iams 196b AGI/Iams 197t AGI/Iams; b AGI/Iams 203b AGI/Iams 204t AU; b Tim Bauer/Austral International 205b AGI/Iams 213b AGI/Iams 214b AGI/Iams 215b AGI/Iams 216 Musee Conde, Chantilly/Giraudon

ILLUSTRATION CREDITS:
All illustrations by Janet Jones except: 49 Iain McKellar; 83 Kylie Mulquin; dog silhouettes and symbols by Rod Westblade, Kylie Mulquin and Robyn Latimer